TRUE
NORTH

TRUE
NORTH

PEARY, COOK, AND THE
RACE TO THE POLE

BRUCE HENDERSON

W. W. NORTON & COMPANY

New York London

For information about permission to reproduce selections from this book,
write to Permissions, W. W. Norton & Company. Inc., 500 Fifth Avenue,
New York, NY 10110

Manufacturing by the Maple-Vail Book Manufacturing Group
Book design by JAM Design
Cartography by Jacques Chazaud
Production manager: Andrew Marasia

Library of Congress Cataloging-in-Publication Data

Henderson, Bruce.
   True north : Peary, Cook, and the race to the Pole / Bruce Henderson.
     p. cm.
   Includes bibliographical references and index.
   ISBN 0-393-05791-7 (hardcover)
   1. Peary, Robert E. (Robert Edwin), 1856–1920. 2. Cook, Frederick Albert,
1865–1940. 3. Explorers—United States—Biography. 4. North Pole. I. Title.

   G634.H46 2005
   910'.9163'2—dc22

                                                              2004026047

W. W. Norton & Company, Inc., 500 Fifth Avenue, New York, N.Y. 10110
www.wwnorton.com

W. W. Norton & Company Ltd., Castle House, 75/76 Wells Street, London
W1T 3QT

1 2 3 4 5 6 7 8 9 0

For George Plimpton,

who suggested this story of polar exploration

for a new generation of readers

———————————

"The Pole discovery is peopled with human romance:

it is part of the epic of man."

—LINCOLN STEFFENS

CONTENTS

PART TWO   TO THE POLE

AUTHOR'S NOTE

———

ARLY IN the twentieth century, an international dispute raged over the discovery of the geographic North Pole, the most prized jewel in the crown of human exploration and a goal sought for nearly four hundred years. Following a rancorous public debate that spilled across the front pages of newspapers everywhere, the issue was largely resolved in favor of one American explorer over another, although each claimed to have been the first at the top of the world, where all meridians of longitude meet and the only direction is south.

In the decades since, strong opinions have developed in some quarters that history got it wrong. According to this revisionist analysis, U.S. Navy civil engineer Robert E. Peary, universally credited with having discovered the North Pole on his final attempt, was untruthful about the distances covered on his "dash to the Pole" and never reached it at all; and the discredited claim of physician Frederick A. Cook to have beaten Peary to the Pole by a year has been accorded increased legitimacy because his detailed descriptions of the North Pole—the first ever published—have been verified by later explorers. If his claim is true, a grave injustice was inflicted upon Cook, who before the great polar controversy bore a reputation as impeccable as that of any explorer of his time, but who ended up being widely debunked and labeled a charlatan.

The controversy has outlasted both men. Today, there are still individuals and groups claiming expertise in polar affairs who are highly partisan in their support of one claimant over the other, on the basis of available information and evidence—scientific, circumstantial, and psychological.

Peary and Cook began as companions drawn by adventure and glory; they ended as bitter rivals. Their desperate efforts to attain the Pole, and, upon their return from the Far North, their equally desperate efforts to secure their place in history were once hailed by journalist Lincoln Steffens as "the story of the century." That was a different century, of course, but it remains an extraordinary tale.

TRUE
NORTH

THE NORTH POLE IS DISCOVERED
BY DR. FREDERICK A. COOK

NEW YORK HERALD

SEPTEMBER 2, 1909

PEARY DISCOVERS THE NORTH POLE
AFTER EIGHT TRIALS IN 23 YEARS

NEW YORK TIMES

SEPTEMBER 7, 1909

1909

A PHYSICIAN FROM Brooklyn and two young Eskimo hunters from a northern Greenland tribe, who together had survived the longest dog sledge journey in history and thereafter spent the meanest of winters hunkered down in an ice cave like Stone Age dwellers, were again staring death in the face. Not heard from for more than a year, they had in some circles been given up as lost, and no search parties were looking for them.

On the final leg of an arduous return journey begun the preceding year, the men had been trekking for weeks up the desolate eastern shores of Ellesmere Island in an effort to reach what served as civilization in these latitudes: Greenland's western coast, where food and shelter were to be found.

When they had emerged from their forced hibernation in mid-February, they fought through one storm after another coming off Jones Sound in the Cape Sparbo region. After each storm passed, they encountered ice tumbled into mountainous barriers, which they could skirt only by cutting through tremendous snow drifts, often while fighting gales that made them stagger like drunkards. Even in the long march northward the preceding spring, they had not experienced such difficult travel. Pulling a single sledge strapped to their shoulders because they no longer had dogs, they lightened the load by disposing of unneeded clothing and equipment.

The Arctic was slowly awakening from its long winter night, which at this high latitude meant six months of no direct sunlight and freezing storms, during which temperatures plunged as low as minus fifty degrees Fahrenheit. On their weeks-long trek under skies that had slowly lightened, they saw no living things on the ice to hunt, no seals or walrus or hare, no beefy musk oxen, not even a lone seabird headed elsewhere. They were at the top of the food chain with no signs of life beneath them.

When the last of their provisions were gone, they began eating things not normally considered food. Half of a wax candle and three cups of hot water were served for one meal. Sections of a walrus hide used as a slicker were cut up, boiled, and eaten for several days; although difficult to masticate and causing a few broken teeth, the hide, while it lasted, eased their voracious hunger. Next they cooked and consumed lengths of walrus line.

As subzero winds cut gashes in the exposed skin of their faces, they trudged onward, every fiber of their weakened bodies quivering with cold and hunger. The exertion fueled by limited sustenance caused them to shrivel; under their furs, they were walking skeletons.

On March 20, they discovered that they were not alone. In the twilight illumination that turned the ice an eerie gray, they gathered silently around the tracks in fresh snow of a bear many times larger than a man. They knew about the white semiaquatic bear found throughout the Arctic region. The physician could recite the scientific name, *Ursus maritimus*, for "sea bear." To the Eskimos it was Nanuk, whom native hunters considered the most prized of all the animals they traditionally hunted. An adult male weighed as much as 1,600 pounds, stood six feet at the shoulders, and grew to eight feet in length. Rising upright on its rear legs, as it did when threatened, it soared to an imposing twelve feet or higher. Bears were often found alone on the drifting ice in the spring and summer, swimming from one chunk of ice to the other, feasting on seals they usually caught on the ice. The Eskimos considered the bear a great lonely roamer, possessing wisdom as well as strength. In addition to being an able swimmer, the polar bear was a capable traveler on solid surfaces, with black footpads on the bottom of foot-long paws that gripped for traction. On the ice, the bear moved with surprising swiftness, able to gallop as fast as a horse for short distances. Shy by nature, it was dangerous when confronted, and stalked its prey before racing in for the kill that few escaped. In lean times, it subsisted on seaweed and grass but was carnivorous by nature, with a taste for seals, birds, and caribou. Although only the females hibernated, while the males remained active during the winter, come spring all "sea bears" were lean and hungry, eager to get on with the eating. Their favored first course: newborn seal pups found cavorting on the ice in early spring. Polar bears had a powerful sense of smell and, when hungry, were known to stalk humans.

The tracks were fresh, meaning that the bear was still in the area and would have little trouble picking up their scent. As yet, they had seen no seals, adults or babies. The bear probably had no better luck. Nanuk would be famished.

It was a sign of the gravity of their predicament that the lurking presence of such a predator registered on the men not as a threat but as an opportunity. Here was a potential food source, but first they would have to do battle with *Ursus maritimus*, the biggest, strongest, and most terrifying of all Arctic creatures.

That evening, they prepared for the coming of the bear. Their plan was to make their prey believe it was the hunter, and not the hunted. A snowhouse was built with blocks of ice cut from the hard-pack surface; there was a peephole on each side and a narrow entryway at one end from which the men might escape or make an attack. On the outside, they built a low shelf upon which they draped remnants of skin and fur, arranged to resemble a recumbent seal on the ice pack. Over this, they rigged a looped line, through which the bear would have to place its head to reach the bait. Arranged on the ground were other looped lines. The end of each line was secured to solid ice. The men sharpened their lances and knives, then went into the snowhouse. One remained on watch while the other two tried to sleep.

They did not have long to wait. First came an ominous crackling sound made by a large creature advancing on the ice and snow. Through the peephole, they saw the little black nose held high— most of the bear's bulk was awash in the whitish background. Then the beady eyes, large head, and extended neck came into focus as the bear approached in slow, measured steps, sniffing the ground toward the furs.

From the men's crouched position, the bear appeared gigantic. Apparently every bit as hungry as the men and without fear, it came straight for the bait. The two natives crept to the entryway, one with a lance and the other with a spiked harpoon shaft, ready to jump out and do battle.

Inside the snowhouse, the doctor jerked the line and the loop tightened around the bear's neck. Another line was yanked, catching a front paw as the bear reared angrily. Within moments, the lance and the spike were driven home into the growling creature, and a fierce struggle began.

When it had become apparent the preceding fall that they would be trapped by winter, the doctor had taken his last four cartridges and hidden them away. The Eskimos knew nothing of them, believing that their ammunition had been expended. These cartridges the doctor intended to use at the last stage of hunger to kill something—perhaps even themselves if their suffering proved too great.

The doctor took one of the cartridges from his pocket, loaded the large-bore, single-shot rifle, and raced outside. He tossed the weapon to one of the hunters, who turned toward the flailing bear and fired at point-blank range. The bear fell, mortally wounded, and the ice shook beneath their feet.

The animal was quickly skinned. Before the butchering began in earnest, the natives hung up the skin atop the snowhouse, carefully laying it out in a lifelike pose. According to legend, the spirit of a dead polar bear that was properly treated by a hunter would share the good news with other bears. The animals would then be eager to be killed by such men, making future hunts successful.

Thick steaks were sliced off the thighs, and, with no thought given to cooking or boiling the meat, the steaming flesh was devoured. More was passed around with bloodied hands until each man had his fill. They then slept, radiating with the inner warmth of full stomachs. When they awoke, they ate again.

They now had an abundance of food, and if they stayed where

they were, by the time they ran low, the seals should be out on the ice in great numbers. The men could then continue their march, hunting along the way to supply their needs. After enduring so much hunger, they were tempted to travel with the promise of adequate nourishment. Yet they had to weigh that benefit against the ice conditions they would be facing as spring turned into early summer.

Situated squarely between them and salvation in Greenland was Smith Sound, thirty miles at its narrowest stretch between Cape Sabine and Annoatok. Their present position south of Cape Sabine prevented a crossing, because the ice in the sound had begun breaking up with the sun's return, and they no longer were hauling the canvas boat they had used last summer to cross gaps of open water known as leads. To make Greenland on foot meant heading farther north along the Ellesmere coast toward the expanse of Kane Basin, where they hoped to find the sea ice solid enough to be traversed on foot. The loop north before heading eastward could add two hundred miles—and several weeks—to their journey, but in this they had no choice.

If they stayed put and waited for abundant game, their fate would be tied to a dangerous race with warmer weather, which could open up so many leads in Kane Basin as to make a crossing without a boat impossible. The onset of fall and an early winter could find them stranded on the Ellesmere shore.

These life-and-death issues weighed heavily on the doctor. The Eskimos were not plagued by any doubt: with Greenland so close, it must be reached at all costs. The doctor decided to honor their well-honed instincts for survival. After more gluttonous eating, the three men set out again, taking with them all the frozen bear meat they could carry.

A new world of trouble soon found them. Unrelenting storms, mountains of ice, fresh snow up to their waists, vicious winds, and impassable snowdrifts impeded their progress and lengthened their course by forcing them to zigzag repeatedly. They reached Cape Sabine after great exertion and long delays, and their food supply was once again exhausted.

Starvation was no stranger to this region, the scene of one of the most tragic incidents in the history of Arctic exploration. In 1881, twenty-four American soldiers, newcomers to the Arctic, set out under the command of U.S. Army Lieutenant Adolphus Greely to conduct scientific observations on the remote northwest coast of Ellesmere. Two years later, after resupply ships failed to arrive, their situation became bleak and the ragtag band retreated south. Following weeks of travel—much of it spent drifting aimlessly on the ice pack of Kane Basin—they made Cape Sabine before being halted by winter. As the weeks passed and food ran out, men began to die. The survivors subsisted on leather from their boots, bits of moss scraped from the rocks, and, eventually, the flesh of their fallen comrades. Alone or in small groups, hungry men—hunting knives in hand—visited the ridge above their camp, where the corpses were piled like logs, and partook of haunting meals that kept them alive. By the time a rescue ship arrived in summer, eighteen men had perished. The six survivors included the leader, Greely, who came under criticism for weak leadership, although poor planning, bad weather, and a lack of sufficient financial and logistical support from the government contributed to the disaster.

Passing through the area, the three travelers grew solemn as they came across human remains, dug up and picked clean by foxes, wolves, and ravens. The two hunters determined that the dead were from their own tribe. Some of the sordid details Cook already knew, but from his companions, Etukishook and Ahwelah, he heard more about the tragic deaths of their people in 1901.

Under a telltale pile of rocks marking a food cache, the carcass of an old seal was found in an oil-soaked bag. It had been caught the year before and placed here by Panikpa, father of Etukishook. Also in the cache was a crude hieroglyphic drawing telling of a loving father's futile search for his lost son and two companions. The meat, along with a pound of salt, had been left as an offering. Eating some now and saving the remainder, they portioned out the salt and eventually devoured every edible part of the seal—meat, blubber, skin—even though it was so rotten that it had the aroma of Limburger cheese.

Heartened at finding the cache, they took it as a good omen.

They pushed farther north, along Bache Peninsula to near Cape Louis Napoleon. Under the ascending sun, soon to offer around-the-clock daylight, nature's incubator had begun to hatch the young of various species; seals, foxes, and bears all experienced the newness of life on the sun-kissed ice cap.

Northern Greenland, home for the natives and the first stepping-stone to home for the doctor, never seemed nearer. Yet they were separated from it by much open water, so they continued north. With the sun upon them and the ice breaking up and the sea beginning to breathe after its winter lock, they still dared to dream they would find a way across.

After two days of hard travel, they found good ice. Turning southeast, they headed back toward the native settlement of Annoatok, which they had overshot because they had been forced so far north. On the back end of the loop their course had taken, they were able to angle toward their destination over steep icy hummocks and through pockets of deep snow.

Inevitably, they would come to open water, which necessitated more detours. When they had eaten all the frozen seal and found nothing to hunt, they began to eat other things again—even their shoelaces and pieces of their boots. On their southward course, they came upon a tall icy ridge. By then, they had so little energy that they had to scramble up it on their hands and knees. At the top, they recognized—not more than a mile away—Annoatok, whence they had departed on their journey a year earlier.

The weary ice men stood weakly and waved, gaunt, dark figures arrayed in rags of fur. Silhouetted against the white backdrop, they were recognized from afar as men in trouble, and dog sledges were dispatched. The three men awaited rescue, huddled together, too exhausted to show any outward signs of joy, although their hearts were beating wildly.

As the sledges pulled up, the dog drivers let out hoots of recognition. Because of their long absence, the three men had been presumed to have perished, and those who saw them could not believe their eyes. The men who had returned from the dead were sights to behold: half human, half beast, rail thin, stringy hair down to their shoulders, and covered with a grounded-in grime that would take more than one immersion in hot water to cleanse.

Ahwelah and Etukishook stood together, facing their tribesmen. They held their distance, and no one said anything at first, but merely gazed in disbelief. All appeared to realize at the same instant that it was not a dream or an illusion, and suddenly everyone seemed to be talking at once.

A tall blond stranger, handsome and rather dashing, stepped forward from one of the sledges and approached the doctor. The two white men were astonished to see the other.

Speaking his own language for the first time in more than a year, the doctor spoke first. "I am Frederick Cook."

The other man looked as if he had seen a ghost. Quickly regaining his composure, he introduced himself as Harry Whitney and added, as if in the parlor of one of his private clubs, "We feel honored to greet you."

The survivors were loaded onto the sledges, and off they went, pulled by howling dogs anxious to return to the village the way horses yearn for the barn. Little was said on the short dash to the village, where the emaciated men were brought in from the cold. A meal was prepared with dispatch by the native women—meat broth, fresh biscuits, hot coffee.

"You have been away for fourteen months," Whitney said when he had a moment with Cook, "with food for two months. How have you done this?"

Cook did his best to satisfy Whitney's curiosity, but at this moment food and sleep were paramount.

Whitney understood, and held off further queries. "Doctor, you are the dirtiest man I ever saw," he said, smiling. "We have a bath ready for you—a tub of hot water, plenty of soap and brushes and big clean towels."

Later, Cook went to the one-room shack he had wintered in a year and a half earlier and left stocked with food and supplies for his return. It was meant to serve, with its priceless store of supplies, as his relief station. He was shocked to find two white men he did not know living in it; all winter they had been partaking of his goods. In addition to the food, there had been skins and ivory tusks worth thousands of dollars. The two interlopers, it turned out, were crewmen from *Roosevelt*, a ship built tough for ice travel and named after the U.S. president, and were on orders of their commander to utilize anything they needed. The skins and ivory had been seized and already taken away.

A bitterness rose within Cook that would not soon abate.

It was April 1909, and *Roosevelt*, having left northern Greenland eight months earlier, was now four hundred miles to the north, and its commander, Robert E. Peary, was leading a large, well-stocked dog sledge expedition northward over the Arctic ice cap attempting to fulfill what he had long considered his rightful destiny: discovering the North Pole.

Isolated from the rest of civilization, Peary had no way of knowing the dramatic declaration Cook was planning to make to the world:

The North Pole had already been reached.

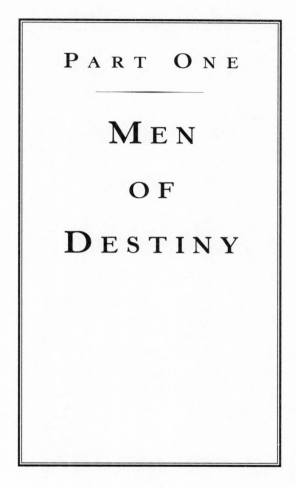

PART ONE

MEN

OF

DESTINY

CHAPTER ONE

CALL OF THE NORTHLAND

FREDERICK ALBERT COOK was five years old when he saw his father in the coffin. The afterimage that stayed with him all his life consisted of two searing details: the under-chin whiskers of his dead father and the mud-colored suit in which he was buried. He would also never forget "the tears and a cold cry which made me shiver . . . at the coffin."

The family lived in an old farmhouse at the fork of two creeks, near Callicoon Depot in Sullivan County, New York. All about them were the rolling, tree-studded foothills of the Catskills, which drained into the Delaware River.

Dr. Theodore Koch, born and educated in Germany, emigrated to the United States in 1848, settling at the foot of the Catskill Mountains, where he began anew his practice of medicine. He changed his surname to the English equivalent, Cook, while serving in the Civil War as a Union Army medical examiner. He and Magdalena Long, also a German emigrant, whose family had fled New York City during an 1850 cholera epidemic, married and had five children—four sons and one daughter. Frederick Albert Cook, born June 10, 1865, two months after the end of the war, was the second youngest.

Although the senior Dr. Cook had a busy medical practice, most of his rural patients paid their bills with homegrown farm goods, and cash was always in short supply. After his death from pneumonia in 1870, years of hardship followed for his family, even though occasionally his widow was able to collect on an old unpaid medical debt in order to buy food and clothing. The boys tried planting crops on the farm of fifteen acres, but most of it was too rocky to till and they had little success. The children received their lessons in a little red schoolhouse four months of the year, and the two older boys found work.

Frederick's inquisitive nature nearly cost him his life at a young age. Fascinated by the lure of a swimming hole, the boy plunged in fearlessly where the water was over his head. He never forgot the ensuing struggle to survive; in the process of churning his arms and kicking, he learned how to swim.

He grew up loving the outdoors and roamed the Catskills, spending nights under the stars and learning outdoor survival skills. Lacking money to buy a sled for winter coasting, he cut young trees and built his own. He soon earned a reputation for building the best and fastest sleds in the region, a skill that served him well in future years.

Eventually, after the oldest brother, William, took a job in New York City, the family moved to Brooklyn, where they hoped to find more opportunity. Deciding that one of her sons should follow in his father's footsteps and become a doctor, Magdalena selected Frederick. To this end, he was kept in school longer than his brothers, although he was still expected to help support the family. He hired on at a wholesale produce market where he started at 2 a.m. Though he often worked until noon, Frederick managed to graduate on time from Public School no. 37. About his formative years, Cook would write that he felt "restless" and had "a yearning for something that was vague and undefined."

After working as an office boy for a real estate company, he started a small printing business, which he ended up selling to buy a milk delivery route. Door-to-door milk service was a somewhat novel idea at the time, but soon he was adding customers. As demand increased, he bought a horse and, with the help of his brothers, built a wagon designed to transport the glass bottles that were coming out on the market. He had several employees and wagons in operation by the time he entered medical school. The early hours of the milk business—starting at 1 a.m. every day—allowed him by 10 a.m. to be in class, where he stayed until 4 p.m. He studied at home each evening and then slept until it was time to begin his milk route, blessed, as he would be for the rest of his life, with the ability to get by on only a few hours' sleep a night.

During a massive blizzard in 1888, New York City came to a standstill, leaving Frederick unable to make milk deliveries or attend class. To replenish the family's coal supply, he rigged up sledge runners on an eighteen-foot boat built by one of his brothers for summertime at the beach, and hitched two horses to it. On the way back from the coal yard, he picked up other customers willing to pay a premium for coal deliveries. He was in the coal business around the clock for a week, and before the specially outfitted boat was retired, a photographer took a picture of him standing with his innovation. The image ran in a magazine as an example of individual resourcefulness during the storm.

For two years, he attended Columbia's College of Physicians and Surgeons at Twenty-third Street and Fourth Avenue, making the commute starting on horsecars that rattled through the streets of Brooklyn before depositing him at the ferry terminal. After crossing the East River to Manhattan, he walked to school. When the Columbia medical department moved more than thirty blocks farther uptown, he transferred to New York University, at the foot of Twenty-sixth Street.

The following year, Cook, twenty-four, became engaged to Mary Elizabeth Forbes. Known as Libby, she was an attractive blonde of medium height and build. Having noticed her previously at church, he was properly introduced to her at a Methodist social. A pioneering woman stenographer—most such positions were then held by men—she worked in the offices of a Manhattan shoe factory. After a short courtship, they married in 1889. Even as Frederick strove to finish his medical studies, their life together was idyllic for a time. Libby soon became pregnant, and they shared the joyful anticipation of the new arrival. Early the following year, Libby gave birth at home to a baby girl, who lived only a few hours; then she herself struggled for a week battling a rampant infection.

In the midst of the ordeal, Cook's presence was required in down-town New York for his final university examinations. He rushed through the tests, anxious to return to his young wife's sickbed. By foot, ferry, and horsecar, he reached their modest rented home in Brooklyn and hurried to Libby's side. He remained with her throughout the night, and the next day labored with their family physician in an effort to save the woman he loved.

As evening approached, there was a knock at the door. A messenger handed Cook an envelope from his school. Inside was a card bearing his full name, and under it a single word. Sitting on the edge of Libby's bed, he showed her the card with the simple inscription "Passed." A smile took shape on her weary face. Libby died that evening, in his arms.

He walked the streets that night with no destination. The gas streetlights barely illuminated his path through a thick fog that draped him like a shroud. He could not comprehend the unfairness of life—his baby and wife taken in rapid succession as he stood on the cusp of a professional career for which he had worked so hard. Miles of Brooklyn's streets passed beneath his aimless steps that night before he returned to the empty structure that had so recently been a home filled with laughter and love.

Emotionally shattered, he agreed to move to Manhattan with his mother and sister. Before doing so, he sold his interest in the milk delivery business to his brother William. Although his wounded heart was hardly into it, Frederick opened an office in one room of their rented house at 338 West Fifty-fifth Street and hung out his shingle. During the next few months, only three patients sought out the services of the newest and youngest physician in the neighborhood.

In spite of growing "anxiety over the disappearing pennies," he found time for further studies. Seeking escape in books on world travel and exploration, he became intrigued with the published works of Arctic explorers. Among his favorites were two Americans: Elisha Kent Kane, a physician who made his first voyage above the Arctic Circle in 1850 and three years later went farther north than anyone had previously gone, and Charles Francis Hall, leader of the ill-fated Polaris Arctic expedition in 1871, who in his years spent in the Far North demonstrated the value of learning the ways of the Eskimos in order to survive the harsh polar climes.

Alone one gloomy winter day in 1891, Cook read in the *New York Herald* about a new expedition to Greenland being planned by Robert E. Peary, who in the summer of 1886 had attempted to cross the Greenland ice cap before being forced back by storms. The article said that Peary, a Navy civil engineer stationed at the Philadelphia Navy Yard, was seeking expedition members, including a surgeon.

Cook knew instantly what he must do. Of his feelings at that moment, he later wrote, "It was as if a door to a prison cell had opened. I felt the first indomitable, commanding call of the Northland."

ROBERT EDWIN PEARY was a young boy when he, too, lost his father to pneumonia. Born May 6, 1856, in Cresson, Pennsylvania, to Charles and Mary (née Wiley) Peary, the future explorer came from French and British ancestry. His paternal side went back three generations to Stephen Peare (from whose name evolved Peary), a man of the sea who once rounded the Horn on his way to the South Pacific. In the New World, Peary's ancestors on both sides formed a long line of "Mainers," mostly lumbermen.

His father became a successful builder of barrelheads and staves in Pennsylvania. Upon Charles Peary's sudden death, at age thirty, his share of the business amounted to nearly twelve thousand dollars, which went to his widow, Mary, a gentle and pious woman who would be left forever melancholy by her husband's untimely death. With her three-year-old son "Bertie" at her side, she packed their belongings and returned by train to her native Portland, Maine, along with her husband's body for burial.

Mary Peary shared the dark shadows in which she lived with her only child, a boy whom she raised more like a girl, something she knew considerably more about. Implanting in him the idea that he was too weak and delicate to play with other boys, she strove to keep

him from their company. On the rare occasions when he was allowed
out to play, she made him wear a sunbonnet to protect his fair, sensitive skin from sunburn. The bonnet, and a lisp that would betray
him all through life during moments of excitement, led to his being
teased by other boys as a sissy and having to engage in fistfights to
prove otherwise. Returning home bruised and battered only reinforced his mother's determination to keep him safely with her.

For Robert, going away to boarding school at age eight was an
important escape from his mother's protective sphere. His letters
home revealed not only his great devotion to her but also his delight
at having "good times playing with the boys in the gymnasium and
out on the baseball ground."

Peary returned home and entered Portland High School in 1870.
That same year, he fell ill with typhoid fever and nearly died. He
was nursed through the ordeal by his omnipresent mother, who
brought to his bedside books on natural history in the hope of raising his spirits. Before long, he would describe the study of nature as
"a never-failing source of happiness to the earnest seeker after wisdom." When he recovered, he crammed a full school year's worth of
study into three months to catch up with his class.

Mother and son lived as if connected through psyche and mood;
however one turned, the other followed. The lack of a male figure in
his life, and the uncommonly close relationship with his melancholy
mother, shaped his emotional makeup. He could be self-assured,
and also emotionally insecure and filled with self-doubt. He could
be social and likable, and by turns stoic and distant.

He worked hard in school and was one of the speakers at graduation. His address about natural history, now a passion in his life, was
entitled "Nature's Mysteries." It included this question: *What would
man find at the North Pole?*

Peary's academic standing earned him a scholarship to Bowdoin
College, in Brunswick, some thirty miles up Maine's coast from
Portland. It was a move he was not to make on his own. His
mother moved to Brunswick, too, so they could continue to live
together. While there is no record of his objection to her move,
some relatives opposed it, believing that it was time for the young

man to be on his own. To such advice, Mary Peary replied, "I am going to college."

Peary chose a civil engineering major and continued on track as a highly competitive student. By graduation in 1877, he was Phi Beta Kappa and ranked second in his class of fifty-two. Instead of setting off to make his mark on the world, however, he agreed to move with his mother to the isolated hamlet of Fryeburg, on Maine's southwestern border with New Hampshire.

Upon their relocation, he was quickly drained of the confidence and verve he had found at Bowdoin. He fought the doldrums with long walks alone in the hills, where his love of nature seemed to revive him. Becoming an eager student of taxidermy, he soon won a reputation for skill and artistry in the mounting of game birds. He was also hired to make a survey of Fryeburg, his first real job.

A notice posted in post offices and colleges around the country in early 1879 caught Peary's attention. Applications were invited from qualified young men for four vacant positions as draftsmen with the U.S. Coast and Geodetic Survey in Washington, D.C. Without telling anyone for fear of embarrassment in the event of rejection, Peary applied, sending in the Fryeburg land survey as a work specimen. The survey by the former star student earned him one of the coveted jobs, which resulted in his leaving home, and his mother finally, at age twenty-three. But six months later, in writing of his broken engagement with a Fryeburg girl, he made it a point to assure his mother of her continued supremacy in his life. "Now it is you and I only, my Mother, and Providence permitting I will make the coming years of your life happy enough to make up in some degree for the sorrow, pain and anxiety. . . ."

Peary eventually grew weary of the realities of his job, which entailed for the most part endless hours of lettering practice in a windowless office of the Coast Survey Building, on Capitol Hill. He wrote his mother asking for permission to quit, explaining he had a "resistless desire to do something," adding, "I wish to acquire a name which shall make my Mother proud and which shall make me feel that I am peer to anyone I may meet." Three weeks passed before she replied. When she did, she advised him to be glad he had "a respectable job" and to be "more contented." That night he penned in his diary, "I bow to her wishes though it may change my entire life."

The following year, Peary was drawn to a public notice that invited young civil engineers to apply for a commission in the U.S. Navy. As before, he did not tell anyone of his intentions, for fear of failure.

After submitting an application and being interviewed by an examining board, Peary was awarded a commission and assigned to the Navy's department of yards and docks. Three years later, having distinguished himself on several construction projects—including overseeing the building of an iron pier in Key West—he was assigned along with other naval engineers to survey a proposed ship canal to connect the Atlantic and the Pacific oceans. He was dispatched to Nicaragua, one locale being considered along with a site in Panama.

With lofty ambitions, he set sail south in 1884. At the ship's rail as they steamed past San Salvador, Peary's thoughts were of Columbus, "whose fame," he wrote to his mother that night, "can be equaled only by him who shall one day stand with 360 degrees of longitude beneath his motionless feet and for whom East and West shall have vanished—the discoverer of the North Pole."

Upon his return from Nicaragua the following year, Peary found in a used-books store an account of a failed attempt by Swedish explorer Baron A. E. Nordenskiöld to cross the Greenland ice cap in 1883. He learned there had been only three ventures of any distance into Greenland's rugged interior, and no one had yet crossed it. The Arctic had interested him since his earliest readings on natural history, and "a chord had vibrated intensely" within him when he had read, as a boy, Elisha Kent Kane's *Arctic Explorations*. Peary now felt "touched again," and devoured all he could on the subject. Deciding he must see for himself "this great mysterious interior," he set out to raise funds for an expedition to Greenland. When he failed, he outfitted himself and bought passage on a sealer with $500 borrowed from his mother, and left in April 1886. The summerlong trip provided adventure, Arctic experience, and some reported success—

upon his return he claimed to have penetrated the ice cap of Greenland one hundred miles inland, farther than anyone before him. In a precursor of debates to follow, doubts were expressed by other explorers—at first privately and later publicly—about the reliability of the young naval engineer's navigation on this trip, and his resultant claim.*

In a letter to his mother, written from Washington upon his return, Peary revealed perhaps his strongest motive for the difficult journeys yet before him:

> My last trip brought my name before the world; my next will give me a standing in the world. . . . I will be foremost in the highest circles in the capital, and make powerful friends with whom I can shape my future instead of letting it come as it will. . . . Remember, mother, I *must* have fame.

Robert E. Peary's course in life had been set.

PHILADELPHIA
Spring 1891

Cook had nearly given up hope of hearing from Peary.

The very day he had read the article about Peary's upcoming journey to Greenland, Cook had posted a letter, stating his medical qualifications and his desire to join the expedition. Two months passed before he received a telegram instructing him to come to Philadelphia for a meeting. He left immediately.

Two inches shy of six feet, Cook combed his ash-blond hair

---

*Dr. Fridtjof Nansen, Norwegian explorer, scientist, future Nobel laureate (1922), and in 1888 the first to cross the frozen continent of Greenland, reported in his book *The First Crossing of Greenland* (1890), "Peary's longitude was only based, as it seems, on some observations of altitude. . . . These so-called 'simple altitudes' are notoriously uncertain for longitude reckoning. . . . The distance of a hundred miles from the margin of the ice cannot, therefore, be considered as established beyond all doubt."

straight back. His most remarkable feature was his eyes: large, expressive orbs that revealed a sensitivity befitting a man trained to help those in need. His nose and ears were oversized, and he had the strong hands of a laborer. His wide shoulders on a sinewy frame suggested someone who could put his back into a chore. A personable fellow, he was quick to smile and had a soft, melodious voice, characteristics that caused people to like him upon first meeting.

When he arrived in Philadelphia and found the Peary apartment overlooking Fairmount Park, Cook rang the bell and waited with trepidation. He wore a black suit and starched white shirt topped with a stiff winged collar around which a wide necktie was trussed in a four-in-hand knot.

A well-dressed woman came to the door, and Cook identified himself to her. She introduced herself as Josephine Peary. Invited in, he followed the tall, poised woman into the apartment, where they came upon Peary in the drawing room.

Peary had met Josephine, the attractive daughter of Herman H. Diebitsch, a professor at the Smithsonian Institute, at a Washington, D.C., party in 1884 when he asked her for a dance. A cultivated young woman of boundless energy known in her youth as Peppy, she had attended business college and served as valedictorian at graduation, delivering what was then a daring address on society's dismissal of women as fully contributing human beings in the workplace. After college, she won through competitive testing a position with the U.S. Census Bureau. Peary courted her as his travels—including his first trip to Greenland—allowed. He proposed marriage in 1887, following a second posting to Nicaragua as engineer in chief, during which he designed a new type of lock gates for the proposed canal, an invention for which he was awarded a U.S. patent. The couple were married in summer 1888. On their New Jersey honeymoon, they took along Mary Peary, determined to maintain her position in the life of her thirty-two-year-old son. Just months earlier, Peary, writing from Nicaragua, had tried to appease his mother's growing irritation over the attention he was paying Josephine: "I have written you as often as I have Jo," he explained, "though not always at the same time. Sometimes I have written to you, the next time to her."

Peary, dressed in a blue wool Navy officer's uniform, struck an impressive figure. Over six feet tall, he had a barrel-chested muscular frame, full head of reddish blond hair, and discolored walrus mustache. His icy blue eyes emitted a stare that could pierce any subordinate.

The two men shook hands.

Cook had reason to be anxious. He had no experience whatsoever as an explorer, and as for any knowledge of northern latitudes, he knew them only from long winters in the Catskills. In fact, the trip to Philadelphia was his first overnight journey outside of New York State. Peary, on the other hand, was an experienced explorer and world traveler, having been on extended trips to Central America and the Arctic.

Peary, too, had his anxieties. After returning from his earlier trip to Greenland and while trying to garner support for another effort to cross the frozen continent, he was devastated to read reports in 1888 that Norwegian explorer Fridtjof Nansen had succeeded in doing just that. Peary was shaken by the news, looking so terribly stricken when he came home the afternoon he heard the news that Josephine thought someone in the family must have died. It sent him into a long depression and filled him with self-doubt. In the years since, he had been trying diligently to get back to the Far North and accomplish something noteworthy, but only in the past several months had he cobbled together the necessary backing for the undertaking. He had raised funds from various sources, including professional groups—Philadelphia's Academy of Natural Sciences would have some of its members along for the ride on the expedition's ship in return for financial support—as well as his own lectures and an advance sale to a newspaper of the rights to his letters from the voyage. Peary had also secured paid leave from the Navy, which currently had him stationed at League Island Naval Base helping design a new dry dock.

The two men sat across from each other, and Josephine served tea.

Peary launched into an explanation of the ambitious aim of his yearlong expedition, declaring that he proposed to determine the northern limit of the continent of Greenland, a geographical mys-

tery at the time. Cook understood that the west-to-east line had
already been taken by Nansen, and that retracing that course would
generate little interest. He thought Peary's idea to make a push into
the unexplored north was a sound one.

Peary segued into a discussion about the techniques of fieldwork,
telling of the surveys he had made in Nicaragua and his earlier trip
to Greenland. He said he considered himself a capable civil engineer, but admitted that acquiring a scientific background of Arctic
regions had not been part of his schooling or training. His plans for
the expedition, he explained, included taking experts in such fields
as meteorology, geology, and biology. What Peary hoped for, he
went on, was that Cook, in addition to serving as expedition physician, could handle some of the scientific work—specifically ethnol-
ogy and anthropology—given his medical school studies.

Medical education at the time included what was considered the
entire realm of science. But Cook believed himself overloaded with
"undigested book knowledge of little immediate use." For example,
one of the most exciting topics of the day in college was evolution,
with biology—then called natural history—the groundwork for all
scientific thought. Students so inclined were well prepared to argue
against every phase of religious philosophy. Cook had absorbed
"much of this insurgency," although the net impact on him was to
make him increasingly tolerant of other religious cultures he
encountered, a valuable attribute when it came to his future dealings with indigenous peoples. Peary advised Cook to read up on
anthropology and in the process assemble books that might serve as
a valuable reference library for the trip.

It hadn't taken Cook long to size up Peary, whom he found to be
"a thoroughly decent fellow and a strong character." He also liked
Josephine, who stayed in their presence for much of the visit,
adding insightful comments. Near the end of the afternoon, the
Pearys, who called each other Jo and Bert and appeared to be an
affectionate couple, invited Cook to stay for dinner, but he declined
because he had an appointment that evening in New York.

Cook felt the meeting was nearing an end and that it had gone
well, but the doctor realized that Peary, nine years his senior, hadn't

made him a formal offer to join the expedition. When they were alone, Peary turned toward Cook with his steely stare.

"The life up there under the Pole is terribly hard," Peary said. "We will be as much out of touch with the world as we would on some other planet. Some of us more than likely will never return. I advise you not to go if there is any fear in your heart."

"I am willing to take the chance," Cook said, showing no outward hesitation but shivering inwardly at the hard Arctic life described by Peary. "This is my great opportunity and I won't be held back by dread of hardships."

Peary had heard what he needed to hear. The two men agreed that Cook would serve as surgeon and ethnologist, for which he would be paid no more than what the other members of the expedition were to be paid upon their return: the sum of fifty dollars for more than a year's work.

Upon their handshake—with a contract to be signed later—Cook became an official member of Peary's inaugural full-scale expedition to the Arctic, where both men, together and separately, were to live out their destinies.

CHAPTER TWO

NORTH GREENLAND EXPEDITION

On a warm, sunlit afternoon in early June 1891, a schooner-rigged auxiliary steam vessel was towed from a pier at the foot of Baltic Street in Brooklyn. Her complement of sails was discolored from age and her wooden decks stained with the oil of countless slaughtered seals and whales.

Under her own power, the fifty-year-old barkentine of 280 tons, her bow and hull sheathed with iron for Arctic travel, swung out into the East River. Up the bustling waterway, ferryboats and steamships saluted the publicized departure with shrill whistles and dipping flags, as passengers on deck waved white handkerchiefs and gave hail and farewell.

Many in the crowd that had appeared dockside for the departure of SS *Kite* were there to glimpse the determined young woman the newspapers had been clamoring about. Never before had an American woman joined an Arctic expedition, and the sentiment of the day was divided: she was either very brave or extremely foolish. And why was her husband allowing her to go on an all-male expedition? Or, more pointedly, why had he agreed to *take* her?

After goodbyes from friends and strangers alike, Josephine Peary had gone to her cabin to find it filled with flowers. Among them was a bouquet from Cook, who had been told by Peary, when he mentioned that his wife would be coming along, that it was to be a second honeymoon for the couple.

If Cook had any reservations about Josephine's participation, he kept them to himself. The same could not be said for other expedition members, all of them young, single men. The idea of sharing what would be close quarters with a married couple for more than a year had not gone over well.

As to the wisdom of taking his wife on the expedition, Peary would explain that she was healthy and enthusiastic and that neither of them saw any reason why she could not endure conditions and environment similar to those in which Danish wives in Greenland passed years of their lives. "First and foremost," Peary acknowledged, was her "desire to be by my side." No doubt it was mutual. He noted, too, that Josephine had a strong inclination for the outdoor life, as when he had taken her "tramping" in the rugged woods of western Maine and she showed that she considered, like him, the open air "the breath of life."

Apart from the ship's crew and nine scientists and professors from Philadelphia's Academy of Natural Sciences along as passengers, the remainder of the seven-member North Greenland expedition party—set to disembark at the farthest northern point attained by the vessel—was composed of men who shared little except an appetite for adventure.

A young Norwegian skiing champion and recent arrival in the United States, Eivind Astrup, who, like the others, happened upon a notice in the newspaper seeking volunteers, was the party's only expert skier. Cheerful and broad-shouldered, Astrup, twenty, was still learning English but already knew about traveling on ice. He was the only member, other than Peary, to have been tested by the severe climatic conditions in northern latitudes.

Another of the flood of young men who wrote to Peary asking to be considered was Longdon Gibson, twenty-six, of Flushing, New York. He was a marksman and experienced hunter and climber. A member of the Brown-Stanton party that had explored the Grand Canyon the preceding year, Gibson had learned boat handling while

shooting rapids. At six-foot-three, solid and well conditioned, he
would add a physical presence to the team.

John M. Verhoeff, twenty-five, a geologist from St. Louis,
admitted in his introductory letter to Peary that he rated his
chances of returning alive no better than one in ten. A Yale graduate, Verhoeff had also studied meteorology. When Peary did not
answer his initial query, Verhoeff wrote again, making an offer not
to be refused: if selected, he would contribute $2,000 to the expe-
dition, an amount that nearly covered the charter fee to hire *Kite*
and her fifteen-man crew.

The final member of the party was Matthew Henson, of average
height and slightly underweight. A twenty-four-year-old Negro of
freeborn parents from Maryland, he was orphaned by the time he
was seven. At twelve he went to sea as a cabin boy, sailing from one
exotic port to the next for five years. Upon quitting the sea, he
worked various jobs—stevedore, bellhop, night watchman—before
settling in Washington, D.C., where he was hired as a stock boy by
one of the capital's most prominent hatters and furriers. He was in
the backroom one day when the owner asked him to find a size
seven and three-eighths pith helmet. Bringing the requested hat to
the front of the store, Henson heard his boss say, "This is the boy I
was telling you about, Lieutenant."

Standing ramrod straight in a U.S. Navy officer's uniform was a
tall man with bushy hair the color of burnt sand. "My name is
Peary," he said as he tried on the sun helmet. "I need a boy to go
with me to Central America, as a valet. Keep my clothes and quarters clean. Must be honest with regular work habits."

Henson jumped at the chance to travel to faraway places again.

After a year in Nicaragua, Henson returned reluctantly to his
stock boy job. Soon, Peary found him a job more to his liking at the
Philadelphia Navy Yard as a messenger. It was there, working for
Peary again, that Henson learned about the upcoming expedition to
Greenland and eagerly volunteered, even though he was a newly-
wed, having married in April 1891. His position, as described by
Peary, would be to serve as his "body-servant."

Peary seemed to harbor no doubts about Henson's fitness for Arctic duty. Henson secretly did, however, wondering whether a man of his race, whose ancestors had lived for centuries in the tropical heat of Africa, could withstand the opposite in climatic conditions. But when confronted in an offensive tone by a naval officer who suggested that no Negro could survive subzero cold, Henson expressed such confidence in his ability to do so that the officer promised to pay him one hundred dollars if he returned "without any fingers or toes frozen off."

As *Kite* sailed into the open waters of Long Island Sound, conversation ceased and all onboard fell silent with their own thoughts.

Josephine, who had come back on deck for their boisterous departure from port, returned to her cabin. Looking at the bouquet sent by Cook, she later wrote in her diary, she felt the first pangs of homesickness with the realization that once these withered she wouldn't see another rose for a long time.

Standing at the rail amidship, Cook understood that the year to come would be an education as well as an adventure. He already had an inkling that "pioneering along the borders of the unknown" could become his chief vocation.

Two days earlier, Peary had presented Cook with a four-page typed contract with "F.A. Cook" penned into nine blank spaces. The boilerplate contract did not describe his specific duties, only that he was to "obey all directions and fully carry out all instructions" by Peary. As Cook read the provisions, he saw that he was not to write or publish any book or other narrative that pertained to the expedition until one year after the "official narrative of said expedition, approved by Peary, had been published and offered for sale." Cook signed "Frederick A. Cook M.D." on the last page underneath Peary's bold "R. E. Peary U.S.N." The signatures were curiously dissimilar. Cook's was cramped and utilitarian, while Peary's had the thick, bold sweeps that would become his lifelong trademark and that could have been caused only by his pressing the point of the pen onto the paper in a conscious effort to make an eye-catching inscription.

Every nook and cranny below deck was crammed with supplies and equipment. Topside, the deck was strewn with boxes and crates—lashed down to prevent shifting at sea—and laden with coal, leaving only narrow aisles. The stench of the old vessel with its oily bilge water was nauseating, and this, along with pitching decks in heavy seas, was to cause severe discomfort among newcomers to shipboard travel.

The expedition's equipment was modest and inexpensive, but they did have a full larder: a year and a half worth of food, including tea, coffee, sugar, milk, evaporated vegetables, compressed pea soup, biscuit, cocoa, and pemmican, a dried food made of meat, fat, a little sugar, and currants packed in tins—long a staple for polar expeditions because it did not spoil. They had only a small amount of fresh meat, which would not keep long aboard ship anyway; they intended to hunt game at their winter camp. They had lumber and timber to build sledges and living quarters, snowshoes and skis, guns and ammo, rubber boots for the ice, stoves and tins of alcohol fuel, extra woolen clothing, cameras and film.

After proceeding cautiously through fogbound seas for two weeks, *Kite* became hemmed in by ice in the Belle Isle Straits at the northern tip of Newfoundland. The ship was secured to an iceberg, and block ice was taken aboard to replenish the water supply. A playful snowball fight broke out one afternoon, as they waited for the summer breakup to progress. On the third day, a narrow passage through the ice suddenly appeared, and *Kite* took it.

For the next several days the vessel was tossed on rough seas, during which time most passengers stayed in their bunks, too sick to eat or move about. By the time the gale let up, they had been pushed far into the Davis Strait.

In the mist off the starboard bow lay their first sight of Greenland, the mysterious land discovered by Norsemen five hundred years before Columbus arrived in America. Although its perimeter was not then known, Greenland would prove to be a great pear-shaped island nearly 1,500 miles long and 900 miles across at its widest. Excepting the southern tip and some rocky fringes, it was all ice up to two miles thick at its center.

Everyone came on deck for the view. Steep, black cliffs two thousand feet high with towering tops covered by sparkling snow rose vertically from the sea. Dwarfing these majestic fortresses from the rear was an ice dome reaching two miles into the sky. In front of the coastal cliffs sat gleaming icebergs of all sizes and shapes—some azure blue and others pure white—waiting to break free and be launched into the sea.

They followed the shoreline north until putting in at the Danish settlement of Godhavn, on the island of Disko, for a brief stop. The highlights of the visit were a European-style dinner as the guests of the governing Danish official and his wife, and a hike up a 2,400-foot summit from which the icebergs dotting the horizon looked like an armada under full sail.

Then it was on to Upernavik, the most northern Danish settlement, consisting of four frame houses, a tiny church, and a scattering of native turf huts built into the hillsides. They were properly greeted by the governor and his wife, and did some duck hunting, bagging several dozen and finding more than a hundred eggs to fry up for breakfast.

With no doctor in residence, Cook was asked to treat the infirm. He took his ship's medical bag and made house calls, even performing minor surgery on one Eskimo—removing a bone fragment from a badly healed broken arm.

The next morning they departed, making their way slowly through the floating ice that marked the entrance to the formidable Melville Bay ice pack. With stops and starts as the ice allowed, they sailed on. Several afternoons were spent by Cook, Astrup, Gibson, and Henson measuring and sawing the lumber for the structure they planned to build at their winter camp.

On July 14, after standing on the bridge as *Kite* butted her way through the ice, Peary went below to warm up. When he came back on deck, he stepped behind the wheelhouse to glance over the stern. The vessel at that moment was reversing its engine—a back-and-forth maneuver was often used by the experienced captain and capable ice master, Richard Pike, to gain forward momentum for the reinforced bow to slice through the ice.

At that instant, a heavy chunk of ice jammed the rudder. The wheel was torn from the helmsman's grip, spinning so wildly that its spokes were invisible. Simultaneously, the heavy iron tiller swung over, striking Peary in the leg.

Josephine reached her husband first. She found him standing unsteadily on his left foot, looking "pale as death."

"Don't be frightened, dearest," said Peary, who later revealed he had heard his leg snap. "I have hurt my leg."

He was carried to a cabin below. Ice-cold from shock, he was covered with blankets and given a shot of whiskey. His boot was cut off and trousers torn open. Both major bones of the right leg were fractured below the knee.

Cook, along with several doctors from the Academy of Natural Sciences, examined the leg. They concurred that the break was a clean one, and it was easily set. The leg was rested in a cotton-padded box with room for swelling. Cook administered an injection of morphine to help Peary sleep.

The next day, after checking for infection, Cook dressed the wounded leg and fashioned a sturdy splint to further immobilize it. He told Peary he would have to remain bedridden and not put any weight on his leg for a month.

The first several nights Peary suffered mightily. More painkillers and sedatives were administered; delirium and sleeplessness followed.

Day and night, Josephine and Cook took turns nursing him. At one point, Josephine asked her husband, withering in pain, if he could tell her what she could possibly do to make him more comfortable.

"Oh, my dear, pack it in ice until some one can shoot it!"

There was hushed talk among expedition members as to the advisability of continuing on, given Peary's incapacitating injury. Even Josephine found herself wishing she could take him "to some place where he can rest in peace." No one dared broach the subject with Peary. In answer to anyone who asked, Cook shared his opinion that their leader would have a full recovery, and by spring—when most of the expedition's work was planned—he should be fine.

In the small hours of July 26, Peary was awakened by Captain

Pike and informed that *Kite* was abreast of McCormick Bay, two miles north of Cape Cleveland, and that because of unbroken ice to the north they could proceed no farther. *Kite* would soon have to turn for home or risk being icebound until next year.

Peary gave the order for his team to disembark and set up winter camp.

When it was time, the leader was carried off the ship, lashed to a plank.

CHAPTER THREE

ARCTIC TENDERFOOTS

COMPARED WITH REGIONS they had seen on their course of more than a thousand miles up the coast, the spot where they ended up was a desolate land. Although they were in position for exploring northern Greenland come springtime, there appeared to be few prospects for game and no signs of natives in the area.

Their first night ashore, a tent was set up and some supplies stacked inside. Everyone except Peary and Josephine rowed back to the ship for another load, but before they could return, a violent storm rolled in and the ship was forced to move farther away from shore. The couple spent the night sitting on boxes in the 7-by-10-foot canvas tent, which the wind tore at and rain leaked through. Josephine feared that every unrecognizable sound outside was a polar bear about to burst in and devour them. They had no weapon with them, and her husband was incapable of outrunning trouble. Not wishing to worry him, she said nothing about her terrible fears. At one point during the long night, she heard some peculiar grunts and snorts coming from the direction of the beach. Cautiously, she peered out. In a section of open water just in front of them, several white whales were frolicking. She was mesmerized by their graceful movements; they seemed to be chasing each other the way children play tag.

Work began in earnest the next day after the remainder of the expedition's gear was unloaded and *Kite*, amid cheerful and enthusiastic goodbyes, turned for home. The prefabricated frame for a two-room structure quickly went up on a rocky, sandy flat adjacent to a stream trickling with glacial runoff. After boarding up and tar-papering the walls, they christened their new home Red Cliff House, after a row of reddish cliffs to the south.

The largest room served as the men's quarters, with five bunks, a potbellied stove, a long table for meals, a workbench, and storage space. The Pearys' room was furnished with a double bed behind draped curtains, a bookcase filled with the expedition's library, and a small table.

They were situated on the eastern shore of McCormick Bay on the isolated northwest coast of Greenland. The bay was mostly covered with ice, thin in some places. Inland, much of the winter snow cover had melted during the summer. When they looked more closely, they were heartened to find flowers and grass, a few birds singing, and signs of small game. In the bay, they spotted seals and walrus, although no one had any idea how to prey upon them.

Arctic tenderfoots dropped in one of the cruelest environments on Earth, they would have to learn how to survive as they went along. Even Peary had no experience this far north—latitude 78 degrees, some seven hundred miles from the Pole. His previous trek to Greenland had been five hundred miles to the south, and he had been gone only five months, through summer into early fall. He had never wintered over in the Arctic.

One of the first things Josephine realized in setting up house-keeping was that they had neglected to bring a broom. Before long she made a makeshift one, using bird feathers. Instead of going to the market as she would at home, she daily went into the supplies storehouse and selected canned goods to go with the next day's meals. She would bring into the kitchen beans or peas or corn or tomatoes, along with peaches or pears or plums or apricots, placing the frozen cans on a shelf next to the stove to thaw out. Flour, sugar, tea, and coffee were delivered to the kitchen in fifty-pound tins. This fare was complemented with the results of any successful hunt, which included everyone's favorite, fresh venison, as well as birds and bear, the latter of which no one liked and was soon dropped from the menu. Also, hot biscuits and fresh cornbread were served daily. The cooking was done on kerosene oil stoves, while the interior of Red Cliff was heated by stoves that burned coal, an ample supply of which had been offloaded from *Kite*.

An integral part of the expeditionary plan was to obtain the assistance of local Eskimos for help in building sledges, traveling across the ice, and hunting, because game was needed for fresh meat as well as for fur and skins for winter clothing. There was also the matter of obtaining trained dogs to pull their sledges.

The Pearys had brought from home two large Newfoundland dogs, although Jack and Frank were so domesticated as to be useless for hunting or any work. The plan, in the event Eskimo dogs were unavailable, was for the men to pull the sledges across the inland ice of Greenland come spring, as had been done with varying degrees of success on previous Arctic expeditions. However, no one was looking forward to that thankless, backbreaking task. They had all heard the dreadful stories about the icy graves of human sledge haulers.*

Cook, as second in command, assumed added responsibilities while Peary was still bedridden. Chief among these was to find local natives and persuade some to camp nearby. Most previous expeditions up the Greenland coast, including those by Americans Elisha Kent Kane, Adolphus Greely, and Dr. Isaac Hayes and all the expeditions of the British, who tended to make the world English wherever they ventured, had dismissed the value in utilizing the knowledge and experience of Eskimos. Peary and Cook agreed that this was a mistake.

A whaleboat was fitted out for a cruise on the bay looking for signs of natives. Gibson and Astrup, expert boatmen and hunters,

---

*The unburied remains of members of Sir John Franklin's expedition, which set out in 1845 to find the Northwest Passage, were found on King William Island in 1859, thirteen years after their demise on an icy trail strapped to overweight sledges—loads of up to two thousand pounds per sledge pulled by British seamen—filled with much useless cargo of their officers. The contents included monogrammed silver plates, blue delftware china, brass curtain rods, the ornaments of ceremonial military dress such as sword belts and gold lace, the silver prize medals of officers won at university for mathematics and medicine, and even a mahogany writing desk.

were included in the party, as was Verhoeff. Josephine and Henson stayed at Red Cliff to care for Peary, who during his confinement to bed had turned into a difficult patient.

The whaleboat passed a rocky island with a huge black cliff. In one of its crevasses was a great rookery of birds, mainly nesting ducks. The party approached quietly. When the birds startled and took flight, the men raised their guns and shot into the moving wall. Their loud reports echoed against the rocks, as waves of birds fell from the sky. They scooped the feathered bodies off the water's surface, taking as many as they could carry aboard the boat in canvas bags.

Before they reached shore, an argument broke out between Gibson and Verhoeff over the number of birds shot. When Verhoeff, who had a cantankerous streak, accused the bigger man of being a liar, Gibson grabbed him by the nape of the neck and tossed him overboard like unwanted cargo.

Pulling into a natural boat harbor with a sandy beach, Gibson made a campfire from lumber scraps. They had been on the water for twenty-four hours with little food and no sleep, doubtless the main reason for rising tensions. As an unhappy Verhoeff warmed up from his submersion, ducks were roasted. They ate like gluttons and slept soundly on the sand around the fire.

Hours later Verhoeff awoke everyone in alarm, saying he had seen a bear in the nearby rocks. Each grabbed his gun and readied himself to defend against the marauder, when out from the rocks stepped a small, dark man. The man, frightened at the reception, darted back behind the rocks. They put down their guns. Hoping to appear friendly, they spoke and laughed among themselves, stoked the fire, and put more ducks on the spit. The man came out and cautiously approached.

"*Chimo,*" he said, with a curious smile. It sounded like a welcome.

He was dressed in a garment sewed together from bird skins, with the feathers worn next to the body for warmth. Over that was a sealskin wrap with the fur on the outside, and a close-fitting hood attached to the neck. He had no visible weapon, not even a knife. How could that be in this untamed territory? Did the native have companions with weapons hiding in the rocks?

Mulling over these thoughts, the men were keenly aware of their vulnerability. They were only four in number and had no large ship with them. Stories of "wild men" this far north did not tell of their friendliness, although there was no record of overt hostility. They sometimes visited ships and were happy with receiving gifts, but usually kept to themselves. They spoke a language different from that of the Eskimos in southern Greenland and in every other way were isolated from other tribes and self-reliant in a brutal environment. At stops *Kite* had made above Cape York, a few of these elusive northernmost natives were spotted, but efforts to interact with them had been unsuccessful.

The visitor spoke some more and smiled. The men spoke back and smiled. Neither side understood the other. But if body language was key, it was positive. The men handed over a roast duck, which pleased the Eskimo. He also seemed to like the coffee he sipped, but spat out a spoonful of baked beans.

The visitor was not much more than five feet tall. Gibson, standing next to the native, towered over him by better than a foot. The native looked up at the big white man in awe. From then on, Gibson made most of the attempts to communicate, as it seemed a good idea to let their biggest man do the talking.

Suddenly, the Eskimo turned and hastily retreated to the rocks and disappeared. It was decided, for reasons of diplomacy and safety, not to follow. When the visitor reappeared, he had a young woman at his side. She was about four and a half feet tall, with long black hair pulled back in a bun. Her skin was the same dark bronze as the man's, and like him she had high cheekbones and almond-shaped eyes. The two approached, holding hands like lovers. The woman wore a similar combination of bird skins and sealskin, along with fox-skin trousers that fit into long-legged boots made of tanned sealskin.

"*Ah-ting-ah?*" she asked one of the men, looking him squarely in the eye. Failing to elicit a response, she moved onto the next man.

"*Ah-ting-ah?*"

When all four men failed to answer, she started down the line again. Food was offered, and gifts, but she wouldn't take anything.

"What does the fool woman mean?" Gibson asked softly.

"She is crazy," said Astrup under his breath.

She continued, more intent than ever to have an answer. Standing before the short and slight Verhoeff, who was closer to her size, she took hold of the lapel of his jacket and said urgently, "*Ah-ting-ah?*" Then, she pushed him back gently and said rather flirtatiously, "*Ah-ting-ah.*"

Verhoeff was dumbfounded.

Gibson had an idea. He stood before the woman, peered down into her black eyes and pointed at her, repeating what she had said. "*Ah-ting-ah?*"

"Manee," she said. Pointing to her husband, she said, "Ikwah."

. All along, Manee had been asking their names. How stupid she must have considered them, Cook thought, men unable to speak their own names.

Cook soon realized *ah-ting-ah* was interchangeable for "What is your name?" and "What is the name of this?" When he held up a rock and said, "*Ah-ting-ah,*" Manee told him how to say it in her language. It was a rudimentary start of communication, but it was a beginning. More words were learned and smiles exchanged.

Soon, Manee and Ikwah went into the rocks and brought forth two little girls; a baby riding on Manee's back in a pouch lined in blue-fox fur, her head covered in a skull cap made of sealskin, and a toddler, dressed in layers like her parents and shyly holding her mother's hand.

In the sand, Cook sketched a map of the bay and showed the position of their headquarters. The diagram seemed fully understood. By means of much sign language, an invitation was extended. The couple spoke to each other, then nodded acceptance. They, their children, and all their belongings were soon in the whaleboat.

On the return trip, a native settlement of summer tents was spotted on a small offshore island. They stopped and found twenty-five men, women, and children and about a hundred dogs in residence. The white men, in the company of an Eskimo family, were readily accepted. They spent several days hunting on land and sea with the locals. Before leaving, Cook invited the entire village to cross over the bay when the ice froze solid, and camp near them.

Eskimo hunters with families moved nowhere without their wives, children, dogs, and everything they owned. Given the nature of life on the ice cap, they could not know when or if they would be able to return from a faraway place to someone or something left behind. Also, importantly, a man and woman formed a partnership for survival. The men hunted, fished, and built shelter, while the women cooked, prepared animal skins, and made clothing. Each needed the other to make a decent life in the harsh conditions.

When they returned to Red Cliff with the first Eskimo family, Peary was overjoyed and congratulated Cook. "If we have near one family," he told Cook, "others will come as fast as we can find use for them."

Each morning a hunting party went out, and, under the tutelage of Ikwah, the results were bountiful—the mounted head of a six-point buck reindeer soon adorned the wall at Red Cliff, and grilled venison became a regular entree. Josephine, with her own Colt .38 revolver and cartridge belt strapped to her waist, eagerly joined them and proved to be an accurate shot, which impressed the men. Ikwah in particular became an ardent admirer. One evening, he put his arm around Josephine, who towered over him. She took it for friendship at first, but it soon became clear that the little hunter expected Peary to honor the Eskimo custom of sharing wives with visitors. When it was explained to him by Cook that white men did not have a wife-swapping custom and that it would not be possible, Ikwah looked very disappointed.

One hunt in late August nearly turned tragic. In the whaleboat, Josephine, Cook, Astrup, Gibson, Verhoeff, and Ikwah came across a horde of walrus resting on ice floes. They had previously picked off walrus alone or in small numbers without any difficulty, but this army of a hundred decided to put up a fight. The snarling beasts attacked from all quarters, attempting to hook their tusks into the sides of the boat, which was in danger of capsizing. The men shot in panicked self-defense, one bullet tearing a hole in the hull above the waterline. Through it all, Josephine coolly reloaded and handed back weapons. When it was over, they had killed scores, although they were able to secure only one carcass weighing about a thousand pounds. With just a small knife, Ikwah skinned and sliced it into hunks that could be carried back to camp.

The sun went down in early October and would not return for months. While constant darkness made travel on the ice very dangerous, it was possible to get across the ice by moonlight a few days a month. With the sea ice on the bay now frozen solid, the Eskimos from the island crossed over—men, women, children, sledges, and dogs—joining the growing community. Gifts were handed out—knives for the men, needles for the women, and a small mirror for the children, who took turns making funny faces in it.

More Eskimos joined in the hunt. They secured seals, walrus, and reindeer, providing meat for food, fat for fuel, skins for clothing. Manee and the other Eskimo women, who knew their jobs as well as the hunters knew theirs, were all willing to work in exchange for the small considerations handed out. They cured skins the traditional way—chewing the side of the skin that had no hair until it was macerated and as soft as chamois—and began fashioning winter clothing. Even with rudimentary tools such as animal bones and driftwood used in the absence of needles, they could put twenty stitches to an inch in the thickest hide; with steel needles, they had the touch of a skilled surgeon. They turned out mittens, stockings, and trousers, all made of fur, and suits of winter skins.

Peary was off the crutches that had been fashioned for him by Cook, and was walking about unaided, albeit gingerly. The leader's attitude improved noticeably once he was able to oversee activities again. He was pleased to have a vibrant Eskimo community at his command and working to help him accomplish his Arctic mission. Even though he liked and admired them, and was less offended by their customs and morals than many white explorers who thought they should be converted to Christianity, he believed they valued life only as did a fox or a bear, purely instinctively. Beyond that, he took surprisingly little interest in learning about their culture and beliefs, or even their language, preferring to let Cook and others interpret for him.

The Eskimos, residing in nearby igloos built for the winter, were allowed access to the larger room at Red Cliff House, now nearly buried by snow but comfortably heated. That winter an informal cultural exchange took place, as each group learned the other's language and exchanged stories. They sang, danced, and smoked together. To Josephine's chagrin, the native women followed their custom of removing the tops of their clothing while indoors (Eskimo men did the same) and nonchalantly sat around bare-breasted.

Cook eagerly undertook his ethnological studies of the natives, keeping detailed notes of his findings. An assiduous student of their language, he kept adding to a list of words and phrases that became his dictionary. He visited their igloos and talked to them about their lives, customs, and legends. Once, when there was laughter and joking about the height difference between one of the taller white men and a much shorter native hunter, an eighty-year-old Eskimo offered, "The difference between men is not skyward, or in the length of gut, but in the way an idea gets into and out of the head." To Cook, this gave a new slant on "the wisdom of all ages." He had never heard it so well expressed.

Immersed, Cook began even to look Eskimo; he stopped cutting his hair and changed from woolens to the warmer winter skins worn by the natives. From them, he found they had no government, council, or even tribal chief. They had no priest and only the most elementary religious conceptions, mostly having to do with evil spirits. They did not believe they were the product of one omnipotent God, although they had their own version of Adam and Eve and the creation. Ancient tradition held that there had once been a great flood that killed all but one man. He was on a mountain afterward and struck a rock with a stick. The rock turned into a woman. From those two all subsequent human beings had sprung. The Eskimo notion of heaven seemed to be based on the element of comfort. Heaven, as the natives described it to Cook, was a place with rugged landscapes such as they were accustomed to, but with perpetual sunshine, clear flowing streams, and unlimited walrus, reindeer, and birds. They had no laws, tribal or otherwise—each family was ruled by the man, who could even decide, with the consent of another married man, to trade wives. If no consent was reached, the men wrestled—and the winner took both women.

That winter, Peary began individually photographing the community of natives. Men, women, and children were brought inside Red Cliff one at a time, asked to disrobe, and positioned in front of a wall next to the stove, which was kept lit. From the middle of the room, Peary snapped pictures of them from the front, back, and side with a camera provided by Eastman Kodak, while Henson supplied illumination from a hand-held oil lamp. In this way, natives with names like Nipzangwa, Oongwah, Klayuh, Tungwee, and Meyuk were photographed from a distance of ten feet. The Eskimos were bemused by the routine, especially when it was explained that their bodies would be compared with those of people from other regions of the world. The prospect seemed fine with them, although a few natives, lost in translation, somehow got the notion that the true purpose of the procedure was to make new people.

Cook, who took physical measurements of each subject, noted that their bodies offered natural defenses against the cold. Parts susceptible to frostbite, such as nose, ears, hands, and feet, were smallish. Also, their frames carried a layer of fatty tissue—muscle delineation was nonexistent—that helped retain warmth. The average male stood five feet one inch and a half and weighed 135 pounds; the average woman was four feet eight inches and 118 pounds. The men wore their hair as long as the women and allowed it to fall over their faces during extreme cold to help protect their skin.

As babies began to be born in the Eskimo enclave that winter, Cook learned that the services of a physician were neither required nor welcome. Survival of the fittest began at birth. When a woman went into labor and was about to give birth, she was placed alone in an igloo with enough oil, blubber, and frozen meat to last for two weeks. If she survived and a baby's cry was heard, others would come in to assist mother and child. If all fell quiet in the igloo, it was sealed up and never entered again.

As for the children who were born, Cook learned that for the first two years the child wore no clothing from the waist down and was carried tucked inside the pouch on the mother's back, held closely against her body warmth. A child nursed for four to six years, or until the mother had another baby; the average period between children was four years. When twins were born, both were killed, because it was considered impossible for the mother to carry and otherwise care for two infants. When a mother or father died and left a child under three years of age, the child was strangled with a sealskin thong. It was seen not as a cruel or heartless deed but as the best and quickest fate that could befall such a child in an unforgiving world. It was deemed critical for a child to have two parents, Cook wrote, "in a land where nothing is alive, either animal or vegetable, for months at a time to support a family. There must be a father to kill seal and a mother to foster the baby till it is old enough to care for itself. The Eskimos, one and all, deplore the custom, but it has descended to them from their ancestors, and they see how necessary it is."

Cook plunged eagerly into all realms of Arctic life. He was taught how to ski and snowshoe by Astrup, and from the Eskimos he learned techniques for building igloos and sledges and how to drive a team of their half-wild, wolflike dogs. He also worked on his proficiency with a rifle. Although most of the men had hunting experience, Cook had never shot a deer or other large animal. One morning when a herd of reindeer came in range, Cook "covered himself with glory," according to Peary, by dropping five of them, setting the record for the most kills in a day.

During the long winter night, the doctor observed that expedition members appeared anemic, with a peculiar greenish tint to their skin. He recognized this as symptomatic of scurvy, the debilitating and often fatal disease that befell sailors, polar explorers, and others on deficient diets. Although at the time there was no unanimous agreement as to its exact cause, some placed blame on external factors like lack of exercise.* Scurvy's advance attack was insidious; pain seized feet and legs, rendering them useless; brown spots cov-

---

*Science once and for all established scurvy as a dietary deficiency disease in 1912. Thereafter, an intensive search began throughout laboratories in the United States and Europe to find the chemical makeup of the deficiency. Eventually, it was proven that the disease was caused by a lack of vitamin C, which was discovered by Hungarian scientist Albert Szent-Györgyi of Cambridge University, for which he won the 1937 Nobel Prize in physiology and medicine.

ered lower extremities, and leg bones blackened; gums turned putrid with sores, and nosebleeds were unstoppable.

Descriptions of the sickness appeared in ancient Greek, Roman, and Chinese writings, although the first documented cases were during the thirteenth-century Crusades. During the Napoleonic Wars, Napoleon's plans included luring the British fleet to the West Indies, where he anticipated that a long engagement would render it scurvy ridden and ineffectual as a fighting force. But the British navy had long provisioned its fleet with substantial supplies of fresh lemon and lime juice, which was found to be a reliable preventative, and Horatio Nelson ordered extra juice rations for all his crews. At the same time, the French fleet, devoid of antiscorbutics, was decimated by the disease and ultimately defeated. Scurvy posed a serious health problem in prisoner-of-war camps, such as Andersonville in the Civil War, and it plagued most of the Arctic expeditions of the nineteenth century, including the Greely expedition of 1881, where it rivaled starvation as a major cause of death.

Examining the Eskimos, Cook found their color normal and no other telltale symptoms. Recognizing that diet was a major difference in the lifestyles of the two groups, he reasoned that the expedition party should eat more like the natives, who ingested their meat raw about two-thirds of the time.

"White men get scurvy. The Eskimos do not," he told Peary, asking rhetorically why they shouldn't learn this vital lesson from the natives.

Peary said he was willing to learn from Eskimos, "but not in food. They eat only meat, mostly raw and disagreeable to us. We must have civilized food."

"In the process of cooking and preserving something vital to our lives is in part destroyed," Cook argued. "The effect on all of us half-witted whites is the same, while the Eskimos are in full vigor. Raw meat is the answer."

"If I must eat raw meat, then I will quit this part of the world," Peary said, ending the discussion.

Cook, on his own, began to include raw meat in his diet.

Cabin fever set in at Red Cliff. Gibson and Verhoeff were still not getting along; the latter had taken a serious dislike to both Pearys; Josephine was increasingly annoyed with the filthy conditions; the men were irritated with her because of the standards of attire and polite behavior her company imposed; and Henson was generally distrusted by the men because they believed him to be a spy in their midst, hurrying to Peary to report whatever he learned from being around them.

To escape the pent-up quarters, Cook often slept outside in his reindeer sleeping bag, made for him by Manee, in temperatures as low as minus fifty degrees. He watched the "cold starry heavens" from an eye slit in the bag and considered the evolution of the universe to free his mind from smaller concerns. On such nights, under "beams of light which had been en route for a million years or more," he learned to enjoy his solitude in the Arctic stillness.

In late January, the southern sky began to lighten. The promised return of the sun brought, Cook observed, renewed hope in all as the world expanded from the four walls of Red Cliff to the great outdoors.

Josephine, who had experienced an "uncanny feeling" during the three months of darkness, celebrated the return of sunlight, appreciating that "everything glistened and sparkled . . . almost like fairy land."

Peary couldn't wait to get moving. In mid-February, he set off with Cook and Astrup, climbing two thousand feet above the head of McCormick Bay to check ice conditions and watch the sunrise of 1892. The trip was also a first test of his mended leg, which held up well. For all, however, the exercise proved exhausting; their heart rates increased alarmingly, and they had difficulty breathing after only moderate exercise. Cook diagnosed their reduced endurance as a product of inactivity during the winter and accurately predicted that after a couple of weeks they would regain their former conditioning.

Josephine eagerly joined her husband in his fieldwork, surveying the unexplored gulfs and bays in the region, as well as studying the natives, whom she initially described as "queer little people" who looked "more like wild animals." She was aghast at their unwashed appearance and oily odor, the latter a "very ancient and fish-like smell" that took some getting used to. An Eskimo's idea of a bath, taken perhaps twice a month, shocked her; the natives cleaned themselves by rubbing the greasy dirt from their body with a bird skin, then hung the skin out to freeze and beat off the frozen dirt with a seal bone. Yet she warmed immediately to their friendliness, even though none had seen a white woman before. "*Suna koonah?*" (which one is the woman?), she was asked by one native woman. Once her gender was established, she was openly gawked at.

With the Eskimo women, it was always the same upon first meeting: they were most curious about her manner of dress. Josephine wore the same long dresses and skirts as she had at home, though she added layers of warmth underneath. She had adopted native footwear, long deer skin stocking with fur on the inside and tan sealskin boots that she found most comfortable and warm. The subfreezing temperatures, in fact, did not bother her; she had been colder in New York City. She accounted for the phenomena as having to do with the unusually dry air in Greenland.

Often, a group of natives—men and women—gathered outside the kitchen window to watch as she prepared a meal. The concept was a strange one to them because they never had a regular mealtime; all ate whenever they were hungry if food was available. Since they ate only meat, either raw or warmed in boiling water, and there was nothing resembling bread or vegetables, the preparation of a multicourse meal was a novelty to them.

Once, an Eskimo hunter came to her and asked earnestly whether all the white women where she came from were lazy, too. Unlike the native women, who did most of the daily work that needed to be done except hunting, she did not bring the ice or water from outside, did not make boots for the men, did not cure the skins of animals killed in the hunt. A native woman attended to all the child care duties as well, kept an igloo's blubber-fuel lamp going day and night because it was the only source of light and heat, and when her husband came in from the hunt and took off his skin boots, she chewed on them to keep the insides soft and pliable. By comparison, and as far as any of them could tell, the only thing Josephine did was play with the pots and pans on the stove.

At times, she felt she was living in another world, cut off from all of civilization. On a stroll one day in the new light of approaching spring, she unexpectedly came upon a blooming daisy. She nearly cried; it seemed as if she had crossed paths with a dear old friend.

A month was spent finalizing the expedition's equipment and developing techniques of travel with teams of men and dogs working in coordination. There was a delay in March because of heavy weather, and in April a supply cache was established on a glacier about twenty-five miles inland. The project involved transporting freight over the ice from sea level to 2,500 feet on men's backs. Cook was in charge, while Peary remained at Red Cliff resting up for the upcoming journey.

Finally, the exploring party of Peary, Cook, Astrup, and Gibson—Verhoeff was left behind with Josephine—shoved off from the new supply depot to probe the uncharted interior, the mission for which the expedition had been formed more than a year earlier.

Within a few miles of the jumping-off point, the Eskimo hunters balked en masse, refusing to venture into Greenland's interior, which they fearfully explained to Cook was the domain of the dead where evil spirits resided. Peary grudgingly sent them back with Henson, who had a painfully frozen heel and would be unable to keep up.

Cook wondered whether the Eskimos knew something they did not: the interior of Greenland was "one of the most damnable regions on Earth," with bone-chilling winds and strange skies pulsating with light. It *seemed* like a land of immortal devils, a place not fit for human life.

The four men pushed deeper into this lonely world. Whenever they stopped, they built an igloo as they had been taught by the natives. They had several close calls when their structures collapsed on top of them. Another time, they nearly suffocated in their sleep when they failed to ventilate the igloo properly and were saturated with the condensation of their breath. Cook would come away convinced that some of the mysterious deaths in Arctic regions ascribed to other causes might have been the result of this sort of failed ventilation, which could cause a man in his sleep to choke to death on his own breath.

They proceeded over ice-sheeted lands with three heavily laden sledges. Everyone except Peary drove a dog team, standing atop the upstander, a step at the back of the sledge, wielding a bullwhip used mostly for intimidation. The dogs, their native handlers gone and under the hand of new masters now, were difficult to control at the start, and the pace slowed to only a few miles a day. Peary walked point, leading the way and getting ahead whenever the caravan stopped for the men to lift the sledges over deep ruts in the ice.

When one of the bigger dogs slipped its harness, it lingered in the rear for several days, dodging all efforts at capture. Finally, Astrup on skis and Cook on snowshoes went out and herded the loner toward camp, where the other dogs, after a day in the harness, were being fed. Peary and Gibson fell upon the deserter with a blanket, and in the process Peary was bitten on his hand.

Since it was not snowing, they laid out the sleeping bags on the snow drifts. Promising to make a hot meal that would put everyone in good humor, Cook used a broken pine ski to light a blazing campfire. He kept his word, "for seldom," Astrup later commented, "had any of us eaten a meal with more satisfaction or with greater delight than that. . . . Dr. Cook has a lucky gift of being able to make good and useful things out of strange materials."

As the storms abated and the men and dog teams worked together more smoothly, they increased their average distance to 20 miles a day. When they reached a spot some 130 miles inland from McCormick Bay, they halted. Here Peary announced he would take only one man with him for the rest of the journey. He spoke of the unknown dangers that lay ahead and asked for a volunteer. Cook promptly stepped forward, with Gibson and Astrup only moments behind him.

The doctor knew he would not be going farther. Peary had spoken with him privately before their departure, explaining that in his absence he wished to leave Cook in charge at Red Cliff. If Peary failed to return from the perilous inland journey, Cook was instructed to do whatever he thought necessary for the safety and well-being of Josephine and the others.

To accompany him, Peary selected Astrup, the group's best and strongest man on the ice. Astrup had made no secret of his idolization of Peary.

After rest and a meal, the two parties headed off in opposite directions. Peary and Astrup, with two sledges loaded with a thousand pounds of supplies pulled by thirteen dogs, headed across the barren ice; Cook and Gibson, with a light sledge holding two weeks of food pulled by two dogs, back to Red Cliff.

Josephine had stayed busy hunting and target shooting with Henson and the Eskimos. Using her six-shot revolver and putting up a tin can forty feet away, the best Eskimo scored three hits, Henson none, and Josephine five.

The days now were long on sun, and large open leads appeared in the bay. The Eskimos took advantage of the return of sea animals to hunt seals, walrus, narwhal, and even small white whales.

On May 30, a dog limped into camp. He was recognized as Devil Dog, a big, strong creature whom Peary, before departing, had designated as the lead dog to bring back the support party's sledge. He was in poor condition, barely able to walk, and evidently had not eaten for a week. The lone deserter caused Josephine and the others to consider the worst possible scenario for the four men who had gone inland against the advice of the Eskimos.

Peary had told those remaining at Red Cliff to expect the support party back by mid-May, but that month had come and gone. Three more days of "increasing suspense" with no news followed, and Josephine found herself filled with "unpleasant forebodings" while being "utterly powerless" in her position.

Her nightmare ended on June 3 when Cook and Gibson arrived with a nearly empty sledge pulled by a single dog. Cook took both of Josephine's hands in his and shook them warmly. He told her that when they had left the advance party two weeks earlier, both her husband and Astrup were in good health and fine spirits, and traveling well.

A longer wait now set in, one that Josephine knew could last two months. In reality, it would seem more like a year's worth of anxiety and worry. "Never in my life," she wrote, "have I felt so utterly alone and forsaken."

Her will was as strong as her husband's, however, and she shared his sense of destiny. They complemented each other; her occasional bouts of depression and pessimism were offset by his unrestrained optimism and high spirits. He lifted her from the depths; she brought him back to earth.

Now, besides wishing for his success and safety, her fervent hope was that he and Astrup would return in time for everyone to go home on the ship due to pick them up at the end of summer. A delay could mean spending a second winter.

Meanwhile, the Eskimos, with no malice intended, assured anyone who would listen that the fate of the two white men on the ice had been sealed by evil spirits—that Peary and Astrup would never return alive from the domain of death.

CHAPTER FOUR

DEATH ON A GLACIER

With the days of summer came rumor of a violent Eskimo uprising. Two native hunters, Kyo and Koolootingwah, were overheard by Henson speaking conspiratorially about killing one of the Americans, though it was not clear just who might fall victim.

In a hushed conference at Red Cliff, an alarmed Henson reported the threat. Josephine dismissed the possibility of a revolt, believing it likely that Henson had misunderstood the Eskimos speaking in their native tongue.

Cook agreed that he didn't think the natives were by nature warlike. However, he had previously had a run-in with Kyo when he had been among those moving supplies inland in support of the exploring party. Kyo had performed so sluggishly and been so uncooperative during the week of work that when it came time to give each native his payment of an empty tomato crate—wood being a prized commodity in the treeless regions of the Arctic—Cook told Kyo, "You get nothing." The Eskimo picked up a gun and threatened to kill Cook. Kyo was calmed by other natives, most of whom agreed with Cook's no-work, no-pay doctrine. Kyo, whom Cook had previously found to be "a soul of kindness," thereafter became "an advocate of hate."

With the safety of everyone at Red Cliff his responsibility, Cook decided it would be wise to prepare for any possible threat. He and the other men began wearing revolvers. The armed-camp atmosphere frightened the entire Eskimo community, which now numbered thirty-four men, women, and children.

Days later, when a window at Red Cliff was opened for ventilation, Kyo was certain that the Americans would start shooting. He ranted that bullets could not hurt him because he was protected by *kokoyah*, an evil spirit. Kyo vowed that if any natives were killed, he would order *kokoyah* to destroy the big ship when it returned and the Americans would die.

Order was restored amid assurances to the natives that no harm would come to them. Cook, in a conciliatory gesture, agreed to trade with Kyo for the wood the native wanted—to make a protective ring around his skin-hulled kayak—in exchange for a sealskin float used to cross open leads.

The days now settled into an easy routine, as only housekeeping chores had to be done. With temperatures in the eighties and a refreshing crispness in the air caused by the nearness of massive formations of glacial ice, the Americans paired off and went exploring, some on day trips and others for a week or longer. Verhoeff violated an expedition rule forbidding members to travel long distances alone. While on a boat trip with Cook and Gibson, he elected to return overland and could not be dissuaded otherwise, even when it was pointed out he would have to cross a formidable glacier alone. Verhoeff made it safely back to Red Cliff only a couple of days behind Cook and Gibson.

The natives enjoyed the summer hunting season in the open waters, where they could utilize their kayaking skills. When Ikwah slew an *oogzook* (a bearded seal), it took him several trips to bring the carcass—four times larger than a normal seal—back to Red Cliff. He then went about slicing into smaller portions the skin, highly prized for boot soles and rawhide rope, and the meat and much valued blubber, used for fuel. Eskimo custom called for any large kill to be divided among the men in a village, whether or not they helped with the hunt. On this day, a man named Kyoshu, crippled by injury and unable to hunt, received a full share.

The first week of July found something new in the diet: a vegetable dish, in fact, the only native vegetable dish in the region. It consisted of smallish purple flowers, which after boiling tasted like stewed rhubarb. By custom, it was eaten by women and children but not by men. Conversely, the men ate the eggs of various birds, something the women and children were not allowed.

On July 13, Josephine set out with Cook for a valley at the head of the bay, near where her husband had gone up onto the glacier and headed inland more than two months earlier. Pulled by some indescribable force, she wanted to be there to greet him when he came off the glacier or, at least—in the event he came back a different route—for him to find at his cache some fresh supplies and her welcoming note.

Henson and Ikwah had gone ahead, and already a tent was up and camp established. Having seen Josephine safely off the trail, Cook bid her adieu and headed back with Ikwah in a pouring rain to Red Cliff, fifteen miles distant.

When clear skies returned the next morning, Josephine took her shotgun and went off in the direction of the nearest glacier, where she knew there were numerous ponds with the possibility of ducks. She saw only two but downed one; the breast made a meal that night, and the rest went into a stew.

She found the setting magical, with the sound of running streams in every direction, clear lakes and ponds, meadows carpeted with moss and wildflowers, the sweet air, all against a backdrop of glaciers and mountains. The seabirds were out in full force, having arrived from southern latitudes. Each morning, snuggled inside her reindeer-skin sleeping bag, she was awakened by a multitude of chirps and whistles.

The next day was dull and foggy, and the mosquitoes so thick that Josephine remained in camp. With the return of warm, clear weather the next morning—daylight was now twenty-four hours long—she set off for the cache that had been established months ago. Henson knew the location up the glacier. At one point, to cut mileage off their trek, they crossed a knee-deep stream that almost knocked them off their feet in near-freezing rushing water.

Once across, they found the cache. Josephine left her note and also cans of milk and fruit, fresh biscuits, and a flask of brandy. She looked northward, in the direction her husband had gone. *Was he near?* she wondered. *Sick or well? Alive or dead?*

They returned to the stream, found that the level had risen, and decided not to chance a crossing. They kept walking, hoping to circle a large lake. But they soon found it was connected to another lake by a deep torrent of icy water that was impossible to ford. They went on until reaching the head of the second lake, which stopped at a sheer glacial cliff. They considered rounding the lake by climbing along the outermost edge of the glacier until they realized that large boulders were continually raining down from above.

Stymied, they decided they had no choice but to backtrack. Unable to locate the exact same spot where they had crossed, they tested the stream in several places, finding it too deep and the current too strong. Each time they retreated to shore, wet and discouraged. They sat on a rock, dried themselves as best they could, and discussed their options.

They had been walking for more than twelve hours with nothing to eat, having had only a cracker and coffee before departing. They had no food or sleeping gear with them. Unless they could make a river crossing, they would have to go the long way—perhaps another twelve hours of hiking.

Josephine suggested they return to the cache and fortify themselves with food and drink before attempting to go farther. This they did, then set off again to find their way back to camp. The hours and miles went by until they were ready to drop from fatigue. Occasionally, they stopped and sat for a few minutes. When one or the other began dozing off, they pushed on.

Climbing up through a rugged ravine, Josephine realized she could go no higher. With trembling legs under her, she was at her limit. They took a breather and started back down, hoping the stream, a few miles away, might have receded. When they reached it about noon, they found that the water level had receded. They were able to get across, and though their feet and legs were numb from the cold water, their camp was only an hour away.

After a good night's sleep, Josephine was sufficiently recovered to go hunting for fresh game the next day, but she returned empty-handed.

Early the next morning, she was awakened by an Eskimo with the exciting news that the ship had returned and was anchored in the bay. Along with a letter from home, the native brought her a note from Professor Angelo Heilprin of the Academy of Natural Sciences—the group of Philadelphia scientists was again aboard *Kite*—telling her that his party was at Red Cliff.

For the next hour or so, Josephine was oblivious to all else as she savored a long missive from her mother. Written as a daily journal, it detailed happenings in the family and the world at large during her absence. When she finished, Josephine's foremost thought was a thankful one—everyone dear to her was alive and well. *Now*, she thought, *if only Bert returns safely*.

Henson was eager for a reunion with the ship's party, but Josephine opted to remain in the valley. The next day, she saw a lone man making his way up a foothill below her campsite. When he came closer, she saw it was Heilprin. It was an exquisite pleasure for Josephine to talk to an old friend—she and her husband had enjoyed the professor's gracious company at home on many occasions. After the isolation of the past year, she drank in conversation with her educated visitor from the civilized world. He brought more letters for her, including one from her brother, Emil, an engineer contractor in New York City, who joined their mother in urging her to come home on the ship whether or not her husband had completed his work.

Heilprin informed Josephine that his orders—from her family and friends—were to bring her home "under any circumstances." She expressed confidence that her husband would return by the end of August, when the ship would have to depart to avoid being frozen in for the winter. While she secretly feared that, if he was not back by then, he might never return, she knew she could not leave for home while there was the faintest chance of his being alive.

"Well, we'll see when the time comes," the professor said.

She worried aloud about how her husband would feel should he show up a week or two after she had left for home. Wouldn't it be "disappointment enough" when he realized he had missed the ship and would have to winter here another year, she asked, "without finding that I, too, have deserted him?"

The professor wanted her to return with him to Red Cliff, but she declined. Heilprin headed back the following morning.

Two days later, Cook showed up at Josephine's campsite with Eskimos carrying supplies. Notwithstanding the resupply mission, Cook beseeched her to return with him to Red Cliff. She relented only when he suggested there was much work to be done in preparation for heading home. She knew her husband would want her to have things ready for their departure.

When Cook and Josephine returned, they found renewed dissension among the Eskimos. Kyo had stabbed his wife in the leg and threatened to kill her daughter, fathered by another hunter. When Kyo had left for a seal hunt, Klayuh ran away with her daughter. When he returned and found them missing, Kyo undertook a frantic search that stretched from the head of the bay to Cape Cleveland in the opposite direction. The other natives, distrustful of Kyo's motive for wanting to find them, conspired to keep him off the track.*

Over the next few days as she clung to hope, Josephine thought of the letter her husband had sent back with the support party two months earlier. He told her that he expected to be back about August 1 but assured her that if he wasn't, it was only a delay and did not portend danger. He explained he had one hundred days worth of provisions—plenty to see him back.

Nonetheless, there was growing anxiety about the fate of the exploring party, not diminished by the continual chatter of the Eskimo hunters about Peary being *sinnypoh* (dead). One native even told Josephine about his dream of only one *kabloona* (white man) returning from the ice cap.

---

*Kyo's bizarre behavior was to continue for years. More than one native hunter suspiciously disappeared on the ice while in the company of Kyo, who thereafter would stake claim to the new widow. His various wives had a way of ending up with cuts and bruises. Finally, he became so distrusted and feared by his own people that one day another hunter approached him, announced dispassionately, "It is time for you to die," and speared Kyo to death.

On August 5, a relief party boarded *Kite* and shipped to the head of the bay. There they set off on foot, scaling the cliffs to the top of the glacier—their scheme being to plant stakes at intervals to aid Peary and Astrup in finding their way home. Everyone, it seemed, felt more comfortable doing something rather than simply waiting. They stopped eight miles inland and drove the first poles into the ice, topping one with a red handkerchief and another with a sign that read: **To Head of McCormick Bay—Kite in port—August 5, 1892.**

As the party moved on, there was a sudden shout from one of its members. Spotted up ahead was a tiny black object set against the white foreground of the glacial top. Then another speck appeared to the naked eye, joined by a dark, elongated shape. Field glasses were aimed—two men in furs and a sledge with dogs in harness were plunging down an icy slope.

As the two men approached, the vision became clearer: Peary and Astrup!

EARLY THE next morning, Josephine, who had made the trip on *Kite* to the head of the bay and remained onboard, was awakened by sounds of the ship being boarded. She knew it was too early for the return of the rescue party, which had planned to be gone considerably longer.

Half-asleep, she heard a familiar gait approaching her cabin. She was afraid to move even when the doorknob rattled. Then she heard his voice, calling for her to open the door—*was she dreaming? was it possible?* She remained in the bunk as if paralyzed until the door was forced open.

Her husband stood before her, looking "well and hearty, safe at last."

There was rejoicing aboard *Kite* and also at Red Cliff, where Peary and Astrup were reunited with the rest of the expedition members. The Eskimos thought the two men were spirits and refused to approach them. Once they accepted them as living humans, the natives gathered around to ask about the spirits of their dead relatives, what they were eating and how they were faring. They were disappointed when informed there had been no sightings of spirits.

Peary and Astrup related details of their difficult travel across the icy wasteland. For days on end, they had endured storms so vicious as to make traveling impossible. The most severe test proved to be the deep chasms in the ice that opened without warning in front of them. More than once they nearly lost the sledge and their supplies, and had to pull up the lead dog by his trace as he dangled helplessly in a dark, bottomless pit.

Five hundred miles from McCormick Bay, they had come to a rocky 3,500-foot cliff, which Peary named for the U. S. Navy. From the top of Navy Cliff, he saw a channel, which he named Peary Channel; he declared it was the northern boundary of mainland Greenland and charted it as such. Beyond that, he saw what appeared to be a vast island to the northeast, which he designated Peary Land. These sightings were the basis for Peary, upon his return home, publicly to stake his claim to having proven the "insularity of Greenland," a major geographical accomplishment that led greatly to the advancement of his reputation as an Arctic explorer.*

The two men had traveled round-trip more than a thousand miles—the longest journey across Greenland up to that time—averaging fourteen miles per day during eighty-five days of marching. Although both had lost weight, they returned in excellent health.

After a few days, Peary was ready for more. Under the threat of heavy storm clouds, he departed in a whaleboat with Josephine, Henson, Verhoeff, and five Eskimo rowers for a photographic and sightseeing excursion. After his long journey, the idea of taking a

---

*Eivind Astrup, Peary's loyal companion, was less certain about what they had seen from Navy Cliff. In a report to the Norwegian Geographical Society after returning home, Astrup made no mention of the northern end of Greenland, nor did he verify the existence of Peary Channel. Twenty years later, explorers Peter Freuchen and Knud Rasmussen found that Peary Channel did not exist. As for Peary Land, it was found to be nothing more than a corner of Greenland. Although Greenland did turn out to be an island—the world's largest—Peary's announcement upon returning home that he had determined the "insularity of Greenland" was premature at best.

leisurely trip "free of the rush and hurry of preparation . . . or anxiety" with his wife had the feel of a "picnic in the woods."

Two days later, they landed on the shore of a small bay that Peary named Bowdoin after his alma mater—new land discoveries gave explorers naming rights, which were considered critical to generating both prestige and contributions from wealthy backers. Verhoeff struck out on his own—"on his proposed trip across the glacier . . . around to Red Cliff," according to Peary, who made no comment about what discussion may have preceded Verhoeff's departure. Peary had previously been a stickler for the rule of no solo hikes of any significant distance. In fact, as winter had approached after their arrival the preceding year, he had established a five-hundred-yard limit around Red Cliff—no one was to proceed farther alone. Verhoeff, the first to break that rule, had taken umbrage at the public dressing down he received from Peary, an incident that had sown the seeds of Verhoeff's discontent with his commander.

Cook was surprised to see Verhoeff back so soon at Red Cliff. The doctor considered Verhoeff "an insurgent type," and although he found the geologist a willing worker, Cook was cognizant of a "suppressed bitterness" Verhoeff directed toward Peary. Verhoeff had already vowed to Cook, "I will never go home in the same ship with that man and that woman."

The next morning, Verhoeff said he was going to collect some mineral specimens at the head of McCormick Bay and would be back in four days. He took supplies to last him that length of time, and a rifle and ammunition.

When Verhoeff did not return, Cook organized a search party, which members of the *Kite* crew joined, along with nine Eskimo hunters. The effort was ongoing when Peary returned. The size of the search party was expanded, and the natives were energized when Peary promised a rifle and ammunition to the man who first spotted Verhoeff.

After six days and nights of searching, Verhoeff's footprints were found atop a glacier twenty-five miles from Red Cliff, along with the label off a tin of food he had taken. No other trace of the strong-willed geologist was found.

The inference seemed clear to both Peary and Cook: Verhoeff, who had previously set the dangerous precedent for himself by traveling alone across glaciers, had probably slipped on the icy surface, perhaps during a furious gale that had hit about then, and fallen into one of the countless yawning crevasses.

Peary was concerned about the record of the expedition, given Verhoeff's disappearance. He asked Cook to write and sign a report about the search, no doubt to ward off any possible criticism that they had not looked long enough. In his report, Cook wrote that Verhoeff's loss was "peculiar, sad and mysterious," but that "his commander [and] companions" had made a "long, systematic and careful search" and done "all in their power to discover his whereabouts."

The party of Philadelphia scientists had brought along many donations for the natives. The Eskimo families were lined up on the beach and given the most valuable possessions most had ever received: pots, kettles, knives, scissors, thimbles, and needles for the women, and for the men, lances, saws, gimlets, knives, timber, and other hardware items. It was repayment for their services for the year they had helped the expedition, and the Eskimos were overjoyed, ensuring that the next expedition to the region would be warmly received.

Peary ordered that a cache of supplies—enough to sustain a man for a year—be established near Verhoeff's last known position, in case he reappeared after the ship had departed. The geologist's prediction in his first letter to Peary that the odds were against his returning alive had proven accurate.

The man with whom Verhoeff did not want to travel home on the same ship did one more thing before *Kite* sailed away.

The glacier where John M. Verhoeff fell was named for him.

CHAPTER FIVE

RULED WITH AN IRON HAND

As *KITE* sailed south against unrelenting headwinds, which made the return trip long and monotonous, Cook, Astrup, and Gibson discussed the hardships of Arctic life. Cook was then of the opinion that the push to explore uncharted regions in the face of such miseries was akin to searching for "a fool's paradise." The three men agreed it was the end of their Far North endeavors.

On the other hand, they were returning fully charged and alive, with a sense of accomplishment for the challenges they had met. Also, they had been deeply touched by the indigenous peoples they had come to know. None would forget life among the northernmost humans on Earth, the most direct, honest, and simple people they had ever met. Beyond having enough to eat and wear, the Eskimos had few cares. "We had from a savage intelligence learned a great deal," Cook recognized, "but wondered if they in turn had acquired much from us."

They headed up the Delaware River to a chorus of ships' horns and whistles and docked at Philadelphia on September 24, 1892. The North Greenland expedition had come to an end.

An overflowing, gala reception was held for the returning explorers at the Philadelphia Academy of Natural Sciences, to which Peary would make his final report on the accomplishments of the expedition. Peary stood tall in his Navy dress blues before more than a thousand guests, including his proud mother. Wearing an elegant black satin gown and cradling a bouquet of red roses, Josephine stood by her husband's side as he was presented to the cheering crowd.

In the course of receiving congratulations from friends and well-wishers, the men who had agreed they were finished with the Arctic began to think differently. "This is true of all frigid explorers" after they returned home and experienced something other than "the ice world," Cook decided. Once duly recovered, "the lure of the Arctic becomes a permanent drawing power for life."

To Peary, the expedition proved the "correctness of [his] theory as to the quality of the personnel of an Arctic expedition," which he thought should consist of "men of youth, perfect health and educated intelligence." He made a point to commend the efforts of each member of the expedition and praised the "soothing presence" of Josephine, her strength when he had found himself "a helpless cripple," and her "valuable assistance" to the expedition.

Peary credited Cook for being "always helpful and an indefatigable worker." To Cook's medical skills "may be attributed the almost complete exemption of the party from even the mildest of indispositions, and personally I owe much to his professional skill, and unruffled patience and coolness in an emergency." As for his work in the ethnological field, Cook had obtained "a large mass of most valuable material concerning a practically unstudied tribe."

Henson, described by Peary as "my faithful coloured boy," was cited for his hard work and being "apt at anything, being in turn cook, hunter, dog driver, housekeeper, and bodyguard." Furthermore, Henson's Arctic service should have dismissed any doubts as to the ability of his race to withstand frigid temperatures. "In powers of endurance and ability to withstand cold," Peary declared, Henson had proven "the equal of others in the party."

As for his own efforts, Peary gladly accepted the accolades that came his way—"my friends were right in saying that I had accomplished a brilliant feat in my long sledge journey"—but believed there was for him still "important work to be done in the north."

Peary began to contemplate another Arctic expedition, its

main intent to "complete the exploration of the northern lands which I discovered last summer," with no intention of trying for the Pole. Coinciding with his desire to mount a new expedition was a proposal by Major James B. Pond, a well-known lecture manager and tour promoter, for Peary to deliver paid lectures around the country. This seemed to Peary an ideal way to raise money for the next trip.

After settling into his new duties at the Brooklyn Navy Yard, Peary petitioned for another leave of absence. Already, there was growing resentment in Navy circles at Peary's frequent leaves. Believing that his request would not be readily granted, Peary enlisted a powerful ally, Isaac Jones Wistar, president of the Philadelphia Academy of Natural Sciences, a former Union Army brigadier general and a prominent Philadelphia lawyer who had made a fortune after the war financing railroad construction. The retired general believed Peary should have the opportunity to carry on with his northern exploration and presented the proposition persuasively to the secretary of the Navy. Soon thereafter, Peary was granted a three-year paid leave beginning in November 1892.

Peary launched his lecture tour in mid-November, opening in Lock Haven, Pennsylvania, for a fee of $100. Two weeks later, on a rainy evening in Brooklyn, he lectured for the same fee in a dimly lit, sparsely filled hall. When the lantern to illuminate his photographic slides failed to work, Peary described in his own words the melancholy setting at Cape Sabine, wintering over at Red Cliff, and his sledge trip across northern Greenland. In the audience, hearing Peary speak for the first time, was a newspaperman from Brooklyn, Herbert Bridgman, who would before long become a mainstay of support for the naval engineer in his Arctic endeavors.

Cook settled into his mother's house in Brooklyn. Because of the publicity he had received as a member of the Peary expedition, his renewed practice of medicine began to prosper, although he found himself "ill at ease as all explorers are in the jungle of city life." His thoughts often wandered to the Far North, and in the months to come it took little coaxing from Peary for Cook to agree to serve as second in command of the next expedition.

Astrup, who had returned to his native Norway, also responded eagerly to Peary's offer to go north again, as did Henson, who, unable to find work in Philadelphia, had fallen on hard times. When Cook learned that Henson was suffering from the lingering effects of snow blindness, he sent money for him to take the train to Brooklyn, where Henson lived as a guest at the Cook home for two months. During that time, Cook arranged for an eye specialist to treat Henson free of charge.

When Henson recovered, he joined Peary on tour. To enliven the lectures, Henson dressed in Arctic furs and, upon Peary's order, burst onto the stage cracking a whip above a team of Eskimo dogs brought back from Greenland. It made for a dramatic entrance with the dogs yelping and jumping about wildly, as Henson, sweltering in the furs, struggled to control them. The show—with "the dogs and sledges and the igloo lights glimmering through the white expanse, as effective a bit of Arctic realism as ever staged"—was soon playing to capacity crowds. St. Louis booked the show for 60 percent of the gross of the gate against a guarantee of $250; Evansville, Indiana, 60 percent of the gate (75 cents for reserved seating) for a matinee and evening performance; Nashville, $300 for two shows; Cincinnati, 55 percent of the gate. Peary filled halls in Columbus, Toledo, Pittsburgh, Trenton, New Haven, and dozens of other cities and towns.

After an appearance in Philadelphia, Henson recognized in the crowd the Navy officer with whom he had made the bet that he would return from the Arctic with his fingers and toes intact. After the presentation, Henson went over and held out his hands. "You see, my fingers are all here."

At first, the officer seemed not to remember.

"The hundred dollars," Henson said.

The officer smiled sheepishly. "Well, let's have a look at you."

Henson sat down, removed his shoes and socks, and wiggled his ten toes. The officer wrote out a check and handed it to Henson with the comment "Hearing from Peary what you people went through, I'd say you earned it."

In the months that Peary toured, he and Cook corresponded. At one point, Peary wrote for information relating to Cook's exhaustive study of the Eskimos for use in his lectures.

In January 1893, Cook responded to Peary's suggestion that he consider renting a hall or tent and lecture at the World's Fair in Chicago: "I have been thinking about your suggestions as to the World's Fair." Cook went a step further as well, proposing his own tour "through such towns and cities as you did not enter. In this way assist in obtaining funds for your next expedition. If you think favorable of this, I will give you a detailed description."

When Peary asked for further details, Cook got down to specifics. "I have two plans regarding the proposed lecturing tour. In both, I wish you to furnish me with the slides and such prints as you wish me to clearly bring out in my lectures." Cook's first idea was to follow the major railroad lines into larger cities and towns that the train served, winding up in Chicago in April. Cook proposed splitting equally with Peary the net proceeds of such a tour. Cook's second plan was for him to travel under Major Pond's sponsorship and "fill such engagements as you will be unable to attend to."

Peary was cool to the notion of Cook's undertaking his own lecture tour, although he continued to advance the idea of the doctor's involvement in an Arctic exhibit at the World's Fair. Cook went to Chicago to investigate the possibilities and returned unenthusiastic. "The rental of a suitable place is unreasonably high and there being so many things to see (at the World's Fair) that I fear it would not prove a successful enterprise," he wrote Peary. Also, Cook had been advised that summer would be the best-attended months at the World's Fair, and since the new expedition's planned departure date was late June or early July, "it would hardly do for [him] to undertake anything like this."

Meanwhile, Cook was appearing before local groups. After delivering a paper on the medical and reproductive practices of the northernmost Eskimos to the Kings County Medical Society in Brooklyn, he was urged by his fellow doctors to publish his findings in book form as scientific literature, along with the measurements, photographs, and other materials he had collected.

Perhaps Cook called on him at a bad time, preoccupied as Peary was with financing the next trip. Seeking permission to publish his

Eskimo research independently, which Cook naively thought would pose no problem, he found Peary in an uncharitable mood. Still stinging from the recent publication of a book by two members of *Kite*'s crew that covered the details of his previous expedition, Peary pointedly reminded Cook that the contract each member of the expedition signed forbade anyone from coming out with a book until one year after Peary's own book appeared.* Until then, Peary said, "not a word can be published by any member of any of my expeditions. Their work is my property for my use, and may or may not be printed." The issue was entirely a judgment call on his part, Peary stated, based upon how the material gathered by others fit into the "scheme" of his forthcoming books.

Cook was "entirely unprepared" for Peary's dictatorial stance—up until that moment, he had found Peary "democratic and cordial" in their dealings. But clearly, Cook had pushed up against a boundary with Peary, who jealously guarded what he considered his turf. In his soft-spoken manner, Cook carefully repeated his intentions, explaining the scientific nature of his publishing interest and the narrowness of the academic audience he would be seeking. In truth, he was not anticipating much financial return from his ethnological study of Eskimos—he had not even received a fee for his talk to the local doctors.

Peary remained silent as he listened, and Cook began to think he might be swaying Peary's thinking.

"I am inclined, Doctor, to extend to you freedom of action, but it is a bad precedent," Peary said when Cook finished. "I cannot do this with others. Every member of my expeditions in the future must be ruled with an iron hand."

The answer was still no.

Cook found Peary's "sudden outburst of selfish autocracy" repug-

*The authors of *Voyage of the Kite* (1893) had signed no such contract with Peary. Although Peary completed his own manuscript before departing on his next expedition, he was not able to make an acceptable publishing arrangement for *Northward over the Great Ice* until 1898. Josephine had better luck with her book, *My Arctic Journal* (1893), for which Peary wrote a short preface telling of his wife's courage and devotion, and a lengthy epilogue, "The Great White Journey," about his long sledge trip across northern Greenland.

nant and knew instantly what he must do, although he said nothing at the time. The preceding month, Cook had finalized plans to close his medical practice and join the next expedition, a decision that left Peary "very glad to hear that you are willing once more to try a hazard of Arctic experiences." But now Cook knew that going on another expedition with Peary would not be possible.

Within a few days, Cook informed Peary by letter of his change of heart: "My Dear Mr. Peary: After a second and more careful consideration of the Arctic question, I have definitely decided not to go on the next expedition. I regret that I have left this to such a late day but trust that it will not seriously inconvenience you."

Peary wrote back from Washington, D.C.: "My dear Doctor: I need not say that I am very sorry to learn of your decision. Your decision will not seriously inconvenience me beyond the fact that it is a personal disappointment. I have letters from about a score of physicians who are eager to go with me."

Even though Peary's handling of Cook's request to publish his Eskimo research put an end to future collaborative ventures between them, the two men remained on friendly terms, continuing their correspondence for a time. In his resignation letter, Cook had volunteered to be of "any service" in preparing for the next expedition. Peary took him up on his offer, asking Cook's advice on several points, such as the type of butter, evaporated milk, and beef peptonoids (to alleviate seasickness) to take along on the trip. Peary also had Cook perform medical examinations on everyone in the expedition party.

Meanwhile, Cook went ahead with his modest efforts to be published. His article "The Most Northern Tribe on Earth," appeared in the *New York Medical Examiner* that year. It opened, "Thinly scattered along the inhospitable shores of northwestern Greenland, from Cape York to Humboldt Glacier, is a tribe of Esquimaux of undoubted Mongolian origin. This tribe is to me the most interesting of any tribe that I have ever seen or read of on the globe." He discussed "more than a few of the peculiarities of this tribe," adding that he hoped the "scientific results" of his studies among these people would be published in book form. However, such a publishing event failed to materialize.

Peary came off the lecture circuit having made, by his count, 168 talks and grossing $18,000. As for raising money elsewhere, he received a $1,000 contribution from the American Geographical Society, and Josephine, who had signed with the Contemporary Publishing Company, of New York, for *My Arctic Journal: A Year Among Ice-Fields and Eskimos*, donated her book advance to the cause. The *New York Sun* agreed to double what it had paid to publish dispatches and letters from the last expedition, and a few thousand dollars more was raised from other sources. Peary knew the total was insufficient to finance the entire expedition, although he had already chartered a ship for the voyage and begun ordering equipment and supplies.

The pressure mounted to be underway in early summer and get as far north as possible during favorable conditions. Otherwise the expedition would have to be delayed for a year, which was intolerable to Peary because he would be wasting a year of his leave.

To address the shortfall, it was suggested that Peary place on exhibit the ship he had chartered, charging the public admission to board the Arctic-bound vessel. Peary at first found the idea "extremely distasteful." However, he soon realized he had no choice but to raise money in any way possible. Thus, as Peary gathered up his expedition members and supplies at ports of calls along the eastern seaboard en route north, the residents of Philadelphia, New York, Boston, and Portland, Maine—thousands at each stop—were afforded the opportunity to visit *Falcon*, a larger and more impressive ship than *Kite*, and "the quarters of the people made up the needed balance."

On the day *Falcon* was to depart Brooklyn, Cook went down to the dock to see the expedition off. Once aboard, Cook found the vessel filled with a last wave of admission-paying sightseers, as well as a contingent of reporters. Addressing the latter with Cook nearby, Peary expressed regret that the doctor was not able, on account of his "professional engagements," to accompany the new expedition. While the reason given was faulty, Peary's lament was likely genuine.

Two weeks earlier, Peary had written his thanks to Cook for the "information and suggestions" provided, and he added, as if having struggled with how things turned out between them, "I am sorry that you are not going with us but I did not feel that I could urge you against your sober judgment."

Peary had a very personal reason to regret not having along on the trip a physician he knew and trusted: Josephine would again be joining him on the expedition, even though she was six months pregnant and would be delivering their first child somewhere in the frozen high latitudes.

A FEW WEEKS after Peary left, Cook went north on another ship.

Some months earlier, Cook had been asked to "advise on the treatment" of a Yale student said to be experiencing hallucinations about the Far North. Cook's remedy was strikingly direct: give the boy his dream and send him north, so as to "feed the brain as you would the stomach." Much to Cook's surprise, the youth's father, James Hoppin, a professor at Yale, contacted Cook about leading a small exploring party that would include his son, Benjamin. Cook deemed such a jaunt better than remaining home. At the professor's behest, Cook went to New Haven for a meeting.

As to the practicality and safety of the voyage, Cook believed Greenland could be visited aboard a seaworthy ship in comparative comfort during the summer. He knew of an available 78-foot fishing schooner, *Zeta*, which could be refitted as a yacht, and estimated the cost of the three-month excursion at $10,000. Hoppin enthusiastically agreed to finance the trip.

When preparations were completed, Cook went by rail to Nova Scotia, where he joined *Zeta* and her eight-man crew, along with three "students of nature" who included the professor's son. Only after they set sail, on July 10, was a public announcement made about Cook's participation, which was described sensationally in one newspaper account as a "rapid and flank movement" on the Peary expedition. Cook felt some jubilation at heading his own seaborne party and quietly relished the idea of crossing paths with Peary in northern Greenland.

Cook had goals beyond visiting the Danish settlements and photographing the landscape, natives, and animals (he would end up taking a thousand images). "I expect to prove by this trip that tourists can go there every year under the proper management, without danger to life or vessel," Cook wrote from Nova Scotia shortly before departing. He also intended, if possible, to bring back a family of Eskimos, which he knew would generate publicity, as few full-blooded Arctic natives had visited America.

Zeta, almost new and strongly built, looked more like a pleasure yacht than a vessel fitted for Arctic travel, and could make eleven knots in fair wind. After cruising up the northwestern shores of Newfoundland and along a stretch of Labrador coastline, they crossed the Davis Strait to Greenland.

They made port at Upernavik, the northernmost Danish settlement, on August 16. Cook had hoped to get as far as Cape York, some four hundred miles north of Upernavik. He considered it a good omen that as yet they had encountered no heavy sea ice and only occasional icebergs, which they easily dodged. However, at Upernavik, the master of the ship, who was also its owner, eyed the cold, stormy weather brewing in the region and decided it was unsafe to proceed farther north because he had no insurance to cover the perils of Arctic travel.

After two days at Upernavik, where Cook was reacquainted with the Danish governor and his gracious wife, *Zeta* turned south and made port at Swartenbaak. A few days later, they sailed on to another landing, where Cook traded natives for several Eskimo dogs—in all, he would in this way obtain six adult dogs and nine puppies. He had it in mind to bring the dogs home and breed them to pull sledges for future explorations, convinced as he was of their value to humans when it came to traveling great distances in the polar regions. Fully grown, an Eskimo dog weighed about seventy pounds and, when harnessed to sledges, could pull at a rate of one hundred pounds dead weight and travel with that load twenty miles a day without much difficulty.

At the next stop, Cook took his small exploring party into a large inlet at Umanak Fjord, with the help of local Eskimos who paddled and steered their dory. Halted about sixty miles from the mouth of the fjord by an expansive, ice-choked valley, they came to a gigantic glacier several miles long and half again as broad. As they watched, pieces of it fell off, forming new icebergs. It was possible to count hundreds of them in all sizes and shapes. Cook realized they had come upon a major birthplace for bergs emanating from western Greenland. Some became grounded not far from their origin, while others traveled hundreds of miles into the North Atlantic.

They commenced a foot search for ethnological specimens and nearby came across an ancient burial ground. Interred in cairns of granite above ground were tools and hunting weapons expertly fashioned from stone, bone, and ivory—no doubt placed with the dead to ease their burden in the spirit world.

Zeta crossed the Davis Strait in a favorable wind and sailed at a leisurely pace down the north coast of Labrador, an isolated and rugged region that offered some of the best wildlife and scenery in all of North America.

They stopped at Rigolet, an active Hudson Bay Company trading post. Here, Cook found a community of full-blooded Eskimos, who were becoming scarce in south Greenland because of decades of intermingling with the Danes. He arranged with one family to take two of their older children to America as a kind of culture exchange; they would be exposed to the ways of the modern world and appear with Cook during lectures as proud examples of the Arctic people and culture. He promised the children's father, a respected elder, to care for them as his own and see to their safe return the following summer.

And so, Katakata, sixteen, and Milsok, fourteen—soon to be known as Clara and Willie, respectively—arrived with Cook in Brooklyn the first week of October.

Not long thereafter, Cook went on tour under the management of Major Pond, with the Rigolet siblings dressed in Arctic garb and his pack of Eskimo sledge dogs, giving paid lectures as a way to promote interest in, and raise funds for, a new expedition he wished to take: this one to the Antarctic.

CHAPTER SIX

THE SNOW BABY

F ALCON MADE THE usual stops up the coast of Greenland, taking on supplies and gathering Eskimos willing to accompany the expedition, until reaching its final destination at the head of Bowdoin Bay the first week of August 1893.

Construction began on a winter structure near where the Pearys, while exploring the area the preceding summer, had pitched their tent in the midst of a fierce rainstorm. During that earlier stay, they had celebrated a wedding anniversary, so they christened their new home Anniversary Lodge.

Before *Falcon* left for home, Peary took a party into Smith Sound to hunt walrus, many of which could be seen out of the water blissfully sunbathing on cakes of ice. With hunters manning small boats that came in at close range, two dozen beasts were quickly slain; weighing on the average fifteen hundred pounds each and adding an abundant supply of fresh meat to the winter larder.

The ship cleared Cape Alexander without difficulty and made it halfway across the sound toward Cape Sabine before being halted by the ice pack, which stretched to the horizon. Forced to turn around, they stopped at scenic Olrich's Bay to hunt reindeer and within hours had downed seventeen.

Upon their return, Anniversary Lodge was completed—a sturdy one-story structure tar-papered on the outside for protection from the elements. The walls were a foot thick, with many windows to let light in until the arrival of the Arctic night. Encircling the house was a veranda, lined with wooden boxes containing canned and dried foods, sugar, flour, coffee, tea, and other supplies.

Inquiries were made of the natives as to whether they had seen any sign of John Verhoeff in the past year. Although the superstitious Eskimos were as reluctant to speak of the lost geologist as of their own missing and dead, the answer was no. The natives did reveal that shortly after the expedition had departed, the supply cache left for the missing Verhoeff was raided by the unpredictable Kyo, who also single-handedly destroyed Red Cliff.

Falcon departed on August 20, carrying the last letters home by the fourteen-member expedition party for a long while. "Everything points to the success which Mr. Peary hopes for," Josephine wrote in closing her book's final chapter, "Greenland Revisited," which was taken back on *Falcon* to be delivered to her publisher. "What the future will bring, however, no one can tell."

One future event could be counted on, and it came to pass inside the Pearys' bedroom at Anniversary Lodge a month after *Falcon*'s departure. For added warmth, the interior walls had been lined with wool blankets, over which family pictures were hung. A bright carpet covered the wooden floor, and a bookcase and pedal sewing machine were within easy reach. From the bed upon which Josephine went into labor, the view out one window was of a great glacier, and from another the high reddish-brown mountains that ringed the picturesque bay like sentinels.

Not long after the first squalls of a newborn were heard on September 12, 1893, a stream of natives began to appear, some from miles away. The visitors were allowed entry while being kept at a distance, since they were uniformly unwashed. They filed through the house quietly, disappointed only when they could not touch the baby to see if she was warm and not made of snow, for she was so white. They came to call her *An-poo-mik-a-ninny*—"the Snow Baby." The blond, blue-eyed infant stared at the shaggy-haired, brown-skinned visitors in furs, and whenever she smiled at one of them, rejoicing resulted, as this was considered very lucky.

She was named Marie, after her only aunt. When it came time for christening, a middle name was added: Ahnighito—for the native woman who, when the Arctic night ended several months after the birth, lovingly made the baby's first fur suit from the softest and warmest fox and fawn skins. Soon enough, Marie Ahnighito Peary, born farther north than any white baby in history, was wearing it for her daily outings with her mother.

Other than the joyous birth, little else on the trip went right for Peary.

In late October, the face of a nearby glacier fell off into the bay with a thunderous rumble, causing a tidal wave that traveled under the ice cap. When the powerful wave hit shore, it washed far beyond the high-water mark, smashing against the rocks the two whaleboats that had been secured for winter. It also engulfed a supply of fuel oil stored in wooden barrels, which were tossed about and slammed down on the rocks, breaking open most of the barrels and spilling their precious contents.

At the time, Peary was twenty miles inland, in the process of establishing a large cache of supplies in preparation for his planned spring journey. When someone rushed out from Anniversary Lodge to tell him about the destruction of the winter's fuel supply, Peary mumbled angrily about the "fates and all hell" being against him, and hurried back to camp to organize an effort to retrieve as much of the spilled fuel as possible.

The lost fuel was a blow. It meant that they would run out before winter's end and be forced to burn walrus blubber and seal oil for cooking and, most critically, to provide interior heat. Although survivable, the loss of the fuel oil would result in much discomfort for all; before the sun returned in the spring, ice several inches thick would form on the inside walls of Anniversary Lodge.

In between new blizzards that kept them inside, Peary and his men made short sledge trips through winter's darkness to surrounding Eskimo communities to secure more trained sledge dogs, and along the way hunted any fresh game they happened upon. Meanwhile, everyone worked on preparing their equipment for the upcoming trip, and the native women sewed tirelessly on the new fur and skin clothing to be worn by the explorers.

Peary elected not to wait until spring. On March 6, 1894, with the Arctic night slowly receding and the hours of daylight steadily increasing, he set off with seven expedition members, five Eskimos, and ninety dogs pulling twelve sledges. The natives, still unwilling to venture onto the interior ice cap, agreed to go only as far as the supply cache.*

Trouble found them almost immediately. A number of dogs fell ill with a dreaded disease the Eskimos called *piblokto*, which could quickly spread through a sledge team and reduce it to a few weakened survivors. Several dogs had to be put out of their misery, and the rest had to work that much harder to pull the heavily laden sledges.

By the time they reached the supply cache, two men were incapacitated, one with a painfully frozen foot and another, Eivind Astrup, whose snow and ice expertise Peary was counting on once they reached the ice cap, with a severe intestinal malady. Neither was able to continue on the journey, and both went back to Anniversary Lodge.

Before the exploring party could again get underway, the weather worsened. Peary was determined to move forward, however, and they did so through temperatures that dropped to forty degrees below zero, winds of up to fifty miles per hour, and a blinding snowstorm. Only when the exhausted dogs were unable to pull any longer did Peary agree to camp and wait out the storm.

By then, another man had a badly frozen heel, which eventually had to be amputated; he was taken back by the team's physician, Dr.

---

*The reluctance of Eskimos to go onto the ice cap involved, in addition to their superstitions about evil spirits, basic common sense. The Arctic natives during the early days of the age of exploration had never quite understood the interest of white visitors in exploring barren, isolated regions. The natives had long survived the harsh climes by learning to follow the game, usually in or near the water, and otherwise trying to make life easier, rather than more difficult. Whenever they saw parties of white men from faraway lands heading off into regions where starvation and death were strong possibilities, they were disinclined to follow.

Edwin Vincent. That left Peary with three companions, including Matthew Henson. The plan to divide the party at Independence Bay in order to explore the new northern lands as well as those to the east now had to be scrapped for lack of manpower.

When the storm abated, the dogs were in a pitiful state. Half of them had been frozen into the snow, some by their legs and others by their tails, and had to be chopped free with axes. Two were dead. Many of the trapped canines had gnawed on their leather harnesses, which had to be repaired.

By the time they set off over the ice cap, two more men were suffering from frostbite, and the party managed only a few miles each day until stopped once again by a storm. For three days they waited; more dogs died, and the men suffered terribly in the cold. Peary had no choice but to turn around.

His 1894 inland journey, for which he had held such high hopes, had gone just 128 miles into the interior of Greenland. He had fallen far short of duplicating, let alone bettering, his 1892 effort. It was a vanquished Peary who returned in mid-April to Anniversary Lodge with his depleted exploring party.

As the men recuperated, Peary audaciously announced that because of his lack of progress exploring the ice cap, he would be staying over another year to try again the following spring. Since there were not enough supplies for the entire group to stay that long, he decreed that he would remain behind with two volunteers, and everyone else would go home on the ship when it arrived in midsummer.

Determined to do something constructive with his time in the region, Peary organized surveying parties to make maps and charts of the Bowdoin Bay area. He also questioned the Eskimos about the location of a possible meteorite, first reported by British explorer John Ross in 1818. The natives called it Iron Mountain, and had long used pieces of what they considered a gift from the skies to make the blades of knives, harpoon heads, and other tools, found to be much stronger than those traditionally made of animal bones.

The Eskimos were reluctant to reveal the location of Iron Mountain because it had been considered valuable—their only source of metal until white traders arrived—and sacred since the time of their great-grandfathers. One finally agreed when Peary offered him a gun in return. They set off across Melville Bay, but the native soon had a change of heart. Peary went through a number of guides with varying degrees of willingness before reaching a site with some bluish rock showing above the snow at the neck of an isolated peninsula not far from Cape York.

Digging several feet into the snow, Peary uncovered part of the meteorite known by the natives as Woman, because of its original curvaceous shape. A smaller meteorite, Dog, was not more than two hundred feet away. Before departing, Peary erected a cairn and deposited a record of his visit. The largest of the three meteorites, a massive projectile called Tent, was located on an island six miles away.

As if cursed for disturbing a holy ground, the two-week trip back was an ordeal they nearly didn't survive. They fought inclement weather, difficult terrain, food poisoning, snowblindness, and hunger.

Falcon appeared in Bowdoin Bay on August 20. By then, dissension was rife among expedition members, with criticism directed at the Pearys for dining privately on better food than the rest were served, and at Peary individually for attempting to win all the glory for himself. The line for volunteers to stay behind for another year was not long.

One person, however, was quite determined to stay. Josephine was initially unswayed by the reasons presented to her against her decision to remain with her husband. However, her engineer brother, Emil Diebitsch, who arrived on *Falcon*, and Peary himself, finally joined to convince her that it was not in the best interests of her infant daughter to remain through another hard winter.

Falcon steamed for home on August 26. For as long as the ship remained in view, Peary looked for Josephine's white handkerchief fluttering in sad farewell. "So ends with the vanishing ship," Peary wrote in his diary a few days later, "the ill-omened first half of my expedition and begins the second."

Peary was left in the company of his faithful companion, Henson, and the youngest member of the expedition, Hugh Lee, who was enticed to stay—according to Lee's diary—by Peary's promise of a federal appointment at home.*

In addition to his feelings of abject failure, Peary experienced loneliness. It was at first crushing, and he found the room he had shared with his wife "cold and cheerless" without her. He slept several nights on the bench in the dining room.

As fall deepened and the daylight waned, Peary fought depression. Only with immense effort was he able to drag himself outside and undertake hunting excursions to restock the supply of meat for winter.

His thoughts inevitably returned to the ice cap, and he began to plan his course of exploration come spring. He directed the men to check and mark with tall poles the two caches that had already been established—the first one 26 miles away, and the farthest one 128 miles out, where, before turning around in April, he had left all the supplies not needed for the trip back. But Henson and Lee returned four days later, having not found the first cache, and without even looking for the second one because of a rising blizzard.

Fearing that if they waited the caches would be buried by snow and never found in the spring, Peary went with Henson on a last-ditch search. It was futile, however: no markers were to be seen in the unending whiteness. All the supplies that had been carefully put aside for the exploring party were unaccounted for.

Without the cached supplies, Peary knew, the only way he would be able to travel any distance in the spring would be to live off the land, a prospect he did not relish, given the uncertainty of game in the interior. The winter took on a nightmarish quality for Peary; through the dark months that followed, he suffered from depression, sleeplessness, and premonitions of failure, even death.

As spring approached and the equipment was readied for another

---

*In his book *Northward over the Great Ice* (1898), Peary credited "Lee and Henson alone" with possessing "the grit and loyalty to remain" with him for another year, while criticizing the other members of the party, who "discovered that Arctic work was not entirely the picnic they had imagined, and . . . had decided to return home." As for Lee, upon his return from the Arctic, he received an appointment as a deputy U.S. marshal.

assault on the ice cap, Peary wrote Josephine. Although the letter began, "It is the eve of our departure for the great ice, and I sit down to write to you what I know I shall later hand you myself," it was a missive intended to be read after his death. He told her the whereabouts of his journals, provided a list of unpaid debts to the Eskimos who had assisted him, and even the location of his keys left at Anniversary Lodge. "Should I not return," he wrote, the structure was to be dismantled, taken back on the ship, and opened to public exhibition—as he had the ship when in need of money—to help support her. He signed off, "Good-by my darling."

Peary left another letter, shorter and more formal, explaining his plans for the upcoming venture, from which he hoped to return on or before September 1. "My movements after reaching Independence Bay and killing and caching as many musk-oxen as possible will depend entirely upon circumstances. It is unnecessary to enumerate possibilities, as once I have put a hundred miles of the Great Ice between me and the Lodge no human help could find or avail us in the event of a catastrophe."

With such a dreary mind-set, Peary left on April 1, 1895, with Henson, Lee, six Eskimos, and forty-two dogs pulling six sledges. The natives initially agreed to remain with the party on the ice cap, but changed their minds and turned back in unison when the supply cache left 128 miles out was not found after another careful search.

Peary and his two companions pushed on. After five hundred miles, they were done—having exhausted themselves and their supplies and being left with only nine dogs. They had made it to McCormick Bay, and the rocky crest Peary had previously named Navy Cliff, but not a foot farther. There were to be no new discoveries this year, and at that point, the challenge became simply to survive. They avoided starvation by eating their famished dogs; a single canine remained when they reached Anniversary Lodge the last week of June.

———

IN PHILADELPHIA, desperate measures were also afoot.

Josephine urgently sought to find the money to hire a ship and crew to go north that summer to bring back her husband and the others. The funds raised by Peary for the expedition had been long spent, and then some. With expenditures the preceding year exceeding estimates, the cost of sending *Falcon* north had been met by the sale of Mary Peary's Maine home.

Prior to Josephine's departure the preceding summer, Peary had told his wife that if she was unable to raise the money to send a ship for him, he would sledge to southern Greenland and take one of the ships that regularly went to Denmark.

Now the prospect of his not coming directly home was beyond her imagination, and she had no idea what kind of physical shape he was in after another winter. She was haunted by the specter of him at some of his lowest moments—when he had been a helpless invalid with a broken leg and when he had returned exhausted from the ice cap. Suppose, she now worried, he was not capable of making a long sledge journey to a southern harbor? In her mind, the only solution was for her to find a way to hire another ship to fetch him.

This time it would not be *Falcon*. After disembarking Josephine, her baby, and the other passengers in Philadelphia the preceding fall, *Falcon* had set sail for St. John's. She never made it. After possibly striking an iceberg off Newfoundland, she went down quickly in a stormy sea with all hands.

Estimating the cost of hiring a ship and crew at $12,000, Josephine set about contacting numerous prominent men, asking for contributions. She made no reference to any rescue of her husband and his men, but more loftily to the Greenland Scientific Expedition of 1895.

One individual who gave her an audience was Morris K. Jesup, an eminent New York financier and philanthropist who was a founder of the Young Men's Christian Association (YMCA) and president of the American Museum of Natural History, which he had endowed with more than $100,000. In his midsixties, he had graying, slicked-back hair and a bushy beard with mutton chops that went beyond his collar. His most striking feature was his intense gaze from deep-set, penetrating eyes.

Josephine explained the work being done by her husband exploring northern Greenland, and his hopes for remaining an extra year. A ship sent to retrieve him the coming summer could take academic researchers northward, she explained, for the purpose of observing and collecting data.

Jesup wanted to know at what cost, and she told him. Their meeting was cordial, and Jesup seemed genuinely interested, but Josephine came away without a bank draft—only with a remarkable vow from the millionaire.

Continuing her solicitations, she received contributions from numerous organizations, some of which would send members on the voyage: the American Geographical Society ($1,000), the Geographical Club of Philadelphia ($760), the American Museum of Natural History ($1,000), Bowdoin College ($1,000), and the Brooklyn Institute of Arts and Sciences ($1,000). In addition, the National Geographical Society organized a lecture for Josephine, which netted $400.

While a substantial amount had been collected, it was not enough, in spite of Josephine's effort. Morris Jesup, who believed in helping people who helped themselves, now made good on his promise to her. He generously made up the difference. A familiar vessel, *Kite*, and her crew were hired and dispatched to northern Greenland.

After much deliberation, Josephine had decided against going north on *Kite*. The past year had not healed the hurt she had felt when her husband chose staying in Greenland over coming home with her and their baby. And what if he again spurned home? For three weeks, she worked on a pained and heartfelt letter to her husband to be personally delivered by the *Kite* captain.

"When you told me your plan a year ago . . . I felt as if you had put a knife into my heart and left it there for the purpose of giving it a turn from time to time," Josephine wrote. "I have reviewed our married life very carefully, my husband, and think I am resigned to the place which you gave me an hour after we were married." Even at such a romantic moment, he had been blunt, telling her she would be number two in his life after his mother. "How it did hurt," she went on, "has continued to hurt and will hurt until the end." She now felt third, she explained, after her mother-in-law and " 'fame' [in] the first place."

"My Bert, my life," she now pleaded, "if you have not been successful won't you be content to put fame in the background and live for me a little . . . ?"

As JOSEPHINE fervently hoped, her husband returned on *Kite*. He brought with him two meteorites lashed down in the ship's hold—Woman, weighing 5,500 pounds, and Dog, 1,000 pounds. Retrieving them had been an engineering feat—the meteorites were moved upon iron rollers over a plank tramway and floated on an ice floe out to the ship, where they were swung onboard with tackles and winches. Bringing home the meteorites was his only real achievement of the trip; tangible trophies in lieu of glorious tales of exploring new territories. Privately, Peary considered it grossly insufficient.

On the voyage back, Peary was dispirited and uncommunicative. When the ship stopped at St. John's, several newspaper reporters, including one from the *New York Times,* boarded. They tried unsuccessfully to interview Peary, who remained in seclusion. They talked to other passengers, such as L. L. Dyche, a professor of vertebrate zoology at Kansas State University, who had gone on the trip to conduct research. Dyche unflinchingly described Peary's most recent expedition as "a dismal failure" and predicted it would be his last.

Peary came home, by his own admission, not himself "physically or mentally," feeling that his "Arctic efforts were ended" and that his "life-work had been a failure." For the first time, Josephine saw her husband "completely crushed."

Notwithstanding their parting of ways, Cook was sorry to hear of his former commander's woes. "Peary's failure is sad news," he wrote to a colleague from the 1891–92 expedition. "He has fought hard and against tremendous odds to accomplish something. He deserves sympathy." Pragmatically, Cook was also concerned that Peary's lack of progress could result in less support for future American explorations and "throw another shadow on Polar work."

When reporters caught up with him in Maine, at his mother's new residence, which she shared with a cousin, Peary showed the world the image of defeat. "I shall never see the North Pole unless someone brings it here," he said. "In my judgment, such work requires a far younger man than I." He had turned forty on his last expedition— "too old," Peary told the reporters, "to snowshoe twenty-five to thirty miles a day for weeks, and to carry a heavy load.

"I am done with it."

CHAPTER SEVEN

"POLAR SUMMER RESORT"

I N THE SUMMER of 1894, Cook again went north. Although he gave well-received public lectures (*"EXTRA! Interesting Lecture, Dr. Cook, Arctic and Antarctic Explorer, Young Eskimo Man and Woman in Full Costume, Team of Eskimo dogs, sledges. Price 75 cents"*) and colorful interviews to newspapers (*"Cook's Expedition: The Great Explorer Proposes to Visit the South Pole"*), during which he explained in detail his plan for an exploring party of a dozen "intelligent, educated" volunteers to penetrate the mysteries of the South Pole, he was unsuccessful in raising the $50,000 he estimated was needed to mount an Antarctic expedition. More than one departure date was announced only to be canceled for lack of funds.

Cook considered the choice of staying home that summer or organizing another short excursion to Greenland. Opting for the latter, he placed advertisements in several publications and signed up some fifty well-to-do passengers paying $500 each. Shortly before the June 1894 departure, one newspaper reported, "Polar Summer Resort: Dr. Cook's Fashionable Arctic Exploration Party."

The junket to the land of the icebergs would be aboard a comfortable decade-old Atlantic steamer belonging to the Red Cross Line. At 1,158 tons and 220 feet in length, *Miranda* was the largest ship ever to set out for Arctic waters.

The passenger manifest suggested a wide range of personalities

and backgrounds—professors and students from Yale, Harvard, and
the University of Pennsylvania; the former mayor of Cleveland; the
ex-prosecuting attorney of St. Louis; the author of *The Ice Age of
North America;* several physicians; a dentist; a taxidermist; a minister; a photographer; the U.S. solicitor of patents; and the thirteen-
year-old son of a U.S. Supreme Court justice.

Two special guests accompanied Cook on the trip—the Eskimo
children Clara and Willie, who were returning home, much to the
regret of the former, according to Cook, for she had "taken very
kindly to the ways of civilization."

Miranda, known as a hard-luck ship for running aground a few
times and being involved in a pair of at-sea collisions, departed New
York on July 7. Even that event did not go well. As the lines were
cast off, the captain signaled the engineers below deck to back
slowly. Instead, the ship lurched forward into the pier with a sicken-
ing thud. Although no damage was done, the incident served as an
"ill omen" to the passengers. A few crewmen shared similar concerns
when rats were seen scurrying ashore after the crash. Although a
landsman beginning a long cruise might consider that a positive
development, old salts take a different view of rats deserting a ship.

The next ten days passed uneventfully.

July 16 dawned bright and clear, and the first icebergs appeared.
Excited passengers spent the day watching bergs of various shapes
and sizes glide by in magnificent procession. The next morning a
dense fog rolled in.

Cook, concerned that *Miranda* had not slowed down enough,
went to the bridge to speak to the captain about the danger of icebergs. While the captain explained how capable he was at avoiding
icebergs, even in fog, Cook only had to look out to see the icy obstacles passing perilously close.

Shortly after eight o'clock that morning, the ship ran into an iceberg that appeared suddenly out of the mist, towering above the
ship. There was a frightful wrenching sound as the ship pitched up
violently, then came crashing down. Passengers and crewmen alike
were sent sprawling to the deck.

Miranda's bow had pieced the iceberg, and was stuck fast.

Fortunately, the ice did not project below the water in front of the berg's steep face, so the blow to the hull was received above the waterline. The starboard side had damage, and some of the deck railing had been ripped away.

Backing astern freed the ship. After all compartments were checked for integrity, *Miranda* put in to the nearest harbor on the Labrador coast for emergency repairs. Once there, the captain decided to seek more permanent repairs at St. John's, Newfoundland—four hundred miles to the south.

Repairs were completed in St. John's by July 29, and *Miranda* again steamed northward. Following several stops along the Labrador coast—Clara and Willie were returned to their family at Rigolet—the ship turned northeast for Greenland. Cook requested that the captain set a double watch for icebergs, which was done without protest.

On August 3, the snowy mountains of southern Greenland rose into view about thirty miles away. They had hoped to make the nearest port after landfall but were kept from doing so by a long stretch of unbroken ice.

For three days, in intermittent fog and rain, they proceeded north along the edge of the ice floe, seeking an opening. The expanse of ice, the proximity of icebergs, and the shifting blanket of the fog combined to impress and frighten the passengers. *Miranda* was occasionally surrounded on three sides by unbroken ice, although with the water calm there was no imminent danger as long as care was taken in the handling of the ship.

On August 6, they worked their way through a field of broken ice and made port at Sukkertoppen, a Danish sealing and whaling village situated on a coastal island in the shadow of an impressive mountain. For three days, the passengers found much to explore along the deep, beautiful fjords. They strolled on surrounding glaciers, hunted reindeer, collected plant specimens, got to know the Danish families who resided there, and met the local Eskimos. After farewells, the ship headed back out to sea.

Seven miles from Sukkertoppen, the ship heaved sharply to starboard after three jarring bumps. At the time, Cook was being served breakfast with other passengers in the dining area, where plates and glassware went flying. As others dashed off to their lifeboat stations, Cook ran to the bridge, where he found more confusion. Even the captain could not immediately account for what had happened.

Cook was surprised at what he did *not* see looming off the bow: no iceberg, which he thought must have been the cause of the crash. Rather, it turned out *Miranda* had struck a submerged reef, which, it was later determined, was clearly marked on the chart in the pilot house. There she was now stuck, with sizable sea swells working to give her a pounding against the rocks.

Once they maneuvered off the reef, a crewman appeared on the bridge with the first damage report from below: the hold had three inches of water, but the portable steam pumps were up and running.

Inexplicably, the captain announced his intention to proceed northward to the harbor of Godthaab, two days away. Cook would not hear of it, and insisted that they return forthwith to Sukkertoppen to assess the damage.

The captain refused. Cook was a man who never seemed hot under the collar and never raised his voice for effect, but in this instance he pushed back. After a heated discussion that some observers thought might end in fisticuffs, the captain finally agreed to turn around.

That decision may have saved lives, because *Miranda* was discovered, on inspection at Sukkertoppen, to have severe damage to her hull that had caused flooding to the ballast tanks. She was still afloat, but for how long no one knew.

Cook realized that if he was to bring his party back safely, outside help was required. To that end, he decided to take a small boat up the coast, where he was told a number of American fishing boats were working the waters.

Several volunteers joined Cook for what turned out to be a rough journey through stiff winds, high seas, and pelting rain. On August 16, after sailing and rowing nearly a hundred miles, they arrived at Holsteinborg, where Cook learned from the Danish governor that several American schooners were a few miles up the coast. An Eskimo kayaker made contact the next morning with the nearest schooner, *Rigel*, of Gloucester, Massachusetts, delivering to the captain a signed letter from Cook telling of the damage to *Miranda* and the number of Americans in his party, and asking, "Will you kindly come to our rescue?"

Rigel, which had spent the summer fishing for halibut on the northern coast of Iceland and had just arrived off Greenland two weeks earlier to finish out the season, anchored at Sukkertoppen on August 20 alongside *Miranda*.

After a conference between the two captains with Cook in attendance, it was decided that both ships should try for Nova Scotia. The prudent course of action, all agreed, was to move the passengers onto the sailing vessel, which would be towed behind *Miranda* at the end of a stout 1,000-foot hawser. In the event the larger ship foundered, *Miranda*'s crew would be transferred to *Rigel*.

Once they were underway, things went smoothly until the second night, when the two ships were in the middle of the Davis Strait— three hundred miles from Greenland—fighting a heavy sea. A ballast tank burst on *Miranda* shortly after midnight, and she blew the signal of distress and lowered a red light that by prearrangement meant the steamer was sinking.

In the dark, pitching sea, the scene for the next three hours was one of high drama. *Rigel* remained attached to the larger ship but with a crewman standing by with an ax ready to sever the line at a moment's notice. Dories made the trip from *Miranda* with members of her thirty-three-man crew, but in the high sea it was a struggle to haul the small boats safely alongside *Rigel*. First came the members of the steward's department; last to arrive was the captain and the rest of his bridge crew, who before departing had lashed the rudder to one side and released the hawser from the fantail of the crippled ship.

Soaked but safe, all hands stood elbow to elbow on the deck of *Rigel* and watched as *Miranda*—her lights still burning, smoke pouring from her stack, and propeller turning—steamed off into the mist, never to be seen again.

Rigel reached North Sydney, on the northeastern shore of Nova Scotia, on September 5, and Cook's party split up. Some wanted no more of ocean travel and purchased railway tickets home. The rest, including Cook, ended up bound for New York on *Portia*, which looked spookily like *Miranda*.

It turned out *Portia* and *Miranda* were sister ships of nearly identical British design. That wasn't all they had in common: one day out of New York, off Vineyard Haven Sound, *Portia* rammed a small sailing vessel.

Rushing up on deck, Cook found a jumble of ripped sails, broken spars, and pieces of a mast from the sailing ship, which had been cut in half with only the stern section still visible. In the next instant, Cook saw two men being sucked under with the wreckage before any assistance could be rendered. Of the five crew members aboard *Dora N. French*, of Bangor, Maine, four were lost.

The extensive press coverage about the ill-fated *Miranda* excursion—complete with questions about the sobriety of the captain and crew—did little to generate interest in more sightseeing trips to Greenland, and Cook remained home the following summer (1895).

His Brooklyn medical practice expanded, and he even took in a partner; still, he found his days very tame compared with those spent in the Far North. Cook's notes on his patients give a glimpse of the tedium of his practice: "Nelson Green . . . spleen enlarged. Frequent nausea, dizziness. Fetid odor of breath, disgusting taste in mouth in morning." And: "Mrs. Green . . . flatulence, constipation. Wants obesity reduced."

Cook was understandably eager to get back to exploring, and he again focused his energies on the Antarctic. As for the North Pole, which had a stronger claim on the imagination of the public than did its southern counterpart, Cook was convinced it would be reached before the end of the century—if not by an American, then by one of the capable European explorers, such as Fridtjof Nansen and Otto Sverdrup, who were making regular forays to the Far North. He did not think there was room for his entry into the race for the North Pole.

The South Pole was another matter, and one potential backer Cook attempted to interest was the industrialist Andrew Carnegie. They met on a wintry day at the Union League Club, a conservative social club at East Twenty-sixth Street and Madison Avenue in New

York City. To Cook's surprise, Carnegie had read several books by Arctic explorers. He was particularly interested in the work of Europeans such as the Norwegian Nansen and the Britons Francis Leopard M'Clintock and John and James Ross (uncle and nephew, respectively). For reasons Carnegie did not make clear, he seemed to have less interest in the accomplishments of American explorers.

Cook hoped to change that.

Carnegie, a diminutive man only a few inches over five feet, had made his journey from rags to riches, and was by then a captain of industry—known as the "king of steel"—and one of the wealthiest men in America.

Cook presented a concrete proposal: to follow up in the Southern Hemisphere on the claimed discoveries of the Wilkes expedition—officially known as the U.S. Surveying and Exploration Expedition (1838–42)—a circumnavigation of the world involving six ships and hundreds of men that charted, among many other areas of the world not yet surveyed, several hundred miles of the coastline of Antarctica. Cook wished to go farther, of course—to the South Pole or as close as possible, with his exploring party.

At the end of the meeting, Carnegie said, "Doctor, I would like to get interested in your ice business. . . . See me next Monday or write me." Cook sought out Carnegie the following week, and they sat in a corner of the same club room. This time, the doctor came prepared with a list of the values of scientific research, and he made a point of talking "utility fast and strong" for the benefit of the businessman before him—a man who, in the steel business, had been quick to adopt modern technological innovations such as the open-hearth furnace and increased managerial efficiency through vertical integration.

At a crucial moment, Carnegie was summoned to another room. When he returned, his thoughts seemed elsewhere. "Doctor, there is so much to be done in this world nearer by," said the industrialist.*

---

*True to his word, Carnegie, after selling his steel company to J. P. Morgan in 1901, retired to devote himself to philanthropy. By the time of his death, in 1919, he had given away $350 million and built libraries and universities, but not a penny for polar exploration.

Cook sensed he had lost whatever momentum had been built.

Upstate New York in winter has "all the ice we will ever need," said Carnegie, who questioned the need for expensive explorations to other icy lands.

Carnegie had clearly missed the point of polar exploration, and for the second summer in a row Cook had nothing to explore and nowhere to go.

CHAPTER EIGHT

BOUNTY HUNTING

FOLLOWING HIS RETURN from the Arctic in fall 1895, Peary resumed his official duties at the Brooklyn Navy Yard. As he regained his stamina and spirits, he went back on the lecture circuit in the evenings and on weekends, telling the familiar tale of his sledge trip across northern Greenland three years earlier.

Peary's narrative came to life whenever he spoke of the meteorites he had unearthed, and particularly of the one great "iron stone" that remained in the Far North, promising that one day he would bring Tent home.

He strove to find a way to make that happen. To augment the funds he raised through lectures and other contributions, he sold round-trip passage to university teachers and students; they would be dropped off at various locations on the Greenland coast to conduct Arctic fieldwork and be picked up on the way back. By the next summer, Peary had enough money to charter a ship.

Returning from his last trip with Woman and Dog had diverted attention from Peary's failure to achieve little else. Woman was the second largest meteorite in any collection in the world, the largest being the Cranbourne meteorite (8,000 pounds) in the British Museum. The meteorites were put on display at the American Museum of Natural History, endearing him to his newest benefactor, the museum's president, Morris K. Jesup, who took up Peary's latest cause with the Navy and helped him secure a summer leave.

Peary sailed aboard *Hope* in July 1896, reaching Cape York in early August. The ice was thin enough in Melville Bay for the ship to push through to the small island where Tent was located. They were able to anchor next to a natural rock shelf that ran down from the meteorite's location.

Racing against the onset of winter conditions, Peary organized an excavation of the site. The stone was then lifted with heavy hydraulic jacks and placed on a trolley. A bridge way was constructed with railroad ties across the rock shelf, and the meteorite was slid down to the ship by winch and steel cable.

At that point, Mother Nature intervened. A sudden and furious southeaster broke up a ridge of icebergs that had been protecting their flank from the pressure of the ice pack. As the ice now closed in for what would surely be a months-long winter captivity for ship and crew, they had no choice but to pull out, leaving the meteorite beached like a giant whale.

Peary came home to further bad news.

The newspapers were filled with exciting reports of one of the most dramatic developments in the history of Arctic exploration. Nansen, using as his base of operations *Fram*, a small ship designed to drift in the ice pack, had left the ship after it had been icebound for two years and marched toward the North Pole the preceding spring, achieving a new farthest-north record of 86 degrees, 13 minutes. Before he was forced to turn around due to storms and melting ice, the Norwegian had stood within 225 miles of the Pole, bettering by nearly 170 miles the record for the highest explored latitude on the globe (83 degrees, 24 minutes, north), set nearly thirteen years earlier by the Greely expedition.* Then overtaken by winter, Nansen had spent nine months in a hut of stones

---

*Mileage hereafter stated as distances to and from the Pole is given in nautical (or geographical) miles. At any location on Earth, one minute of latitude is equal to one nautical mile, and one degree equates to sixty nautical miles. A nautical mile is some 800 feet longer than a statute mile, or approximately 1.15 statute miles.

and walrus hide. Unable to find *Fram*, a wandering Nansen happened upon the ship of an English explorer, Frederick Jackson, who returned him safely to Norway.

For Peary, it was a painful reminder of Nansen's trump of his earlier effort, when the Norwegian had been the first man to cross Greenland. After his initial disappointment, Peary seemed galvanized by the competition. Using the January 1897 occasion of his receiving an American Geographical Society award, Peary declared the goal of his next expedition as "the conquest of the North Pole." He would launch his effort, he explained, from a base in northern Greenland, where he would be prepared to stay five years, if necessary. He estimated the cost at $150,000.

"Nansen has wrested from the Stars and Stripes the record of the highest north which it had held for a dozen years, and has placed the Norwegian flag far in advance," Peary said with his usual dose of patriotic fervor. "The Pole is certain to be reached soon; it is only a question of time and money, and not so very much of the latter, and unless we are alert we shall be left in the rear. . . . I know there is not an American man or woman whose heart would not thrill with patriotism to see the realization of this project, and know that it was American money, intelligence, energy and endurance that had scaled the apex of the Earth, and lighted it with 'Old Glory. . .'. No man could . . . without personal exertion or discomfort, obtain a more royal and imperishable monument, than to have his name written forever across the mysterious rocks and ice which form the setting for the spinning axis of the Globe, the North Pole."

Peary found the reaction to his plan "immediate and emphatic." Within a month, the American Geographical Society offered its full support, with the understanding that Peary would continue to solicit other backers.

The Navy had other plans for Peary. His request for a five-year leave to undertake his first assault on the North Pole was rejected, and orders were cut for his transfer to the shipyards at Mare Island, California.

Peary found the forces against him in the Navy "determined, concentrated, and bitter," and none of the strings he had previously pulled worked this time. Within two weeks of his scheduled exile to the west coast, Peary by chance was introduced to Charles A. Moore, a prominent New York politician, who caught the explorer's enthusiasm about his planned assault on the Pole. Moore, who had supported William McKinley in the presidential election months earlier—New York State's thirty-six electoral votes went to McKinley in his race against William Jennings Bryan—made an appointment with the secretary of the Navy to lobby on Peary's behalf. When Moore explained the nature of his request, the secretary said, "*Anything* but that." The subject of Peary's duty status had obviously become a sore point at the highest levels.

Undeterred, Moore walked across the street and received an immediate audience with President McKinley, who had been sworn into office only weeks earlier. "You remember," Moore pointedly asked McKinley, "that you said to come to you if I ever wanted anything?"

McKinley nodded. As a former longtime member of Congress and twice governor of Ohio, he knew about paying back political favors.

"I want Lieutenant Peary of the Navy granted five years' leave in order to continue his great work in the north."

Obvious relief passed over McKinley's face. He had been anticipating having to deliver on a much larger favor. "Is that all? . . . Of course I'll do it."

McKinley dictated a memorandum, which Moore, who could not resist the temptation, hand-delivered to the Navy secretary a few minutes later. Peary's orders for Mare Island were revoked straightaway, and a month later he was detached from his official duties for five years' paid leave.*

Before turning his attention to his polar expedition, Peary had

*Peary's five-year leave on President McKinley's orders was granted effective May 25, 1897. Although Peary had been in the Navy more than fifteen years since his commission in October 1881, he had already been on leave (seven years, one month) nearly as long as on duty (eight years, five months)—a highly unusual imbalance that continued throughout his naval career.

unfinished business in northern Greenland. Again partly financed through the sale of passage to scientists and other sightseers—including a couple who wished to spend their honeymoon at Godhavn—Peary put together a party and chartered a ship for the specific purpose of retrieving Tent. Josephine and their now four-year-old daughter, Marie, went along on the summer journey. In the process of loading the meteorite onto the ship, a U.S. flag was draped over it at one point, and Marie dashed a little bottle of wine against it, christening the rock that had fallen from the heavens in a fireball, Ahnighito, her own Eskimo name.

Leading meteorite authorities agreed that the recovery of the Cape York meteorites—including Ahnighito, which weighed nearly forty tons, by far the largest in any collection in the world—was a valuable find. From the beginning, it seemed, Peary's motives were not altogether altruistic. As if to ensure clear and undisputed title, he made a point of acquiring from a Danish official a bill of sale for the meteorites, although there is no evidence anything of value was received by the Danes or local natives in return for the meteorites. He also required the passengers on *Hope* to sign a statement concerning the recovery of the meteorite being "entirely confidential" and agreeing that the incident could simply "be covered by the statement that I have the meteorite on board" and nothing more. Although Peary had previously spoken colorfully about the meteorites' having been responsible for the rise of the natives to the iron age of tools and weapons, he subsequently justified his removal of the buried treasures by noting that the "savage stress of [the] natural environment" of the Eskimos allowed "them no room" for any real appreciation of their "celestial guests."

Peary presented the third and largest meteorite to the American Museum of Natural History, where it went on display with the others in the cavernous Seventy-seventh Street lobby. He did not, as the press and public generally assumed, make gifts of the meteorites. Rather, they were on loan subject to a buyer being found by the museum or by the sales agent he had retained to sell other valuable Arctic artifacts—furs, skins, ivory, narwhal tusks, and similar souvenirs obtained in trade with the Eskimos for such staples as coffee, biscuits, and candy—he was now diligently bringing back on each trip. In most cases, he avoided being assessed any duty on his property by having all items marked as museum pieces. Peary eventually placed what was then an astronomical price on the three sky stones, known by the Eskimos for generations as *saviksue* (great irons): $50,000.

That summer Peary also brought back Eskimos, alive as well as dead, and left them all at the American Museum of Natural History. Asked by an assistant curator of the museum, an anthropologist, to bring him one live Eskimo to study for a year, Peary instead delivered six: two of his best hunters and sledge drivers from Smith Sound, who had helped him secure the big meteorite, the wife of one of the hunters, and three youngsters. They had been promised by Peary, according to one of the natives, "nice warm houses in the sunshine land, and guns and knives and needles and many other things."

No such promises had to be made to acquire the remains of recently deceased natives, some of whom Peary had personally known. He simply ordered their fresh graves opened, and their bodies and the implements they were buried with—to aid their lives in the spirit world—gathered up and placed in big barrels for transport to the museum. The remains, which included a hunter named Qujaukitsoq, his wife, and young daughter, all of whom died during an epidemic, were sold by Peary to the museum as anthropological specimens.

Room was made for the six Eskimo visitors in the museum's basement. In an early October heat wave, they soon became sick. Within a few months, after being taken to a farm in upstate New York to recuperate, four were dead, succumbing to pneumonia brought on by strains of influenza to which they had no resistance. Only two boys, Uisaakassak and Minik, survived.

One of the dead was Minik's father, Qisuk, whose remains—along with those of the other Eskimo dead—were returned to the museum, where plaster casts were made of the bodies and brains, the bones cleaned, and the skeletons mounted for display. To assuage the grief of the eight-year-old boy, a mock funeral was staged for his father. Inside the coffin was a log.

Although short of his fund-raising goal, Peary made preparations to depart in summer 1898, hoping that publicity would generate additional interest among potential backers. On the morning of February 16, 1898, Peary brought in the morning paper and glanced at the headlines. The day before, the battleship USS *Maine* had been blown up by a mysterious explosion and sunk in Havana Harbor, killing 260 American sailors. *Maine* had arrived in Havana a month earlier to protect U.S. citizens and property after riots in Cuba's struggle for independence from Spain. With anti-Spanish sentiment inflamed ("Remember the *Maine!*")—only later did it come out that the deadly explosion was an accident and not an act of sabotage— Peary expected his leave to be canceled by the Navy, but it was not.

He decided against volunteering for the war that everyone knew would soon be fought, and continued with his Arctic planning. He was, after all, forty-two years old, and he genuinely believed this would likely be his last chance. He departed on July 4, 1898, aboard *Windward*, two months after war with Spain was declared by Congress.

Peary's war was not with foreign powers but with the North Pole.

CHAPTER NINE

DESTINATION ANTARCTICA

STEAMING OFF CAPE HORN in storm-tossed seas aboard *Belgica*, a converted sealer outfitted with a scientific laboratory, photography darkroom, and the latest equipment for studying ocean currents and marine life, Cook knew nothing about the outbreak of hostilities with Spain. In fact, he would not learn of the Spanish-American War until after it had ended.

After returning from the luckless *Miranda* cruise, Cook had settled into his medical practice in Brooklyn. Although he lectured periodically about Greenland and Eskimo life, and still harbored hopes of exploring the Antarctic, he found his expanding medical practice demanding ever more of his time. For a number of years, his home and office had been situated in a modest brick building at 687 Bushwick Avenue, a quiet and fashionable neighborhood known for its many doctors' offices. Cook made his house calls in a buggy pulled by a handsome white horse. He seemed the image of an established family physician doing precisely what he wished to be doing. His home was kept by his mother-in-law, Mrs. Forbes, and her three grown daughters were regular visitors. Before long, Frederick was courting one of his late wife's sisters, Anna, a schoolteacher. None of this, however, had kept Cook from dreaming of exploration. One day he read an article in the *New York Sun* quoting a cabled dispatch from Antwerp about the delayed departure of the

Belgian Antarctic expedition. The group's physician had resigned, and Cook knew "in a flash" that this was his opportunity to do what he wanted. He at once cabled his willingness to join the expedition, and within hours he received a message of acceptance with instructions to meet the ship at Rio de Janeiro.

Coverage of Nansen's long drift across the polar sea filled columns in newspapers and periodicals, as did the bold plans of a Swedish engineer, Salomon Andrée, who was about to launch an attempt to cross the North Pole in a hydrogen-filled balloon.* Other Arctic expeditions from Europe and America were also reported to be in the planning stages. Exploration of the Far North was again a hot topic, yet Cook was about to head in the opposite direction. About his southerly destination—"the dream of my life"—he could not have been more excited, and he eagerly set about organizing the equipment and supplies he had been accumulating for an Antarctic expedition.

Cook and Anna Forbes had by late 1897 announced their engagement, and perhaps she thought the former Arctic explorer was ready to settle down. She was to learn that nothing was further from the truth. However, Cook did come to harbor reservations about leaving his fiancée, given her precarious health. Fearing a grave illness— even tuberculosis—he took her to a specialist, who gave his assurances that Anna's condition was not serious. Still, Cook hesitated at the last minute, missing the departure of a ship on which he had reserved passage, baffling his mother and sister, who had shown up dockside to bid him farewell. Three weeks later, notwithstanding Anna's wish that he stay home, Cook boarded another ship bound for South America.

In Rio, Cook waited anxiously for two weeks. Upon the arrival of

---

*Andrée and his two companions disappeared over the ice cap, never to be heard from again. Their bones were found in the Arctic thirty years later at their last campsite, along with a record of their progress, contained in recovered diaries and scores of pictures developed from long-frozen film. After escaping from their careening balloon, they had set out to walk two hundred miles to nearest land, but never made it. The cause of their demise has never been determined, although a likely one was carbon monoxide poisoning from an improperly ventilated tent.

Belgica, he was introduced to the international crew. The chief scientist was Romanian and the second scientist a Pole, five crewmen were Norwegians, including the first mate, named Roald Amundsen, and the remainder were Belgians. Communication would at times prove tricky, with French the principal language in the officers' cabin, German and French in the scientific labs, and elsewhere a hodgepodge of English, Norwegian, French, and German.

Cook learned that in addition to being appointed physician, he was to serve as anthropologist and photographer. The commander of the expedition was Adrien de Gerlache, a Belgian naval officer who had received the approval of the Royal Geographical Society of Brussels and funds from the Belgian government to make detailed scientific studies of the sea and lands within the Antarctic Circle for one season, returning *Belgica* to a South American port in time to avoid being trapped by the long winter.*

After several stops on the wild, eastern shore of South America, *Belgica* put in at the archipelago Tierra del Fuego, off that continent's southernmost tip. In this picturesque setting, they lingered for a month, mapping the area's coastline and studying its wildlife and aborigines, the vanishing Yahgans and the giant Onas, who were more than seven feet tall. It was summertime in this latitude, and Gerlache, a gentle and scholarly man who was more scientist than military officer, was enthralled by the vegetation and rock formations. He encouraged the crew to collect and categorize plants, rock specimens, and fish, many of them species never before seen, while he took soundings of the water's depth at various locations and marked them on his charts.

Finally, they steamed away from the breathtaking views of the snow-covered Andes into Antarctic waters, which Cook soon judged to be a breeding ground for the world's worst weather. Caught in a terrible gale accompanied by driving sleet and snow, *Belgica* battled

---

*The Antarctic Circle is marked by the approximate latitude of 66.5 degrees south, considered the northern limit of the area within which the sun does not rise or set for at least one day each year. The same definition marks the beginning of the Arctic Circle at approximately 66.5 degrees north of the equator.

up each massive wall of water only to plunge into a trough before starting the climb to the next crest. Icy waves cascaded over the decks, and the ship heeled and rocked until it seemed close to foundering. The surfaces above deck were coated with ice, and the men crawled on their hands and knees to move about.

Clinging for their lives to the bridge, Cook and Amundsen heard a scream that made them "shiver because of its force and painful tone." Fearing an accident in the engine room, Amundsen rushed below, while Cook struggled aft to the quarter deck to investigate. Looking astern, Cook saw in the water a young sailor, Carl Wiencke, who had managed to grab a line as he was falling overboard. Cook began reeling in the line and was soon assisted by several crewmen and the master of the ship, Georges Lecointe. As Wiencke was drawn closer, his grip on the line began to loosen. In the raging seas, it was impossible to launch a rescue boat. In an uncommonly brave act, Lecointe, a Belgian artillery officer who had served in the French navy, ordered himself lowered overboard in an effort to secure a lifeline around the struggling sailor. Lecointe sank immediately and resurfaced locked in a fierce fight for his own life, which he nearly lost. Wiencke, who had turned bluish in the icy water, was sucked under the ship by the current, and disappeared with what Cook later described as a "death mask on his face." *Belgica* circled the area for an hour, but there was no sign of their shipmate. Wiencke, one of the youngest sailors on board, had many friends in the crew, and his loss was deeply felt.

Proceeding southward, they passed the South Shetland Islands, and the Antarctic continent soon came in sight.* Since this region was partly unmapped, they spent time tracing the outlines of the coast—valuable information for future mariners as well as geographers. A landing party consisting of Amundsen, Cook, and the ship's two scientists went ashore to explore inland.

They camped the first night in a snowfield overlooking a glacier and endured a storm that struck without warning. When the weather

---

*Antarctica is a landmass covered in snow and ice, unlike the region at and around the North Pole, which would prove to have no solid land but only endless sea and ice.

cleared in the morning, they set out to establish a camp at a higher elevation. Cook and Amundsen, leading the way, came to a series of impassable crevasses at about 1,600 feet. Deciding to scale up a sheer ice face in an effort to bypass the gap, Cook and Amundsen roped themselves together. Amundsen was impressed with Cook's practical skill and calmness, and willingly followed behind the experienced explorer, who used a hand ax to cut steps in the ice. After several failed attempts, they succeeded in getting across. At one high over-look, they could see a distance of fifty miles. Cook unfolded an American flag he had placed in his pack and unfurled it in the breeze; it was the farthest south Old Glory had ever flown. After a week of exploring, the party was summoned back to *Belgica* by urgent blasts of the ship's whistle. An opening in the ice to the southwest had been spotted, and Gerlache wished to be off. Once underway again, every-one took turns on deck, marveling at the countless penguins, cor-morants, gulls, albatross, and other seabirds.

In mid-February 1898, *Belgica* emerged at the south end of a pas-sage that emptied into the Pacific Ocean. Winter was rapidly approaching, and it was still a long way to their destination on the Antarctic coast south of Australia, where four men were to be landed in the region of the South Magnetic Pole.* They were to establish a winter camp, while the ship and remainder of the crew returned to civilization. The exploring party—again to be com-posed of Amundsen, Cook, and the expedition's scientists—was to be picked up by *Belgica* come spring.

Belgica's course was adjusted to the west to make up for lost time. Soon they were fighting another terrific storm, this time with the added danger of icebergs looming in all directions. Throughout the

---

*In both the north and the south, the magnetic poles are far removed from the geographic poles, and the former were attained many years before the latter. The magnetic poles are the two points on Earth that either attract or repel a compass needle—because of the con-vergence of Earth's magnetic field—and they are constantly moving. The North Magnetic Pole, since its discovery by James Ross in 1831 off King William Island at some 70 degrees north by 96 degrees west, has moved hundreds of miles north. At the time of the *Belgica* expedition, the South Magnetic Pole was located more than a thousand miles from the geographic South Pole.

day, the captain kept the vessel in the lee of a long ridge of bergs that provided shelter from the wind and swells. During the night, the watch officer lost track of the blocking bergs, and when the sun came up they were becalmed in a small basin, surrounded by towering icebergs. In the darkness and heavy weather, the vessel had been pushed by the sea and wind through an opening between icebergs, miraculously without being dashed to pieces. With no immediate means of escape, *Belgica* dropped anchor and waited.

That evening, the wind shifted, and two icebergs parted. Thanks to deft maneuvering by Captain Lecointe, *Belgica* was extricated from its predicament.

This close call in increasingly wintry conditions, which would only worsen as the season advanced, did not deter the expedition commander, Gerlache, from pushing onward. They had not gone far when their westward course was blocked by an impenetrable wall of ice. At the same time, a strong gale came up from the north, pushing them steadily south toward a field of broken ice. "The instinct of any navigator accustomed to the Polar seas would have been to use every effort to get away to the north and into the open sea," the first mate, Amundsen, later attested. "This we could have done." But Gerlache, realizing that the season for Antarctic navigation had passed and that there was no hope of reaching their original destination, wanted at least to secure a farthest-south record. Eying an opening in the ice to the south, he persuaded Captain Lecointe to head in that direction. According to Amundsen, who was not asked his opinion on the bridge that day—and naval discipline required him to keep silent until asked—the two commanders "could not have made a greater mistake." He added, "I saw and understood fully the great danger they exposed the whole expedition to."

Indeed, what Amundsen feared soon happened. By the time they had ridden out the storm, *Belgica* was a hundred miles inside the ice field, and the pack ice had closed around them in all directions. The narrow channel they had taken through the ice no longer existed. After four days of searching for an escape route, everyone reached the same conclusion: there was no way out of the ice. The situation was all the more perilous in that *Belgica* was neither equipped nor supplied for winter. There wasn't enough winter clothing for the entire crew, nor enough lamps to keep all the quarters lit.

Cook and Amundsen, who had similar interests and experiences— Amundsen not only was "schooled . . . in fighting against the hardest elements of nature" but had also studied medicine for two years in Norway—nonetheless reacted differently to *Belgica*'s plight. To Amundsen, at home in the rigging of a ship at sea, being stuck in the Antarctic Circle was "a truly dreadful prospect," while Cook, who knew about wintering over in harsh climes, was more philosophical: "To be caught in the ice is, after all, the usual luck of polar explorers." Yet Cook well knew what to expect: a life "of hardship, of monotony and isolation, full of certain dangers and uncertain rewards."

Belgica soon became wedged into the ice pack, hopelessly pinned between two large icebergs. Their position was 71 degrees south by 85 degrees west; some 300 miles south of the Antarctic Circle but still 1,100 miles from the South Pole. Halted well short of a far-thest-south record, the men of *Belgica* were destined to make a greater contribution to the history of exploration: they would become the first to spend the long polar night in the Antarctic.

Amid the grinding of ever-shifting ice against the hull, they set-tled in for winter. *Belgica* would not remain stationary, but would slowly drift in whichever direction the floes moved.

Their duty now, everyone knew, was to prepare for the coming of perpetual darkness. All spaces had their coal supplies refilled from the ship's hold, and some structural changes were made for safety and comfort. A blacksmith shop was built on deck amidships and a stove added to one of the berthing compartments. Storm windows and doors were put up to keep out the worst of the weather. Snow was shoveled up high around the hull for insulation against bone-chilling winds, and a gangway was secured to the port side.

Meanwhile, the scientific staff stayed busy. There was much life in the sea below and on the pack ice, and the Romanian naturalist eagerly studied everything. One ship's officer, Lieutenant Emile Danco, realizing that *Belgica* was caught in the zigzag drift of the ice, carefully recorded the movement, which had never been docu-mented. In the diminishing light, Cook experimented with photography using German and French cameras with Zeiss lenses and glass plates. Since no exposure meters had been purchased for the photo lab, he had to learn how to estimate light correctly, and ended up taking some striking images. When the supply of chemicals for developing was gone, he tried fixing the negatives in a bath of prussic acid and found that it worked surprisingly well.

One night when the clear sky was filled with stars, Cook decided to sleep outside. He unfolded his sleeping bag in a sheltered spot not far from the ship, buried himself in the warm furs, and went to sleep. During the night, the wind shifted so that it blew directly into the bag. By morning, Cook's hair and beard were stuck by frozen condensation to the fur of his sleeping bag, and the back of his head was so solidly sheathed in ice that he was unable to move.

Amundsen awoke early that morning and went out to hunt. He saw a dark outline on the ice and, thinking it was a seal, raised his rifle and took aim. At the last moment, he realized that something about this seal looked strange. Investigating, he found the doctor eager to be chopped free from his icy bed.

In such close quarters, the crew developed either intense dislikes for one another or warm attachments. For Cook and Amundsen, it was the latter. In the young Norwegian, Cook saw someone with "more sense than most," a man who had done a great deal of reading and put what he had read to good advantage. "You have a good head for observation on your shoulder," he told Amundsen, who soon became Cook's regular companion and right-hand man. If Cook had found a willing student in Amundsen, the Norwegian found a patient mentor in Cook, seven years his senior. They went on forages across the ice fields, during which the experienced explorer never stopped teaching and encouraging.

The sun disappeared at midnight on May 15, not to be seen again for more than two months. Soon thereafter, wind storms became so severe and continuous that it was impossible to spend much time outside, and no one got much exercise. From then on, there was little for the men to do but idle away the time with talk and day-dreams, most often of home and loved ones.

As the weeks passed, the men grew listless and ill tempered.

They complained about the lack of planning that had caused them to be trapped for the winter, about the officers, about each other, about their chores, about the moisture that condensed around their bunks, and about everything else.

The first to report to sick bay was Lieutenant Danco, suffering heart problems. Beyond ordering bed rest, there was little Cook could do for him. The weakened Danco seemed to rally near the end, and his last words to Cook were optimistic: "I can breathe lighter and will soon get strength." He died on June 5. "His life . . . steadily . . . sunk with the northerly setting of the sun," Cook wrote in his journal. Danco's health had been adversely affected by the "prolonged darkness," the physician believed, which had "disturbed [his] equilibrium" and sent him to "a premature grave." The body, sewn into a sailcloth bag, was borne by sledge to a spot where a hole had been cut in the ice. A low moon lit the grayish night sky as a few remarks were spoken; then the body, with weights attached to it, was offered to the deep.

The death of the most popular officer on the ship weighed heavily on the crew. "The melancholy death, and the incidents of the sad burial of Danco, have brought over us a spell of despondency which we seem unable to conquer," Cook wrote on June 8. "I fear that this feeling will remain with us for some time, and we can ill afford it." According to Cook, a "spell of shivers" hung over the crew. "We are constantly picturing to ourselves the form of our late companion floating about in a standing position . . . under the frozen surface and perhaps under the *Belgica*."

Next to die was Nansen, the ship's cat. Always affectionate and eager to be stroked, the cat became irritable, ate little, and seemed to be in a stupor just before its death. The passing of their pet further depressed the men.

The first to break was a French sailor, Ernest Poulson. He appeared on deck one morning stark raving mad, swinging a knife and injuring several crewmen before leaping over the side and dashing across the snow. Amundsen gave chase, while Cook treated the wounded. When Amundsen caught up with Poulson, he was dead, having fallen on his own blade.

During the funeral procession that followed, the men were frightened and sobered, and even the officers were stunned to silence.
Before they headed back to the ship, Cook climbed atop a hummock
and got everyone's attention.

"Men, we're going through a bad time," Cook said into the howling wind. "I am sure that with enough thought and planning we'll
get out of it. But we must maintain level heads. We must be strong.
Otherwise, we will all die."

With that, Cook turned to Amundsen and exhorted his friend to
sing. Amundsen broke into a Norwegian sea chantey, and the men
joined in on the march back to the ship, momentarily distracted
from their predicament.

Two weeks later, a sailor climbed the mast and shouted, "Open
water!" pointing to where there was only unbroken ice. In his hallu-
cinatory excitement, he lost his grip and fell to his death on the
main deck. Another burial followed.

In addition to the obvious mental stress, Cook began to notice
worrisome physical symptoms among the crew. Gums grew spongy,
eyes and ankles showed puffiness, faces were pale and oily. Reports
of headaches, insomnia, indigestion, and loss of appetite were wide-
spread. Any exertion brought shortness of breath, and some men
were troubled by rheumatism. The doctor checked pulse rates and
found them irregular. One day a man's pulse would be strong and
vigorous; the next day, weak and twice as rapid. Strong young men
were wasting away. Cook diagnosed "a form of anemia peculiar to
the polar regions." A precursor to scurvy, it was a condition he had
seen before among the members of the first Peary Arctic expedition,
although the crew of *Belgica* had it far worse.

Cook was convinced the sun offered therapeutic value that was
missing in their lives. As a substitute, he experimented with the
light of an open fire. A man placed naked in front of an open fire,
soaking up the heat and rays for an hour or more, could go from
having a weak pulse to a normal one. One of the first to receive this
treatment was Captain Lecointe, who felt so ill and weak that,
resigned to his death, he had prepared his will. In addition to what
the sailors called the "baking treatment," Cook prescribed a diet of

fresh meat not only for his patient but for the entire crew. "We must have fresh meat or we will die, all of us," he said. But there was no longer fresh meat in the ship's larder.

Cook and Amundsen tried cutting a hole in the ice and fishing, but to no avail. They then took harpoons and clubs and crossed the ice fields to where they had seen a community of penguins. They were docile creatures and easy to kill, so much so that Amundsen felt remorseful. Since the meat was needed, Cook had no problem with the distasteful chore. Next on the menu was seal, as Cook and Amundsen went out to hunt seals basking on the ice.

Back at the ship, they boiled and broiled the meat. Although the flavor was strong and took some getting used to, Lecointe devoured everything put in front of him. After a few weeks of Cook's daily artificial sun treatments and a diet of fresh meat, Lecointe had recovered so completely that he was back at his duties. The men were heartened by what they considered a miracle, and everyone eagerly ate the meat— even those who had previously refused because of the taste—and rushed to get in front of the open fire sans clothing. Fewer showed up at sick call, and spirits were noticeably uplifted. As the symptoms abated, the men exhibited increased energy and less depression.

On July 22, after an absence of some seventy days, the sun appeared. Everyone was anticipating the happy event, and men were crowded into the rigging and crow's nest and waiting at elevated spots on the ice from which to watch. That first day only a slice of the sun appeared and stayed visible just a few minutes; however, it was a joyous event that marked not only the return of the sun's rays but also tangible hope for escape from their ice prison.

As the amount of sunlight increased daily, Cook and Amundsen "entered into a co-partnership . . . to make new and more perfect traveling equipment." They started with building a sledge of their design from hickory planks and other materials Cook had brought aboard. Most polar sledges of the day were heavy and cumbersome platforms weighing 150 pounds; their solid wooden runners often split from the shock of travel over the uneven surface of the pack ice. Cook believed that lightness, flexibility, and added strength were required. The styles of the two men complemented each other;

Amundsen could easily identify the defects of certain equipment, and Cook had a way of coming up with an improved design, which they worked side by side to construct. Their finished sledge weighed 75 pounds, with a framework of seasoned hickory curved to shape and braced with cross struts. The runners were shod with iron strips. To the upstander was fixed a movable framework that supported a double-walled tent over the body of the sledge. Portions of the frame could be removed and used as framework for a canvas boat; until then, the canvas doubled as a tarpaulin. Next, they worked on crafting a tent that could withstand the worst storms and weighed only 12 pounds, required just one pole, and could be set up by one man in a few minutes. They also fashioned boots made of penguin skins, and improvised seal-oil lamps from a design Cook had learned from the Eskimos.

As Cook and Amundsen became fast friends, they found they had both held in high regard Eivind Astrup; Amundsen had gone to school with him, and Cook had befriended him on the 1891–93 Peary expedition. They shared remembrances tinged with regret, as Astrup was now gone. A *New York Sun* article, datelined Oslo, had reported the sad news on January 22, 1896. Astrup had started out on skis a few days after Christmas to visit friends in a town fifty miles away, taking with him only a single day's ration. When he had been gone three weeks with no word, his alarmed friends formed a search party and came upon his frozen corpse in the wilderness.

To Cook and Amundsen it seemed incongruous that the strapping young man from the rugged mountains of Norway, who had grown up skiing in all weather and terrain and survived far worse conditions in the Arctic, would perish so close to home on a pleasure outing. His friends, including Cook, with whom Astrup had stayed in Brooklyn for a time after the latter's return from his second Peary expedition in fall 1894, knew that Astrup had gone back to Norway the following year still brooding over the unfairness and ingratitude shown by Peary, the man he had once idolized. Peary had openly rebuked Astrup for deserting him in 1894 rather than volunteering to spend a second, unplanned year in the Far North. It was a charge that left Astrup feeling humiliated and betrayed.

On his own, Astrup had made a monthlong survey of the Melville Bay area on his last expedition with Peary; subsequently, he wrote a detailed report published by the Norwegian Geographical Society. The Paris Geographical Society hailed Astrup's work as "the principal result of the expedition." To Peary, the lavish praise was a personal affront. In his own book, in which he included Astrup's entire Melville Bay survey, offering it as work done under his tutelage, Peary discreetly labeled the young Norwegian's independent literary efforts—which went counter to Peary's longtime policy of restricting the publication of any expedition accounts other than his own—as a "discourtesy."*

What was not known was whether illness, injury, or depression had played any role in Astrup's demise. Cook and Amundsen speculated aloud—*why hadn't he taken more supplies and been better prepared? Unless he never intended to reach his destination.* Had despair and gloom worn him down? Or was it something else? A jilted romance? Perhaps a serious health problem? Cook and Amundsen, unable to embrace any reasonable explanation for his death, were left to wonder.

While awaiting the breakup of the ice pack, Cook and Amundsen went on sojourns to test the new equipment. To their mutual satisfaction, everything worked as designed. During one outing, however, they were trapped for a time on an ice floe that had broken off from the pack before finding their way back.

Although ice conditions in the region grew increasingly unstable through spring and summer as the ice shifted and cracked, the vessel was still held fast in the ice pack. Late August and early September brought the lowest temperatures yet, and any hopes of the early melting and breakup of the ice in which they were stuck were soundly dashed.

As more months passed, supplies of food and fuel grew alarm-

---

*Astrup, who died before Peary's *Northward over the Great Ice* (1898) was published, did complete his own treatise of his Arctic experiences. In *With Peary near the Pole* (1898), published posthumously in Norwegian and English, Astrup questioned some of Peary's reported observations and claims from the 1892 ice cap journey the two men had taken.

ingly low. Despondency swept through the crew like a pox. It did not seem fair: they had made it through the winter but still *Belgica* could not move.

Fall passed slowly; Christmas 1898 arrived; then the new year began. There were no holiday festivities. The prospect of being stuck another year loomed, and everyone knew what that would mean.

One day, Amundsen thought he saw from the crow's nest a basin of water about half a mile from the ship. He and Cook went out to investigate. When they returned, Cook announced to the officers and crew that as the surrounding ice melted and broke up, the basin would expand and lead to open water. It seemed at the time a brash statement.

"The rest of us thought nothing of it as, naturally, water would form here and there," Amundsen later reported. "Somehow, though, to Dr. Cook's restless mind this basin seemed an omen of hope. He declared his firm conviction that the ice would break, and that, when the opening came, it would lead to this basin. . . . He proposed what sounded at first like a mad enterprise."

Cook proposed digging two shallow trenches—one from the bow and the other from the stern—connecting the ship to the basin. If, as he suspected, the ice fractured along the manmade lines, he reasoned, *Belgica* would find open water. Amundsen backed Cook's plan before the officers and men.

A sign of the crew's growing desperation was that they went along with the idea, which everyone understood would tax their strength and endurance, already weakened by the year of captivity. There was also the shortage of warm clothing—only enough to put a few men on the ice at a time. Amundsen proposed making clothing out of some extra wool blankets. He and the ship's carpenter cut out the patterns and sewed them into baggy suits. When the crew dressed in them, everyone burst out laughing and a few men rolled on the deck. The suits had been made from red blankets, and the men looked like a collection of Santa's elves.

For three days, the men labored with picks, axes, cleavers, shovels, and any other useful implement they could find, chopping through the ice, several feet thick in some places, to open water. By the time the trenches were completed, it was clear there was a complication. With winter approaching, the sun was no longer as intense as it had been, and its heat was not enough to keep new ice from forming in the trenches. Perhaps if they had dug the trenches a couple of months earlier, it would have worked, but now it was too late.

Since the sun could not be counted on to break up the ice, Cook concluded that they would have to cut their own channel directly to the basin. From the commander to the lowliest seaman, all hands agreed they had nothing to lose, and so *Belgica*'s crew went back to work with their tools. They also ignited sticks of tonite, an explosive more powerful than dynamite, to break up ice, which averaged four feet thick. The strenuous work continued around the clock in eight-hour shifts, with scientists, officers, and crewmen toiling side by side.

After a month, they were done. One night, everyone turned in, with the plan to put out lines in the morning and pull the vessel through the narrow channel. Upon awakening, they were shocked to see that the channel banks had been pushed together during the night by the pressure of the ice pack. This demoralizing circumstance did not last long, however, as a shift in the wind soon opened up the channel again. No time was lost in getting multiple lines hitched to the bow over the side, and the men slowly dragged *Belgica* forward into the basin, where finally, for the first time in a year, the ship sat afloat. Men cried at the sight, and spontaneous cheers went up.

For a time, they seemed no closer to making their escape. Then: "The miracle happened—exactly what Cook had predicted," Amundsen reported. "The ice opened up and the lane to the sea ran directly through our basin! Joy restored our energy, and with all speed we made our way to the open sea and safety."

Belgica had drifted in the pack ice more than one thousand miles, roughly following along the 70th parallel to a longitude of 101 degrees west.

Eager to continue his research among the Indians on the isolated coast, Cook disembarked in South America, and *Belgica* headed home across the Atlantic. Within a month Cook had worked his way into Uruguay, where at Montevideo a letter from home caught up with him, providing him with the sad news that his betrothed, Anna, had passed away. Her health had improved for a time, he learned from her family, but upon speculation as to the loss of *Belgica*—not heard from for more than a year—she "seemed to pine away."

Cook returned to Brooklyn in June 1899 to an empty house and a shuttered medical practice. He managed to revive the latter out of financial necessity and, while still in mourning, went to work on a book about the *Belgica* expedition. As time allowed, he finished a 400-page narrative, *Through the First Antarctic Night*, which was published in the first year of the new century. The book, the only account in English of the *Belgica* expedition, found a readership interested in polar exploration. In its dedication, Cook wrote,

TO THE LITTLE FAMILY, THE OFFICERS, THE SCIENTIFIC STAFF, AND THE CREW OF THE "BELGICA," WHOSE FORTUNES AND MISFORTUNES MADE THIS STORY OF THE FIRST HUMAN EXPERIENCE THROUGH-OUT A SOUTH POLAR YEAR; TO THESE MEN, WHOSE CLOSE COMPAN-IONSHIP AND STURDY GOOD-FELLOWSHIP MADE LIFE ENDURABLE DURING THE STORMS, THE DARKNESS, AND THE MONOTONY OF THE ANTARCTIC. . . .

With publication of *Through the First Antarctic Night*, Cook was recognized as the only living American to have explored both the Arctic and the Antarctic. Although he tended to downplay his critical role in the escape of *Belgica*—whereas Amundsen credited his "ingenuity" for having "saved the day"—Cook went back on the lecture circuit under the auspices of Peary's promoter, Major Pond, who labeled the physician-explorer "as modest and unassuming as he is accomplished" and added, "Among Arctic explorers I do not regard any one as more bold [or] more to be depended upon for accuracy of statement."

For services rendered during the Belgian Antarctic expedition, Belgium's King Leopold II awarded his nation's highest honor, the

Order of Leopold, named for his father, the first king of the Belgians, to Cook—the only non-Belgian in the *Belgica* crew so decorated.

Other polar expeditions were planning to set off both northward and southward, and Cook's name came up several times as a possible participant. Responding to one inaccurate report, Cook told a newspaper reporter, "I have been exploring for many years now and I think I'll give somebody else a chance."

With that, Cook went back to being a family doctor.

CHAPTER TEN

THE ICE MAN

NORTHERN GREENLAND
1901

In the shadows of the ship's cabin illuminated by a flickering oil lamp, Cook could see that Peary had aged beyond his forty-five years. The doctor's impression of the figure before him was of "an iron man, wrecked in ambition, wrecked in physique, and wrecked in hope."

Cook knew of Peary's activities in the intervening years mostly from the dispatches that appeared from time to time in newspapers, although some details had recently been filled in for him. He learned that Peary's current expedition—the one so boldly billed as an attempted "conquest of the North Pole"—had been eighteen months old when he was last heard from a year earlier. Peary had given his position as the southern coast of Greenland and reported plans to push north. When nothing more was heard from him, Josephine, in many ways as fiercely determined as the man she married, had boarded *Windward*, a relief ship sent the preceding summer by the newly formed Peary Arctic Club, a group of a dozen or so wealthy subscribers brought together by Morris Jesup to provide financial support for Peary's explorations. Along with her daughter, Marie, Josephine headed north to find her husband. Since then, nothing had been heard from her party either.

Peary's backers feared the worst for the man upon whom they had pinned their hopes and reputations, as well as their funds. They had asked Cook to go north as second in command of a new relief mission, explaining that they wanted someone who knew the region and the language of its natives to direct, if necessary, a rescue of the Peary party. "Peary is lost somewhere in the Arctic," said Peary Arctic Club officer and *Brooklyn Standard-Union* publisher Herbert Bridgman, who in 1892 had been in the audience for one of Peary's Arctic lectures and had since become a fervent supporter. Bridgman knew and respected Cook and urged him to join in the search because, he said, "we need the benefit of your judgment." From his experience with polar travel—including that of being stuck in unfavorable ice conditions—Cook surmised that Peary might simply be holed up and out of touch while awaiting more favorable conditions for travel. However, since the voyage was represented to him as an errand of mercy for a fellow explorer, Cook accepted, joining without compensation and providing his own equipment.

When Cook had arrived August 7 off Etah harbor aboard the sealing ship *Erik*, he saw the relief ship, *Windward*, close-in at anchor.

Josephine had indeed been reunited with her husband here, nearly a thousand miles from the Pole, although not before becoming a virtual prisoner of winter when *Windward* froze in the ice pack 250 miles south of her husband's winter encampment. It had been a long, trying wait for Josephine before conditions allowed him to join her.

Soon after *Windward* had arrived the preceding summer, a young Eskimo woman came aboard. To Josephine's horror, Allakasingwah boasted of being the wife of Pearyasksoah (Big Peary). Ensconced in a papoose on the native woman's back was a baby boy whose blue eyes and mop of reddish hair left little doubt as to his paternity. Allakasingwah, who greeted her man's white wife as a kind of tribal sister, was more receptive than Josephine to the concept of sharing. Josephine recognized the native woman from a picture in her husband's book, *Northward over the Great Ice,* published just prior to his latest departure. The image of her stretched out naked on a rocky outcrop had looked innocent enough; indeed, she was only in her early teens at the time. In retrospect the picture, captioned "Mother of the Seals (An Eskimo legend)," provided ample evidence of what had transpired after Josephine returned home aboard *Falcon* in 1894, leaving her husband behind to continue his work.*

While Josephine did warm to the innocent, childlike "Ally" during the winter—even caring for the young woman when she fell dreadfully ill—the fact that her husband had given his mistress a child deepened her resentment of the affair. In January 1899, Josephine had given birth to a second child, a girl she named Francine. In a letter delivered that summer by a relief ship, she had written her husband of the joyous news. Tragedy struck seven months later when the baby died of cholera. That her husband had sired a healthy child of another woman when her own hadn't survived seemed the final cruelty.

When confronted, Peary had been unapologetic about his liaison with Allakasingwah, and Josephine found herself in the position of having to accept it, however reluctantly. In any case, the relationship would not end any time soon—in fact, Ally would bear Peary a second child. He had revealed his feelings about such matters as early as 1885, when he wrote in his diary after his first Greenland expedition, "If colonization is to succeed in the polar region let white men take with them native wives, then from this union may spring a race combining the hardiness of the mothers with the intelligence of the fathers. Such a race would surely reach the Pole if their fathers did not succeed in doing it."

Soon after disembarking, Cook had come upon Josephine. They had not seen much of each other since returning from the earlier expedition that wintered over at Red Cliff. She looked every bit as regal as he remembered: tall and willowy, with a long, graceful neck and chiseled cheekbones and chin. As a concession to the difficult conditions she had endured for more than a year, her brunette

---

*Peary first met Allakasingwah when he took some ethnological photographs of her family during his 1893–95 expedition. In his own hand, Peary wrote about the meeting, "The girl, then just beginning to develop into a woman, evinced extreme reluctance to having her picture taken, and only a direct order from her father accomplished the desired result." Peary described her glowingly as the "belle of the tribe" and soon thereafter was taking her to his bed.

hair had been chopped unfashionably short. Otherwise, she was ready for a wintry stroll in Central Park, with her black cape-style coat that buttoned down the front, a jaunty cap worn at a tilt, and flat-heeled boots.

Cook told her why he had come, and also the sorrowful news from home. Peary's beloved mother had passed away at her Maine home the preceding winter. Cook was correct in thinking that Josephine would want to be the one to tell her husband.

Whatever difficulties had arisen between the Pearys had seemingly been put aside by Josephine. Her most urgent concern appeared to be for her husband's health, and she urged Cook to examine him promptly. She also beseeched Cook to persuade her husband to return home on *Windward* with her and their daughter.

Exhorting her husband to leave the Far North was unlike Josephine. Even while wintered in aboard *Windward* and still separated from him, she had written him a note she directed the Eskimos to deliver as soon as conditions allowed, imploring that he not try to reach the stranded ship in the dead of winter for concern it would "interfere with [his] work." Although Josephine had steadfastly supported her husband's polar efforts through all the heartaches of a life lived so much alone, she also expressed in the same letter her deepest longing: "Oh, Bert, Bert. I want you so much. Life is slipping away so fast—pretty soon all will be over."

She told Cook that her husband was a "physical wreck" and that his coming home, where she could "love and nurse" him, offered the only hope for his regaining his strength. "He must come home," she said.

Now standing before Peary, who had reluctantly agreed to be examined, Cook found himself in a comfortless cabin before the man who had taken him to the Far North for the first time a decade earlier. He was still a larger-than-life figure, considered by some to be the best "Ice Man" in the world, and yet Cook could see the "aging effect of his failing physique."

Peary slowly unbuttoned his clothing. As he did, his hands quivered.

Burnt by years of exposure to frigid winds, his face wasn't bronzed as much as broiled in patches. A different pallor loomed underneath his outerwear. To Cook, Peary was a remarkable gray-green with a tinge of yellow.

Since entering the cabin, Cook had felt there was something odd about Peary that he wasn't able to identify. He still had the strange mannerism Cook had observed upon their first meeting: the constant twitching nostrils. That, combined with the big teeth, which looked wolfish whenever he bared them, suggested a wild animal about to pounce. Cook finally realized what it was: gone was something from the eyes, a keen, youthful alertness that Peary had always projected. It had been replaced by what could only be described as a vacant gaze.

Cook observed that Peary's weight was subnormal and his muscular development uneven; in the doctor's opinion, both were due to poor diet. The muscles in the arms and chest were good, but the skin was hard in texture, hung in folds, and lacked the quick response of healthy skin. His reflective reactions, tested at his knees and elsewhere, were blunted.

To Cook, all outward appearances suggested some morbid disease.

Examining the eyes, Cook saw signs of some recent inflammation not only of the eyeballs but of the surrounding soft tissue as well. Asked about it, Peary said he suffered from night blindness. *Is it getting worse?* Cook inquired. *Yes,* came the answer in a hoarse whisper.

To a series of similar questions, Peary responded that he had little appetite and complained of bad digestion and shortness of breath.

Cook continued his examination, which he later noted in detail:

The teeth were in bad shape with caries and pyorrhea. There were premonitory symptoms of scurvy in his gums. The membranes of nose and throat were undergoing some atrophy. The gastric intestinal tract at all times refused to function normally. . . . The heart action was irregular and responded too rapidly to mild physical exercise. . . . The arteries were hard indicating progressive organic degeneration. . . . There were varicose veins of serious importance in both legs and a peculiar distension of small veins in other parts of the body.

Peary was quick to ascribe his infirmities to the stress of his current circumstances, but Cook did not concur. While the symptoms and signs found in Peary were common for brief periods to all polar explorers, Cook saw in him a worrisome chronic effect. It was his medical opinion that Peary suffered from a "well marked and deep seated anemia."

Near the end of the exam, Cook made a shocking discovery. Peary's feet were horribly crippled by old ulcers, the result of repeated frost bite. In addition, eight of his toes had been amputated under less than ideal conditions, leaving painful stubs that had refused to heal. Cook was stunned, for he knew what this meant.

The physician stepped back and told Peary he could dress. "You are through as a traveler on snow on foot," he said, "for without toes and painful stubs, you can never wear snowshoes or ski."

Peary made no comment. He had lost his toes the first winter of the current expedition. After departing from home in July 1898, Peary had planned to sit out the long polar winter, and when it ended early the following year, to push farther north two hundred miles to establish an advance base at Fort Conger. But that first December, he happened across the camp of Norwegian Otto Sverdrup, who claimed to be mapping the region.* The accidental encounter did not go well, although the lack of cordiality came entirely from Peary. Sverdrup, starting what would turn into a four-year undertaking, asked whether Peary would be so kind as to take his men's outgoing mail. Peary agreed on the condition that "nothing should be made known with regard to the [Sverdrup] expedition itself." Peary had no intention of carrying news about another explorer's business in the Arctic. Peary came back to camp agitated, convinced that Sverdrup was going to make a try for the Pole.

---

*In 1903, when Sverdrup reported that he had circled and mapped a vast new island west of Ellesmere, which he named Axel Heiberg, Peary countered that he had seen it first. Peary claimed he had seen the new territory in 1899, while standing atop Ellesmere's great inland glacier, and that it appeared to him like mountains in the misty distance, which he named Jesup Land. Curiously, Peary had not documented the sighting in his official report. Sverdrup had accurately charted the new land; Peary had not. Sverdrup's claim was accepted; Peary's was rejected.

"Sverdrup may at this minute be planning to beat me to Conger," Peary told Matthew Henson, who once again had come north with his longtime employer. "I can't let him do it!" Peary increasingly believed the Arctic to be his private domain and regarded with suspicion any man whose ambitions might converge upon his own. Henson pointed out that it would be best to wait until spring because it was "stormy and damned cold on the trail." Peary would have none of it. He ordered an immediate push north. On an insane journey through cold as intense as minus sixty-nine degrees, Peary, Henson, and the expedition's physician, Dr. Thomas Dedrick, made it to Conger. Once there, Peary removed his shoes, and several of his toes snapped off at the joint. The doctor removed the rest of the deadened toes. Peary was strapped to a sledge and taken back to camp. He remained in terrible pain for weeks. When he was able to walk, it was with difficulty and in a shuffling stride.

Cook had come upon Peary's darkest secret: the loss of the toes was a formidable handicap, meaning that he would find it hard to walk alongside the dog-driven sledges as Arctic explorers customarily did. Instead, he would take up space on the sledges that was ordinarily reserved for provisions and equipment. It was not an image that would have gone over well at home with his supporters or the public.

Cook now understood just how correct Josephine had been in her dire assessment of her husband's health and why he had to cease his activities. Cook strongly advised a period of recuperation at home. Peary scoffed at the notion. He had ample provisions to get him through another season and one more year of leave from his naval duties, he explained. He intended to stay and make another attempt for the Pole.

Cook warned Peary that if he remained in the Far North and his anemia grew worse, it could prove to be very harmful to his health, perhaps even fatal. "Have you learned nothing in ten years?" Cook asked. "Your present condition is directly due to long use of the embalmed food out of tins."

Peary rose to his full height, and his face reddened, as Cook knew it did before an outburst of his notorious temper. Peary's great chest heaved. "That is all bunk!" he cried. The fire had returned to his eyes.

The subject had been a sensitive topic between them since their earlier expedition together when Cook first observed that Eskimos did not get scurvy and anemia. The reason, he decided then, was that the Eskimos ate liver and raw meat.* At the time, Peary had rejected the notion of learning dietary lessons from the Arctic natives. Now the old impasse had been revisited, and even Cook's mention of his success treating severe anemia with diet on *Belgica* left Peary unconvinced.

While he would not take Cook's advice, Peary did ask a favor. Shortly before Cook's arrival, Peary had dismissed Dedrick as expedition physician; a series of disagreements between them had developed into a rift. After the arrival of *Erik*, Peary had ordered Dedrick home, but the doctor had taken his belongings and moved inland. Peary now asked Cook to go ashore and persuade his fellow physician to return home on the ship.

Cook found the young doctor living in an Eskimo hut. He learned that Dedrick came from New Jersey, where he practiced medicine and also published a small newspaper. Although he had no previous Arctic experience, Dedrick seemed to have adjusted to the harsh environment and was well liked by the Eskimos, with whom he lived. His being in such close quarters with the natives and providing them with ongoing medical attention had upset Peary and led to their final split, Dedrick claimed.

Dedrick told Cook he did not believe he should go home as long as the Peary party remained and the potential existed for future illness and injury. "I intend to do my duty and not desert human beings," he said.

Cook persuaded Dedrick to accompany him back to *Erik* for further discussion. Peary refused to meet with Dedrick, however, and designated as his stand-in Herbert Bridgman, who, along with sev-

---

*Cook's initial recommendation, based on Eskimo eating habits, for a diet high in liver came some thirty-five years prior to an article in the *Journal of the American Medical Association* describing the successful use of liver in the treatment of pernicious anemia.

eral other Peary Arctic Club members, was traveling as a passenger on *Erik*. When it became clear that Dedrick could not be induced to return, Bridgman consulted with Peary, then informed the doctor that his salary of $1,800, due him for services rendered, would be forfeited. Bridgman added a potential death sentence: "You understand that you will not be given one ounce of food from this ship."

Nor was he. Cook gave Dedrick some furs, ammunition, and food from his own store. Before his departure, Cook last saw the young outcast doctor heading back to his stone hut on the lonely, dark coast of Cape Sabine, the scene, twenty years earlier, of the death by disease and starvation of most members of the Greely expedition.

Peary's announced his plan to have Cook replace Dedrick as expedition physician, but Cook explained he could not do so unless his medical colleague voluntarily resigned from his official position.

Before getting off the ship, Dedrick left a letter addressed to Peary, promising, "You will never by any voluntary act of mine be deprived of my medical services nor of a helping hand so long as you remain in the Arctic. If I am not to remain at your headquarters, you can depend on my being at the nearest possible point that I can effect a landing and maintain life."

That same day, August 24, *Windward* sailed for home with Josephine and six-year-old Marie aboard. Josephine stood tall and proud as she bade her husband goodbye, although she knew full well that she was, in effect, abdicating for the time being her position to the young Eskimo woman.

After *Windward*'s departure, *Erik* weighed anchor and took the Peary party forty miles across Smith Sound. Upon landing Peary, Henson, their Eskimos, dogs, and sledges, *Erik* departed south for home with Cook and Bridgman aboard.

That winter of 1901, on the shores of Smith Sound, tragedy struck.

When the details reached Cook in Brooklyn, he was sickened by what he perceived to be the blatant disregard for the welfare of the natives, without whom white men stood little chance of surviving, let alone accomplishing their bold Arctic endeavors. Dedrick, Cook would learn, had remained at Etah, living with the Eskimos. As the winter and polar night advanced, Dedrick got news that the Eskimos with Peary were sick and required medical assistance. Dedrick immediately set out on foot across the dangerous sea ice of Smith Sound. When he reached Peary's camp, Peary refused to allow the physician to attend to the afflicted Eskimos and ordered him out of the camp. Before departing, Dedrick asked for some coffee, a little sugar, and a few biscuits for his return journey. These Peary refused him. After Dedrick left and with no physician in attendance, six of Peary's Eskimos died in fever and pain. It was, Cook believed, a dark page in the history of Arctic exploration.

Come spring, Peary, hobbling on his deformed feet when not riding on a sledge, made another push north. At that point, the surviving natives were disinclined to work for him, and his original contingent of fourteen had dwindled to four when he started across the frozen sea ice north of Conger. Those who accompanied him did so with the promise of rewards.

On April 21, 1902, Peary, stormbound for days and making little progress over rough ice, gave up and turned south with his weary band. His farthest north point was 84 degrees, 17 minutes, 27 seconds—still 343 miles from the Pole.

Peary was back at Cape Sabine the next month when *Windward* arrived to return his party—and Dedrick—to civilization after four years.

Among the news brought by *Windward* was that of a new farthest-north record. In the international race to the Pole, such records made front pages everywhere, as one explorer after another returned from the north and made his claim to fame, however fleeting it proved to be. Each advance was the one to beat, and today's record soon became tomorrow's footnote. Captain Umberto Cagni, of the duke of the Abruzzi's expedition, now claimed the farthest-north record: 86 degrees, 34 minutes. Bettering Nansen's previous record by some twenty miles, Cagni had gone 137 miles farther than Peary.

"Next time I'll smash that all to bits," Peary told Henson.

"Next time!"

CHAPTER ELEVEN

ROOF OF THE CONTINENT

WHENEVER HE RETURNED from his latest far-flung adventure, Cook reopened his medical practice on Bushwick Avenue. In spite of his long absences, many former patients drifted back, and new ones sought him out, drawn in part by the publicity generated by his travels and writings.

At age thirty-six, Cook fell in love again. Her name was Marie Fidele Hunt, a voluptuous twenty-four-year-old brunette with a roundish face and deep-set brown eyes. She had recently been widowed by the death of her husband, Willis Hunt, a prosperous homeopath from Camden, New Jersey. She was left with a four-year-old daughter, Ruth, and some financial resources. Marie had shown up on Bushwick Avenue to visit friends—the family of a physician, Dr. Robert Davidson, whom Cook also knew. The Davidsons lived a few doors down from Cook, and it was in their parlor during an evening social—as the Davidsons' daughter, Lotta, played the piano—that Marie and Frederick first met. A romantic at heart, Marie long remembered the piece being played, Schumann's sweet and moving "Träumerei," as the "most beautiful thing that has ever been written." In the presence of the well-known but modest doctor and explorer, Marie felt "hypnotized." She and her daughter soon packed up and departed Camden, moving in with her sister's family in Brooklyn. Smitten by the charms of this warm, vivacious young woman who made no secret of her interest in him, Cook became a regular caller.

Marie and Frederick were married at New York Avenue Methodist Episcopal Church on June 10, 1902, Cook's thirty-seventh birthday. After a short honeymoon in Saratoga Springs, they settled into an elegant home they purchased together across the street from Cook's longtime residence. The three-story stone mansion at 670 Bushwick Avenue had room aplenty for the young family (Cook adopted Marie's daughter, Ruth) as well as a study and a surgery, for which Cook acquired the latest equipment, including one of the city's first X-ray machines used in private practice. He replaced his horse and buggy with one of the first four-cylinder, air-cooled Franklin automobiles to be built, beginning what turned out to be a lifelong love of motoring. Cook soon had a reputation for speeding, because he was often seen driving in excess of ten miles per hour and taking corners precariously on two bicycle-style wheels as he hurried to appointments.*

That same summer in faraway Alaska, a U.S. Geological Survey team headed by Alfred Brooks, the government's top geologist in the region, was exploring an unknown area around Mount McKinley. Several months later, Cook read a *National Geographic* article about their experiences. The highest mountain peak in North America had been discovered only six years earlier, in 1896, by a gold prospector, W. A. Dickey, who named it in honor of President William McKinley. Its height was estimated to be twenty thousand feet, although the summit had not yet been scaled. The government surveyors, who had reached the twenty-five-mile-wide base of the mountain, discussed a number of possible approaches to the summit. McKinley was set in the rugged Alaskan Range, surrounded by numerous peaks that exceeded thirteen thousand feet and hundreds of miles of some of the wildest country in the world—which explains

---

*The first four-cylinder Franklin was sold on June 23, 1902, to New York sportsman S.G. Averell, who paid $1,200. In 1904, a lightweight, air-cooled Franklin made it from coast to coast in 32 days, 23 hours, and 20 minutes—obliterating the record of 65 days set the preceding year—a triumph that sent demand soaring for the wood-and-aluminum framed automobiles.

why the mountain had not been spotted earlier. In the article, Brooks suggested that anyone attempting to scale McKinley should have "long training in frontier life and exploratory work." Believing that he qualified, Cook, growing restless again, began to formulate a plan for how the great mountain might be conquered. He eagerly discussed his ideas with Marie, whose enthusiasm and support for her husband's life as an explorer would never wane.

Cook made the decision to devote himself "for a time" to mountaineering. One motive, clearly, was to not leave his new bride for the years that polar endeavors often required; an assault on a mountain, successful or not, was done in a single season. Also, he had come to consider polar exploration and mountaineering "twin efforts which bring about a somewhat similar train of joys and sorrows." He believed that the mountain climber and Arctic explorer "in their exploits run to kindred attainments."

While overseas in 1900 to receive the Belgian government's award for his service to the *Belgica* expedition, Cook had met one of the most famous mountaineers of the era, Edward Whymper, who in 1865 had become the first to scale the Matterhorn. The expedition cost the lives of four of Whymper's companions during the descent, considered the most dangerous phase of any climb. The old Englishman, who in his historic climb had beaten a group of Italian climbers to the top by just three days, sought to interest Cook in mountaineering, convinced that his polar expertise would serve him well. The two explorers shared their wide-ranging experiences, discussing various methods and equipment for traversing snow and ice.

Cook searched for ways to combine his own polar techniques with those of the emerging sport (among Americans) of alpine climbing, in which no relays of supplies or advance lines are put up and everything is carried on the climber's back. His experiments in the Antarctic with Amundsen, using lightweight sledges and tents, had convinced him of the importance of traveling fast and light. At approximately 63 degrees north, McKinley was the most Arctic of the world's tallest mountains; scaling it would require crossing the largest glaciers outside of Greenland and the Antarctic, then climbing steep slopes packed with perpetual snow and ice while avoiding cliffs and avalanches.

With the mountain set in such difficult, isolated terrain, transporting men and supplies would be an arduous task. Cook anticipated carrying supplies on horseback as far as possible, but once the terrain became too treacherous—and certainly once the climb started—there would be no beasts of burden to carry the load. If the climbers were to reach the summit, they could not be weighted down with blankets, heavy tents, canned foods, and other supplies.

Cook visited a Manhattan sporting goods store and ordered a custom tent of his own design from proprietor David T. Abercrombie. Shaped like an octagonal pyramid and made of exceptionally light Shantung silk, it was unlike any tent Abercrombie had ever made. Weighing only three pounds, it could be folded up and put into a good-sized pocket. The tent required no pole and could be supported by the handles of ice axes.

Cook also had in mind a new kind of sleeping bag for use on the climb, one that would not be dead weight when not in use. He worked with Marie, a capable seamstress, and they came up with a novel design: three robes that could be buttoned together along the edge to make a bag. The eider duck skin robes—lined in camel's hair—could be used as ponchos separately or together. The climbers ended up carrying no other coats or jackets, since the sleeping robes provided all the protection and warmth they needed.

Marie asked to join the expedition, making it clear she wished to accompany her husband on adventures just as Josephine Peary had done. Cook was not sure about including his wife on the climb, but he was delighted to take her to Alaska, even though the region was still so untamed as to be without railroad service.

In May 1903, they closed up their Bushwick home, placed Ruth with relatives, and took the Northwestern Limited to the Pacific Northwest, where the expedition was assembling. Other members of the team were to include Columbia student Ralph Shainwald von Ahlefeldt, twenty-one, the bespectacled and urbane son of a wealthy paint manufacturer and a veteran of one Arctic expedition; Robert Dunn, twenty-six, a Harvard graduate who had made two trips to the Klondike; Fred Printz, a tobacco-chewing Montana horse packer who had been employed by the government survey team that explored part of the McKinley region; and two jack-of-all-trades, Walter Miller and Jack Carroll, to assist with the horses and supplies. Shainwald and Dunn had made substantial contributions to help defray expenses; the balance of the funding came from the Cooks and an advance from *Harper's Monthly* for a series of articles to be written by Cook about the expedition.

In Seattle, they spent several days selecting and buying food and supplies, and fifteen horses were purchased from a Yakima Indian. For the overland journey to the base of the mountain, Cook planned to bring along flour, sugar, bacon, coffee, and other supplies favored by prospectors, including kerosene for fuel. The climbing party, however, would travel much lighter—more like an Arctic expedition—with pemmican, biscuits, condensed milk, tea, and alcohol fuel to melt snow for water. Each man would carry a forty-pound rucksack with provisions for ten days, an alpine ax, and a new rope made of horsehair, which Cook considered an improvement over the silk rope of alpine climbers that when wet became heavy and slippery.

They boarded an Alaskan coastal steamer, *Santa Ana*, and cast off the first week of June, taking the ship's regularly scheduled route north through the Puget Sound. After several stops to drop off cargo, *Santa Ana* left the placid inland waters and entered the Gulf of Alaska.

Mount Fairweather soon rose on the northeastern horizon, then Mount St. Elias and Mount Logan—towering over nineteen thousand feet, the second highest peak in North America. They put in at Valdez, a newly incorporated city nestled at the foot of the Chugach Mountains that had become a debarkation point and supply center for the Klondike goldfields. Although the recipient of three hundred inches of snow annually, Valdez had an ice-free port that remained open year-round.

One cloudless dawn as they steamed up the gulf, McKinley came into view. From a distance of 250 miles, it appeared to Cook to be a "mere tooth of ice biting the arctic skies." Some 100 miles farther north, the steamer pulled into Tyonek, a row of log huts and Alaska Commercial Company warehouses set on a sand spit. The backwater settlement consisted of twenty Indian families and a handful of white residents. *Santa Ana* anchored half a mile offshore.

They soon began pushing the horses over the side. The current was so strong that the horses nearly exhausted themselves before scenting land and swimming for it. Once ashore, they trotted to the nearest field and grazed contentedly.

The Cooks had journeyed five thousand miles to get here, and yet the enormous task of reaching the base of McKinley was still ahead of them. Realizing this, Frederick and Marie had a serious talk about the anticipated hardships of the overland trip to come. She decided against going any farther. Rather than stay in desolate Tyonek, she elected to return on the *Santa Ana* to Valdez and "limit her exploring ventures to [that] more congenial coast."

The Indian ponies turned out to be only half broken, and most had never carried a load. Two days of training were required before the frisky animals submitted to their occupation as packhorses, each loaded with 150 pounds of supplies.

On June 25, the expedition party, composed of "the wildest kind of dreamers," moved out for the mountain that even from a distance of more than a hundred miles appeared mysterious and "kept one's attention pointed."

They hauled with them a small boat. When they reached the Skwentna River, they crossed over and split the party. Cook and Miller headed upriver in the boat with some of the supplies, while the rest of the party, including some Indian helpers hired at Tyonek, led the horses through forests and marshes.

Cook soon ran into trouble with the boat, which went high and dry on a vast mud flat. Fearing that a rising tide would fill up and swamp the boat before it could rise from the sticky clay, he and Miller devised a way to raise the boat atop planks. They spent a fretful night, but in the morning the tide came and easily floated the boat. Then they had the opposite problem: for a long stretch, the water became too swift for paddling and too deep for using poles.

They poled and towed, rowed and pushed, averaging twelve miles a day.

On July 8, Cook and his companion pitched camp on a small island below a canyon that had been designated as the rendezvous point. There was no sign of the packtrain, even though the boat trip had taken several days longer than planned. Later that day, however, they heard voices and soon spotted the rest of the party bringing the horses along the riverbank.

The weather was oppressively hot and humid; it had rained non-stop since they left Tyonek, and everyone was soaked to the skin. Mosquitoes, out in great numbers, added to their miseries, and men and horses began to show signs of strain. Some of the men quarreled. The writer, Dunn, who had a sarcastic streak, was often the instigator; Cook finally chastised him for talking "too much and all the time too loud."

As character flaws emerged under pressure, Cook said little but remained the leader by example, often assigning himself the most difficult and dangerous tasks. Dunn, in his writings, did not spare Cook the criticism he leveled at all the other members of the party—"[Cook's] ways and person irritated me," including, it seemed, his refusal to use tobacco, "and that makes me uncomfortable." Even so, Dunn later wrote of Cook, "I think he would face death and disaster without a word. . . .*

After a night's rest, the party again split up and proceeded another twenty miles. The Indians, anxious to return to their coastal fishing grounds, were sent back with enough supplies to sustain them on their return journey.

---

*Dunn had been recommended to Cook for the expedition by the newspaper editor Lincoln Steffens, even though the latter found Dunn incorrigible and antisemitic—having "no respect for anybody or anything"—and had fired him from his reporting position. Dunn, upon his return home, wrote five articles about the expedition published in *Outing Magazine* between January and May 1904. Dunn chided Cook, called Doc in the articles, for, among other things, saying too little and smiling too often. "Not much will be done in Northern exploration until it gets in the hands of some one Napoleonic, brutal perhaps, but with a compelling *ego*. . . ."

More rain, heavy underbrush, rapid streams, and steep slopes slowed them down. The horses suffered bruised and lacerated legs from the brush. Worried about the wear and tear on the animals, Printz suggested a full day's rest, and Cook agreed. For the next week, they worked the horses only three hours a day until they recovered.

From two thousand feet, they began a steady climb and soon passed the tree line. On the open ground, longer marches were possible. Just above three thousand feet, they reached the first glacial shelf, where they found abundant caribou, moose, and mountain sheep, which they hunted successfully without interrupting their forward progress.

On August 11, they reached the top of a bluff as the sun was setting. The view was of a "great waving sea of evergreen forests" behind them and of the "unknown world [of] glacial rivers . . . and big mountains" in front of them. They also got their first unobstructed view of the top of McKinley, with the upper four thousand feet visible. McKinley's steep contour, "shingled by plates of ice," revealed a surprise: a double system of peaks (northern and southern), which they had not seen from earlier sightings and which had not been previously reported. Of the awe-inspiring view, Cook wrote, "Here was the roof of the continent; the prize of our conquest, seemingly within grasp." With much enthusiasm in the air, they pitched camp and prepared a hot meal.

Three more days of travel took them to within fifteen miles of McKinley's crest, where they camped. A violent storm struck, forcing them to take cover inside their tents. Before dawn, they were lying in pools of chilly water from a rapidly rising stream and had to break camp in the dark and move to higher ground. Come daylight, their position looked favorable for an assault on McKinley from the southwest.

As they approached, Cook considered several possible routes to the summit. The northeast side showed a long ridge with a gradual ascent, but had several miniature peaks that seemed to block the way. The western face presented its own obstacle: above twelve thousand feet, it appeared to be a solid cliff of pinkish granite, so steep that snow did not collect on its surface. The southwest approach looked the most promising, although it was interrupted by a spur that would have to be avoided.

Cook had planned to reach the base of McKinley by the first of August, but owing to unpredictable weather and terrain, and because the horses had to rest even when the men were fit for more travel, they were three weeks behind schedule. The climbing season would soon be ending, giving way to winter. Temperatures had dropped to forty-five degrees, and rainstorms were blowing down the mountain, swelling the countless glacial streams and making crossings more difficult.

They had taken fifty-four days to cover a "tortuous course of five hundred miles through swamps and forest, over glacial streams, up and down mountain sides, through a trackless country." They were at last in position. Before beginning the climb, however, everyone agreed on the wisdom of resting for two days and undertaking final preparations, which included baking a batch of hardtack biscuits for the climb.

They broke camp with the five strongest horses carrying supplies and climbed into a high valley, where they waited out a sudden downpour, then pushed over a series of jagged moraines to the top of a glacier. Their first extended trek over ice proved difficult for the horses. That night, they pitched camp at seventy-three hundred feet.

Much snow fell during the night. Leaving the horses and supplies behind with one man, the rest of the party proceeded up the mountain another thousand feet until stopped by a chasm of cliffs that dropped two thousand feet.*

When the party reassembled, some members left with the horses to return to a lower camp, while others remained on the glacier with Cook, who was intent on searching the area for another route upward. In this he was unsuccessful and finally had to accept "defeat for our first attempt" and head back down.

---

*Unbeknownst to Cook at the time, this was the approximate location where a party led by James Wickersham, a U.S. district judge from Fairbanks, had turned around three months earlier after making the first attempt to climb McKinley. Facing this dead end, Wickersham decided that only a "flying machine" would allow a man to go any higher up the mountain.

The entire group circled twenty-five miles around the base of McKinley to approach from the west. Separating from the supply party at a lower elevation, a climbing team crossed a glacier through bright sunlight that would have blinded them had it not been for the smoke-colored goggles of Cook's design. At eight thousand feet, they broke above the cloud cover and "burst into the arctic world, with all its glory of glitter and frost."

Cook led the way through deep snow to nine thousand feet, where they pitched camp. The temperature had abruptly dropped to ten degrees below freezing. In the tent, they turned their robes into sleeping bags, lit the alcohol lamp, made tea, and ate pemmican, as outside a great wind rushed across the glacier. Throughout the night, they could hear the explosive crackling of avalanches breaking loose all around.

On August 29, they made their first assault on McKinley's main peak. They hoped to reach the top in five days and return two or three days later. In order to do so, they cached everything they did not absolutely need, and in his rucksack each man carried ten days worth of food.

The ascent began easily enough, following an old avalanche path, although to a man the climbers staggered under the weight of the packs. When they paused to stamp footholds and catch their breath, they leaned their backs against the steep slope. Without warning, Shainwald lost his balance and began to slip. Instinctively, Cook went for him and somehow managed to jockey him into a safe position. It was a close call—had Shainwald fallen, he would not have come to a stop for thousands of feet.

On they went, and up. Having to focus all their energies on the work of the climb, they proceeded in silence. In another few hundred feet, they were halted by a slope ranging from forty to sixty degrees that refused to provide traction. Now came the difficult job of chopping steps in the ice. Equally strenuous was the effort to clear more than a foot of soft snow just to find stable ice into which a step could be cut. Cook led off, using short, powerful strokes to slash the three-inch blade of his crosshead ax into the solid ice, as he had done when he and Amundsen had made the first technical ascent in the Antarctic. Once he had cut a new foothold, he tested it with one foot, while keeping most of his weight on the other foot. In this way, they advanced step by step up the mountain, against a freezing wind and driving snow.

Everyone took turns clearing the snow and cutting steps—one hundred at a time before giving way to the next man—except for Dunn, who had inexplicably left his ice ax behind that morning. "I hadn't given [it] a thought," explained Dunn, who was carrying a willow pole from one of the large camp tents. No one volunteered to trade his trusty ax for a walking stick.

The setting sun forced the climbers to find a place to make camp for the night. Unable to locate level ground large enough for the silk climbing tent, which could accommodate four men with no room to spare, they were compelled to clear away the snow and cut into the ice to make a suitable flooring. They made tea, ate pemmican, and slept that night at ninety-five hundred feet.

The following day, they found the slopes even steeper, and their staircase of steps newly cut into the ice turned into more of a step ladder. After they tied themselves together in pairs, Cook led the way up a steep face.

They camped at nearly eleven thousand feet, again having to chop a floor into the ice for the tent to keep from rolling off their perch in their sleep. Everyone was exhausted and disappointed by the difficulty and slowness of the climb, which was taking twice as long as planned.

The act of lighting the alcohol burner brought cheer, and warm tea further raised their spirits. Soon, they were joking and laughing. Not long after settling down for the night, someone peeked out of the tent and said breathlessly, "My God, look at that!" Everyone came out of the tent to see the sight that had stirred such a reaction. The usual cloud cover had abruptly cleared—and there, seemingly within touch, stood the great summit (McKinley's northern peak) they were aiming for, "its glittering spurs piecing a dark purple sky nine thousand feet above us."

Scores of avalanches could be seen crashing down the sides of the peak with "trains of rock and ice followed by clouds of vapour and snow." The reverberating sound was a "chaos of awful noise."

Without a word being uttered, each climber understood that was where they were headed. The frightening scene unfolding before them "made one's marrow shrink."

Back inside the tent, no one slept for the longest while. Bundled as they were in the warmth of their bags, they were not cold, and yet they shivered.

In the morning, they climbed from the tent to see an entirely different scene. The peak above them shone a vivid blue and seemed less intimidating in the golden light of dawn. Immediately above them, however, they could see a series of rock-and-ice obstructions that appeared impenetrable.

Dunn immediately announced that no further progress was possible. Cook was not yet prepared to accept defeat. They had food for several more days, and if they could find a safe and sure line of attack, there was still a chance for success. After breakfast, he said to Dunn, "Don't pack up. Come along." Dunn refused to join him and began packing up for the descent.

With Printz, Cook scouted the terrain above. Within a short distance, the ridge upon which they were camped led steeply to a granite cliff that looked climbable, but that was just for starters. Not far away, there was a steep ridge stretching for several thousand feet which appeared impassable.*

With their way blocked and the season for mountaineering at this latitude closed, it was time to leave. They came down the mountain rapidly, not wanting to be caught by winter at high altitude, and were reunited with the packtrain.

Rather than returning by the same way they had come, Cook insisted on forging a new route that allowed him to study McKinley's contour from various angles. They encountered an uncharted 6,000-foot pass that cut the central axis of the Alaskan Range, and crossed over it. As they did, they were the first to look across the range from its heart, seeing both the east and the west horizons.

---

*Cook's assessment was more right than wrong. Not until 1954 was this steep ridge climbed, and then only with the utilization of a complete array of modern twentieth-century alpine equipment.

The trip back proved as difficult as their ordeal in reaching the mountain. At the end, racing against worsening weather and with their supplies nearly gone, they constructed rafts from cottonwood trees and floated down the Chulitna River. Before boarding the rafts, Cook decided against shooting the "good, faithful animals" they had so relied upon, ordering the release of the seven surviving horses—the rest had either wandered off or been destroyed after breaking a leg or becoming seriously ill. The grass was good here, and it was hoped that when deep snow came the horses could feed by digging under it.

While rafting down the Chulitna, they came to an impressive glacier, which Cook named Fidele—Marie's maiden name—and another large one farther south, which he christened Ruth, after his stepdaughter. The northeastern slopes of McKinley drained into both glaciers. To determine whether the mountain might be climbed from this direction, Cook walked up to six thousand feet. What he saw looked promising, but there was no time for further exploring.

The party floated into what served as civilization—a river trading post at Susitna Station—on September 25, exhausted and near starvation, almost shoeless and their clothes in rags. They had made history as the first to circumnavigate McKinley, an achievement that would not be duplicated for half a century. In three months, they had walked seven hundred miles and traveled three hundred miles by boat and raft, adding greatly to the knowledge of Alaska's rugged interior.

"McKinley offers a unique challenge to mountaineers . . . its ascent will prove a tremendous task," Cook wrote upon his return home. "It is the loftiest mountain in North America, the steepest mountain in the world, and the most frigid of all great mountains. The prospective conqueror of America's culminating peak will be amply rewarded, but he must be prepared to withstand the tortures of the torrids, the discomforts of the North Pole seeker, combined with the hardships of the Matterhorn ascents multiplied many times over."

Cook was already thinking about *next time*.

CHAPTER TWELVE

FARTHEST NORTH

UPON PEARY'S RETURN from the Arctic in 1902, he lost no time in having surgery on his mangled feet, for he realized the truth in Cook's dire prediction that his handicap was a barrier to future polar work. For his surgeon, Peary selected one of the country's most eminent physicians, Dr. William W. Keen of Philadelphia. During the Civil War, Keen had served as a field surgeon in the Union Army. In 1883, after undertaking advanced medical studies in Europe, he edited *Gray's Anatomy*. Four years later, he performed the first successful removal of a brain tumor in the United States. In 1893, Keen was a member of a top-flight surgical team that secretly operated on President Grover Cleveland—in the salon of a private yacht as it steamed up Long Island Sound—to remove a cancerous lesion from inside the president's mouth.*

---

*Cleveland decided on secrecy because of the nation's ongoing turmoil as a result of the Panic of 1893, a period of railroad failures, mortgage foreclosures, and low gold reserves. The surgery was performed in July, only days after a major stock market crash. Despite all efforts to keep the news from leaking out that the president had cancer—his doctors believed that even if Cleveland's life was spared, he would be left with a severe speech impediment—the story broke in the *Philadelphia Press* a month later. It was strongly denied by the White House. By then, Cleveland was speaking normally, thanks to a rubber plate fitted in his mouth to replace his missing left jawbone. The cancer operation was a success; Cleveland died of old age in 1908.

After a pair of operations in the Arctic under trying conditions, Peary had been left with his two remaining little toes, which projected beyond the stumps of his missing toes. Dr. Keen evened things off a bit by amputating the last joint of the little toes. He slit the skin at the front of the feet and drew forward tissue from underneath and behind the toes, then stitched together the flaps to make a cushion for the stumps. It was the best that could be done with what remained, and upon this makeshift design Peary would walk in a peculiar shuffle for the rest of his days.

Peary's return to his official duties in Washington, D.C., was unheralded. Seemingly forgotten by his fellow naval engineers, even by those with whom he had previously worked, he felt as if he "had wandered back like a lost cat." Still, owing to his seniority and after passing two promotional examinations, he rapidly advanced to the post of commander in the Civil Engineers' Corps. His new assignment in November 1902 was in the Bureau of Yards and Docks at the Navy Department. A month later, he was sent abroad to study European types of troop barracks, and he wrote a lengthy report of his findings.

To his dismay, Peary found that public interest in his polar efforts had waned with his long absences and repeated failures to reach his well-publicized goal. Even some of his ardent supporters in the Peary Arctic Club were discouraged by his expensive, unsuccessful efforts. The response to his new call for funds to mount another attempt on the Pole was tepid at best. Never one to give up easily, he undertook what he referred to sarcastically as one long, continuous "black march" to raise money for his next expedition by lecturing, writing, and otherwise laying siege to anyone presumed to possess ample means.

In an effort to find financing, Peary wrote letters of solicitation to members of his Arctic club as well as to potential new backers. His tone could be blunt and stern at times, as when he wrote in January 1903 to a member guilty of lukewarm support, "Ever since my return from the North last fall, there has been an undercurrent of dissatisfaction in the Peary Arctic Club at letting the work of the Club drop before the Pole was attained." Peary's pitch to the wealthy could also be polished, as when he offered something that all their money could never buy: immortality. "The names of those who made the work possible will be kept through the coming centuries floating forever above the forgotten and submerged debris of our time and day," he wrote in one letter of solicitation to club members. "The one thing we remember about Ferdinand of Spain is that he sent Columbus to his life-work."

The plan Peary presented began with his own commitment to "throw [him]self into the work for two more years, and make a supreme effort which shall crown all past efforts with success," if he could have "suitable equipment." At the top of his shopping list was a new ship. Not just any ship, but a "first-class" one of his own design. He wanted a vessel capable of going farther north through the ice-jammed channels between Greenland and Ellesmere and delivering the expedition party to the edge of the frozen Arctic Sea, thereby eliminating the long, exhausting sledge trips previously undertaken to get to that point. With such a head start on his last journey, Peary pointed out, the length of his sledge trip to the north would have taken him *beyond* the Pole.

Since no such ship existed, it was necessary, Peary argued, to build one. Nansen's ship, *Fram*, had been built for polar service, but as a sailing ship with auxiliary steam power she was largely at the mercy of the winds and currents. Her unique design allowed her to drift safely while stuck in the ice; as the pressures on her wooden hull increased, the vessel lifted above the compression rather than being crushed like an eggshell. There *Fram* would stay perched until the ice melted or broke apart.

Peary envisioned a ship that could make her way at will through and around icy barriers. To do so, she would need powerful engines, reinforced hull, and sturdy rudder and screw assemblies that would not be easily damaged.

The Peary Arctic Club was officially incorporated in April 1904, along with a charter that spelled out the group's original mission to provide the wherewithal to "aid and assist in forming and maintaining certain expeditions" under Peary's command "with the object of continuing his explorations." Before the membership rolls were filled out, they would include the president of Chase Manhattan Bank, the founder of the Great Northern Railway, the chairman of the Erie Railroad, the founder of the Remington Typewriter Company, and other company directors, bank and insurance company presidents, manufacturing and transportation magnates, and lawyers. The club had two immediate goals. The first had nothing to do with building a ship; rather, it aimed at "the altering of public opinion so that existing prejudice against Arctic work would be lessened." This "work of propaganda was done with the greatest amount of finesse" by Peary's powerful supporters, and soon magazine and newspaper articles appeared that placed his new Arctic plans "in the most favorable light possible." Within months, there had been a "complete reversal of the public's estimate of the value and national prestige to be gained" by the discovery of the North Pole, and Peary was again seen as the man for the job.

One prominent citizen quick to get aboard the Peary bandwagon was the new president of the United States, Theodore Roosevelt, at forty-two the youngest man to reach this office. Elected vice-president in 1900, Roosevelt had, with the assassination of William McKinley, become president on September 14, 1901, while Peary was in the Arctic. A lifelong advocate of "the strenuous life," Roosevelt was a hunter and explorer in his own right. In Peary, he saw a man much like himself—rugged, determined, courageous.

The second goal of the newly rejuvenated Peary Arctic Club provided for the "construction of a vessel that would place Peary and his party at a base on the shores of the Polar Sea." The price of such a ship was estimated at $100,000.

With a down payment of half the total amount required in order to begin construction, the banker Morris Jesup put up $25,000. When contributions fell short of the mark, James Colgate, a member of the wealthy New York family, wrote out a check "with characteristic promptitude and generosity" that "rounded out the $50,000." The Peary Arctic Club entered into a contract with McKay and Dix of Bucksport, Maine, one of the finest shipbuilders in the world. Timber for the vessel was ordered in August 1904.

That same month, Josephine gave birth to a healthy boy named for his father. A few days later, Peary's three-year paid leave commenced. With the backing of President Roosevelt, his request had been rapidly granted. For the first time, the Navy described in his leave orders the exact nature of his Arctic mission. "The attainment of the Pole should be your main objective," wrote Charles H. Darling, assistant secretary of the Navy. "Nothing short will suffice." However, the government would not be financing any of the undertaking.

By all accounts, 1904 was a great summer for Peary, with the birth of a son and a ship, another extended leave to pursue his dream, and the completion of a summer cottage on his beloved Eagle Island, in Casco Bay off the coast of Portland, Maine. He had fallen in love with the place, named after the eagles that once nested there, when he first saw it at age seventeen. He had bought the island for $500 with his first earnings shortly after college. With a three-room house now on the island, he would spend summers there with his family as often as possible—recovering from his latest journey or simply escaping the humidity of Washington, D.C. The island became nothing short of a sanctuary for Peary, and throughout his life he thought often of its serenity and woodsy beauty during difficult times.

In mid-September 1904, the Eighth International Geographic Congress convened in New York City, with representatives from around the world in attendance for two days. Cook delivered three major papers at the conference: one about his circumnavigation of Mount McKinley, another on the *Belgica* expedition, and a third comparing the environs of the Arctic and the Antarctic, something he alone among the world's explorers was qualified to do. With Peary in the audience, Cook was one of the stars of the event, receiving enthusiastic ovations and extensive coverage in the press.

Peary had, upon Cook's return from McKinley, written his fellow explorer and former colleague, "I congratulate you on the work which you did on Mt. McKinley, and am sincerely sorry that you did not attain the tip top. I hope you may tackle it again and win out."

For Peary, exploration had become more about winning or losing, and less about any of the scientific disciplines. It was at the last ses-

Robert E. Peary at the time of his
last Arctic expedition, 1909.
(The Ohio State University Archives)

Josephine (Diebitsch)
Peary with her pet
Newfoundland in
northern Greenland,
1891.
*(National Archives at
College Park, Maryland)*

Belgica trapped in the Antarctic, 1897.
(The Ohio State University Archives)

Crewmen digging trenches in the ice to free *Belgica*, 1898.
(The Ohio State University Archives)

Frederick A. Cook at the time of
Mount McKinley ascent, 1906.
(The Ohio State University Archives)

Cook's Mount McKinley climbing party scaling the heights.
(The Ohio State University Archives)

With Cook aboard, schooner
John R. Bradley sailing to
northern Greenland for his
final Arctic expedition, 1907.
(The Ohio State University Archives)

Peary with sledge dogs
aboard his support
vessel, *Roosevelt*, headed
for northern Greenland
for his final assault on
the North Pole, 1909.
*(The Ohio State University
Archives)*

Eskimo couple who assisted
Cook's expedition in northern
Greenland, 1908.
(The Ohio State University Archives)

Peary's sledges heading
northward, 1909.
(The Ohio State University Archives)

Making sledge repairs,
Peary's expedition, 1909.
*(The Ohio State University
Archives)*

Peary's teams topping icy
hummock on northbound
journey, 1909.
*(The Ohio State University
Archives)*

Cook's North Pole photograph, April 21, 1908; Eskimo companions, Etukishook and Alwelah, next to igloo, above which flies Old Glory.
(The Ohio State University Archives)

Cook's triumphant reception in Copenhagen, September 1909; at right, U.S. minister to Denmark, Maurice Egan.
(The Ohio State University Archives)

Marie (Fidele Hunt) Cook and her two children, Ruth and Helen.
(The Ohio State University Archives)

Robert E. Peary aboard *Roosevelt*, 1909.

(The Ohio State University Archives)

Frederick A. Cook, 1907: True discoverer of the North Pole?

(The Ohio State University Archives)

sion of the geographic conference that he announced to the world
his intention of making a "final" North Pole expedition. Peary's
remarks came at a dinner during which he was presented with an
award from the Paris Geographical Society. "Next summer I shall
start north again after that on which I have set my heart. Shall I
win? God knows. I hope and dream and pray that I may."

Once the keel of his new ship was laid in October, Peary brought
Josephine and their two children to Bucksport, where they moved
into the town's only hotel. Every morning he went to the shipyard
and stayed until nightfall, overseeing the construction down to the
smallest detail. When work was completed six months later, final
payment to the shipyard came from a $50,000 contribution made by
banker George Crocker, a founding member of the Peary Arctic Club.

Other donations rolled in from contributing members; the list
now contained sums from seventy-three of some of the most affluent
men in America: $20,000 from Thomas H. Hubbard, a prominent
New York civil attorney, trustee of Bowdoin College, and director of
Southern Pacific Railroad and Western Union; $5,000 from an
anonymous Wall Street banker; $1,000 from candy maker John S.
Huyler; and another $25,000 from the always supportive Jesup.
Show business even got into the act: two benefit performances at
Brighton Beach near Coney Island by a wild west show raised
$10,000. Every dollar was needed, because after the new ship was
paid off, equipment and supplies would cost another $40,000.

In a shrewd gesture, Peary's request to President Roosevelt—
relayed through Jesup, a personal friend—to name the ship after
him was accepted. Christened by Josephine with a bottle of cham-
pagne frozen in a block of ice, *Roosevelt* was launched on March 23,
1905, before five thousand onlookers lining the shore, the largest
gathering in Bucksport history. The new ship plunged into the
water for the first time, then rose and shook herself as the spectators
cheered. With her momentum, the vessel slid across the narrow
channel and, rather ignobly, became stuck in the mud on the far
side. A few days later, after *Roosevelt* was towed to Portland, Maine,
installation of the machinery was started, and in two months she
was completely fitted out.

Roosevelt, like Nansen's polar ship, was designed to rise above the pressure of the ice pack to avoid damage to her hull. At 614 tons, she was slightly larger than an oceangoing tug. Her wooden hull— up to thirty inches thick, braced inside with struts and sheathed on the outside with steel—was built to be strong as well as flexible. She was narrow but somewhat stubby for easier maneuvering in ice- jammed seas: 166 feet long at the waterline, 35 feet abeam, with a draft of only 16 feet so as to get close in to shore. Her bow was sharply raked for ramming the ice. The propeller blades were detachable, and the rudder could be lifted and swung up onto the deck to prevent damage, should the ship become stuck in solid ice. With oversized propellers and shaft, and an unusually powerful engine fed by multiple boilers, *Roosevelt* was more battering ram than sailing ship, making her the world's first icebreaker. Fitted with masts, she carried small fore and aft sails to take advantage of favoring winds and conserve coal, also as a contingency in the event of irreparable damage to the propulsion system. Powerful deck equipment—windlass, steam capstan, and winch—was installed to provide the muscle for freeing the ship from trouble, including hauling her off the bottom when aground. Quarters for the crew and expedition members were located on deck; space below was reserved for the storage of coal and supplies.

As with everything on the ship, Peary had given considerable thought to the design of his sea cabin. Extra roomy and with an adjoining private bathroom, it was paneled in yellow pine painted white and had a wide built-in bunk, writing desk, office chair, bookcases that contained Arctic titles along with novels and maga- zines, wicker chair, and chest of drawers. On the wall were etchings of Morris Jesup and President Roosevelt, the latter autographed. Various flags were displayed: a silk U.S. flag made by Josephine, which Peary had carried with him to the Far North several times; the flag of his college fraternity, Delta Kappa Epsilon; the flag of the Navy League; and the peace flag of the Daughters of the American Revolution. Above the headboard of his bed was a picture of Josephine; atop the dresser sat a framed picture of the cottage on his beloved Eagle Island. On his bunk was a fragrant pillow made by his now eleven-year-old daughter, Marie, containing pine needles from the island. Also in his cabin was a player piano, which would become a "pleasant companion," and two hundred rolls of mechanical music from classical to ragtime.*

After a well-publicized day cruise for wealthy backers that raised more money, *Roosevelt* left her anchorage off Manhattan's West Thirty-fourth Street on July 16, 1905, and steamed down the Hudson River. Peary stood amidships like a proud admiral, "bowing to the plaudits that came from all sides"—the tooting whistles of passing ships in the half-mile-wide river and, once *Roosevelt* entered New York Bay, volleys of cannon fire from forts and sailing clubs lining the shore. At his side were Josephine, their toddler son, Robert E. Peary Jr., their daughter, Marie, and several members of the Peary Arctic Club, including Herbert Bridgman.

Peary had recently been asked by a reporter whether he expected to find land at the North Pole, as some experts believed. "It would not surprise me at all to find it there," Peary said. "Either a polar continent or a collection of islands. However. . . . I do not expect to find an open sea as some scientists have predicted."

When it was time, a tug came alongside *Roosevelt* to take the family members and visitors ashore. Before departing, Bridgman led a brief and moving farewell ceremony, during which he publicly assured Peary that he had the full membership and resources of the club behind him in his patriotic cause.

"I am going now in God's name," said Peary.

TWO MONTHS LATER, *Roosevelt* butted her way into the frozen Arctic Sea and anchored off Cape Sheridan, on the north coast of Ellesmere Island. In spite of boiler troubles for much of the trip that robbed her of half her engine power, the stalwart ship had accom-

---

*It would be a blessing for Peary that he made his private cabin so comfortable. For the remainder of his Arctic exploring career (his last two expeditions), he would spend a total of two years living aboard ship, compared with seven months traveling on the polar ice pack.

plished her mission, fighting through usually impenetrable ice-
clogged channels to deliver Peary to a site 300 miles farther north
than any of his previous winter encampments. Come spring, the
expedition would begin approximately 450 miles from the Pole.

Preparations for the long Arctic night began immediately.
Eskimos had been brought aboard at various stops up the coast of
Greenland, and hunters were sent out to augment winter food supplies with fresh meat. They returned with quantities of musk oxen,
caribou, and hare.

While men worked at bringing supplies from the holds on deck,
others went ashore to build a large boxlike structure in which emergency supplies would be kept in case the ship caught fire and had to
be abandoned or was otherwise suddenly lost, forcing them to survive on land until rescued.

A week later, the catastrophe for which they were preparing
nearly occurred. An ice floe came into sight pivoting around the
cape, moving in their direction. Broken off from mountainous glaciers, floes spend their existence drifting in the northern seas. They
are more or less level on the surface, but underwater they range in
thickness from twenty to a hundred feet.

The huge floe broke through the thin sea ice and pushed aside
smaller floes in its path, and kept advancing until one massive corner of it, rising higher than the ship's rail, plowed into the starboard
side. It was the "crucial moment," according to Peary. "For a minute
or so, which seemed an age, the pressure was terrific. The *Roosevelt's*
ribs and interior bracing cracked like the discharge of musketry; the
deck amidships bulged up several inches . . . and the masts and rigging shook as in a violent gale." All hands knew if the hull split
open, they would have precious little time to abandon ship.

Then, with a "mighty tremor," *Roosevelt* broke free from the pressure of the ice and slowly rose upward until her propeller was out of
the water. It was exactly what her hull had been designed to do in
such a situation, yet it was extraordinary to witness. A portion of
the floe rode under the ship, broke off against the weight, and dis-
persed its energy against smaller floes until beaching on the nearby

shore. *Roosevelt* was intact, but stranded high and dry on the ice. She would not float again until summer.

After that, things settled into a comfortable routine. Food was plentiful and well prepared in the galley, the quarters stayed warm and dry, and the crew had time to read and play cards. Some men were engrossed in accounts of earlier Arctic expeditions, borrowed from the ship's library, and spoke among themselves about how appreciative they were not to have to endure the same hardships others had faced in northern latitudes.

Peary had arrived north on a brand-new ship and with a new strategy as well. He was giving up on his long-espoused theory that the only way to reach the Pole was with a small party, which required fewer supplies and therefore involved less complicated logistics than a large party. His new plan called for thirty men and more than a hundred dogs to be divided into supply parties that relayed food and fuel from one depot to the next, pressing ever northward and in support of his own party. Confident that his plan would succeed, he had already proudly dubbed it the "Peary System." In fact, the multiple-party relay system had been tried out half a century earlier by the English explorer Francis Leopard M'Clintock, although with men rather than dogs pulling heavily laden sledges.

In mid-February, as the polar night gave way to increased hours of daylight, the advance party left *Roosevelt*, followed by the other teams sent out at intervals. In just twenty miles, they crossed the eighty-third parallel, and soon afterward they left solid land and started over the frozen sea ice, setting up well-marked caches every fifty miles.

Peary was exuberant to be launching the expedition a month earlier than his last one, and so much farther north, for already he was only sixty miles shy of the highest latitude he had ever attained. From here, he estimated, they could make it to the Pole and back in one hundred days, averaging ten miles per day.

"The battle is on at last," Peary wrote in his diary on March 2. "We are straightened out on the ice of the Polar Sea heading direct for our goal."

When Peary broke camp, his longtime companion Matthew Henson, on his sixth Arctic expedition with Peary, was already ahead leading the pioneer party of three sledges, hacking out a trail through the icy hummocks that laced the frozen landscape. The pioneer party had to select the best route and render it passable for the other sledges. For that reason, they had the pick of the dogs and carried the lightest loads. This was the toughest and most dangerous job; the pioneer party could be cut off by the shifting ice from the supply line or even a safe route back.

After the pioneer party came the main body, split into five subdivisions, not including Peary's, each led by an American.* As they advanced along the trail, one party would drop out at intervals of fifty miles—after depositing supplies and marking its cache—then head back over its trail and pick up supplies that had been brought forward by a subdivision behind them, relaying those provisions north to the next team. Peary's plan called for him, at the opportune moment, to slingshot past the others with his own party for a dash to the Pole. On his return, he was to follow the same trail back, subsisting on the supplies that had been cached along the way.

For two weeks, they marched up and over broken ice, zigzagging where necessary to avoid open waters. Then, on March 25, midway between 84 and 85 degrees north, they came to a standstill at what they named the Big Lead, a body of open water too large to be bypassed. Several subdivisions caught up with one another, and together they waited for a way to cross. After an agonizing week, the lead closed with new ice, and the sledges dashed across.

They soon faced a gale that made travel impossible. When it abated after six days, Peary determined their latitude to be 85 degrees, 12 minutes, and found they had drifted on the ice pack more than seventy miles to the east. Henson again went out to lead the way, while two Eskimos with empty sledges were sent back to bring forward supplies. The Eskimos returned in twenty-four hours

---

*Also along on the journey were Robert Bartlett, thirty, a seafaring Newfoundlander and the skipper of *Roosevelt*; Ross Marvin, twenty-five, a trained engineer; Dr. Louie Wolf, the expedition surgeon; and two crewmen from *Roosevelt*'s engine room.

to report new impassable leads to the south; they were cut off from the caches that had been established, and from the support parties behind them. The Peary System had collapsed.

The remaining sledges were now nearly empty of supplies, and there were no caches ahead. Peary dumped all the equipment that was not necessary and followed on Henson's trail to the north, realizing that his chance for the Pole was gone but desperate to come home with at least a new farthest-north record.

On the second day, Peary met up with Henson. Between them, they had seven Eskimos and six sledges. The combined party went north. As the dogs gave out, they were killed and fed to the other dogs, and the sledges abandoned.

After being stymied on April 20 by what Peary described as a "perfect mesh of open leads" that appeared to make further progress impossible, he reported they somehow made a "forced march . . . between these leads," then slept a few hours. Upon awakening, he took an observation shortly before noontime.

Celestial observations require visibility to measure the sun's progress in the sky. By measuring the angle of the horizon to the sun as it rises to high noon, a capable navigator can determine the number of degrees, minutes, and seconds of latitude at local noon. No such determination is possible when the sun is not visible, as is often the case in polar regions.

Peary was the only one in the party who could use a sextant to fix a position. Henson, although he had spent his formative years at sea, did not know navigation or the mathematics required to make computations, only "knot and splice seamanship." The Eskimos had no reliable way of marking position; for them, it usually came down to how many days they marched or being within sight of familiar land. Henson often assisted Peary by writing down the numbers he read off, which could be difficult for the person working the sextant with numbed fingers.

Following his observation, Peary calculated their position at 86 degrees, 6 minutes, north—by thirty-three miles a new farthest-north record. "We had at last beaten the record, for which I thanked God," Peary wrote in his journal, "though I felt that the mere beating of the record was but an empty bauble compared with the splendid jewel on which I had set my heart for years."*

Looking at the "thin and pinched" faces and shrunken bodies of his companions and the "sagging jaws and lusterless eyes" of the sledge dogs, and fearing that the ice pack might have opened up leads behind them, Peary felt he had "cut the margin as narrow as could reasonably be expected." He ordered their return march to the south.

Henson, who usually took his orders from Peary with little or no comment, could not believe it, inasmuch as Peary had just told him they were less than two hundred miles from the Pole. "We can make it! Somehow, we can make it."

Both men could see to the north a stretch of clear ice with no leads or obstructions as far as the horizon—perhaps extending even to the Pole? Peary pointed out to Henson that the ice pack was continuing to drift steadily to the east; he had determined their longitude to be 50 degrees west, which put them due north of the coast of Greenland. If they continued northward, they would also keep drifting to the east where they would end up "God only knows."

Peary's eyes narrowed and his lips quivered below his ice-encrusted mustache. "I give the command to retreat, and I'm breaking my own heart."

They headed south at once, breaking new trail the entire way. Their desperate march for land stretched into weeks. Peary walked for as long as he could until, weak from hunger and exhaustion and his feet paining him greatly, he climbed into a sledge to ride, something polar explorers rarely did unless injured.

---

*Although there was written documentation of his earlier observations on this journey— times, angles, mathematical equations—no detailed notes of the record-breaking farthest-north observation was ever produced by Peary, nor was such proof found in his journal and other notes when they were first made available to outside researchers more than eighty years later. Peary also failed to document the daily mileages and conditions faced the last three days of his northward march. On the basis of previous positions that he did record, however, the weary men and dogs would have had to travel some ninety miles on those missing days to achieve the latitude record Peary claimed. By comparison, Nansen had traveled just under seven miles per day to make his farthest-north record of 86 degrees, 13 minutes, north (1895), and the duke of the Abruzzi's party had made nine miles a day (1900). On these issues of latitude and mileage, Peary would ask the world to take his word for it.

At one point, stuck on a drifting floe and with only the thinnest ice providing an escape route over a lead, they stripped themselves of extra gear and carefully walked and slid along in their snow-shoes—feet apart to better distribute their weight—until reaching stronger ice. Midway, trying to lighten his load, Peary discarded one of his parkas on the ice. Henson, following behind, picked it up. When they were safely across, Henson returned the parka to Peary with a grin. "They tell me it's cold in these parts."

Near starvation, they began eating the dogs, roasting them over fires made of broken-up sledges. (When asked upon his return about the palatability of dog meat, Peary said, "One who can eat hog meat or craves the delicacy of Limburger cheese can have nothing to say against dog. To be sure, the hind leg of an overworked dog is a little tough and rank sometimes.")

When there were but two canines left, a musk ox herd appeared as if dropped from heaven in their path. They killed seven, feasted, and found the strength to locate *Roosevelt* near Repulse harbor.

Although some of the supply parties were still out on the ice pack, they all eventually found their way back to the ship. Not a single man was lost, and of the 121 dogs that began the trip, 41 returned.

Notwithstanding his claim to have gone farther north than any-one in history, Peary was dismayed by his failure to reach the Pole. The conditions for travel that season had been deplorable; the ice had started disintegrating and melting too early in the year, and continuous storms had forced delays and cost them valuable time. *Nothing short will suffice*, the Navy Department had warned him of his effort to reach the Pole; and miserably short he had fallen. "To think that I have failed once more," a melancholy Peary wrote in his journal, "that I shall never have the chance to win again."

After returning to *Roosevelt* and allowing himself and the others to recuperate, Peary, knowing it would be weeks before the ship could break free of the ice pack, set out with a sledge party, traveling west along the northern shore of Ellesmere Island, a region known as Grant Land. When he reached the cape at the end of Ellesmere, on June 24, he named it Colgate, after his wealthy supporter and Peary

Arctic Club member James Colgate. In so doing, Peary disregarded the prior claim of Sverdrup, who had dubbed the region Lands-Lokk (Land's End) four years earlier. Peary crossed Nansen's Sound—without renaming it—to Axel Heiberg Island, which Sverdrup had named for one of his own supporters; claiming "to have found no other explorer's cairn, Peary renamed it Jesup Land. Three days later, he climbed the 1,600-foot headland Sverdrup called Svartevoeg, and named it Cape Thomas Hubbard. From that vantage point, Peary later claimed, he had seen through his field glass a landmass nearly one hundred miles to the northwest in the frozen Arctic Ocean. Upon his return home, Peary would name this "distant land . . . above the ice horizon" Crocker Land, after his banker benefactor who had been instrumental in financing previous expeditions. In this flurry of honoring his principal backers by naming—even renaming—geographical discoveries after them, was Peary thinking about his past adventures? or perhaps a future one?

When *Roosevelt* finally left for home, the season was late for traveling through the heavy Arctic ice, and the return voyage proceeded through nonstop storm activity. Any other ship would most likely have been stuck for the winter, if not sunk. But *Roosevelt* limped along, entering New York harbor on Christmas Day 1906, with her ironsides punctured like a tin can, her massive propeller sheared, rudder shredded, sternpost torn away, and emergency pumps going constantly. Naval officers who visited her in dry dock could not believe a ship in her condition had made it home.

In the north, when things had looked most dire from the bridge of *Roosevelt* as they fought rolling seas on the crippled ship, Peary seemed to regain his verve. He turned to Captain Bartlett and said evenly, "We have got to get her back, Captain. We are going to come again next year."

PART TWO

TO
THE
POLE

CHAPTER THIRTEEN

"A CRAZY HUNGER"

THE SUBJECT OF sensational newspaper reports that he had two months earlier led the first expedition to reach the summit of Mount McKinley, Cook addressed a "breathlessly appreciative audience" of five hundred members of a Seattle mountaineering club two weeks before Thanksgiving 1906.

Upon returning from his earlier climbing trip—Alaska geological surveyor Alfred Brooks hailed Cook's discovery of the 6,000-foot pass through the central axis of the Alaskan Range as more important than the scaling of McKinley—Cook had undertaken a campaign to field a second attempt to reach the highest point in North America. Things came together in early 1906, when he was promised $2,000 from Herschel Parker, a Columbia physics professor who wanted to make the climb, and $10,000 from the son of a millionaire saw manufacturer interested in hunting game in the Alaskan wilderness. Cook offered him the opportunity to do so in the untamed territory around McKinley after the climb. The balance of expenses was again covered by the Cooks and an advance from *Harper's Monthly*. (Cook would estimate the cost of his two McKinley expeditions at $28,000.) In addition to Parker, Cook signed up a topographer, Russell Porter, who had made one Arctic expedition; Belmore Browne, an artist and amateur climber; cook Samuel Beecher; and two veterans of the earlier climb, horse packer

Fred Printz and Walter Miller. Printz recommended a fellow Montanan, Edward Barrill, to help with the horses, and Cook hired him. The expedition assembled in Seattle that May and boarded a ship for Alaska. There was no talk this time of Marie's coming along. She had given birth to another daughter, Helen, the preceding May, and she stayed behind to care for her "babies."

Cook once again divided his party into two groups—one riding with the pack train and the other going upriver by boat on a power launch suited to the swift, shallow rivers that meandered from their sources beneath the Alaskan Range to the ocean. When everyone arrived at the rendezvous point, the boat was beached and the entire party went overland on horseback.

By the time they reached a point eighteen miles from McKinley, where they encountered steep cliffs blocking their way, one member of the party was ready to call it quits. Professor Parker, who had shown himself to be the "rankest kind of tenderfoot" in the field, declared the mountain unclimbable and expressed his desire to end the attempt and return home. After they set up camp, Cook surveyed the area for other approaches, but found none.

Porter was left in the field to map the area, and Cook returned with the others to the boat and headed back. Crossing an inlet during heavy seas, the boat—its propeller bent and rudder broken—was nearly swamped. While Cook fought to keep the sputtering engine going, Browne and Printz steered with an oar as the rest of the seasick party huddled under a tarpaulin.

On August 1, they reached Susitna Station, where they came upon a party of prospectors who had been forced to stand upright for days on partially submerged rocks in the middle of a stretch of rapids after their boat broke up. In spite of his own exhaustion, Cook worked for hours ministering to the injured, including one half-drowned man who had arrived in camp near death.

Parker, who later acknowledged the "heroic efforts" of Cook in saving their own boat party from disaster, was soon homeward bound on a passing steamer. Others also scattered; Browne, Miller, Printz, and Beecher took off together to shoot big game for museum exhibits. When a wire arrived that the millionaire's son would not be showing up for his hunt, Cook decided to take the launch and work his way back toward McKinley, heading for a large glacier he had discovered on the last expedition and named for his stepdaughter, Ruth. His companion was the no-nonsense Barrill, a powerfully built bear of a man who towered well over six feet.

Two months later in Seattle, for his first public remarks as to how McKinley had been climbed, Cook brought to the appearance Browne and Porter. The artist and topographer provided colorful descriptions of the difficult trek to the base of the isolated mountain—"that day we had to swim the river sixteen times"—then introduced the expedition leader for the rest of the story.

To a hero's ovation, Cook stepped to the platform. When the applause died down, he explained that while mountaineering was a new hobby of his, it held much in common with polar exploration. Facing freezing winds, the difficulty of taking along enough food, the struggle to survive far removed from assistance or rescue, traveling on ice and snow across uncharted paths, and seeing Mother Nature in her foulest moods—all were formidable obstacles shared by the two endeavors.

When he and Barrill had left the boat and continued on foot, Cook explained, they each carried a fifty-pound backpack. They had food for two weeks, an alcohol stove, fuel, a silk tent, sleeping bags, a horsehair rope, and ice axes. They also brought along three aneroid barometers, two thermometers, a prismatic compass, a watch, and a 5-by-7 camera with six film packs. It was not their intent to try to ascend North America's tallest mountain, Cook admitted; that effort had been given up for the season. Rather, he and Barrill set out to find an approach and possible line of attack to the top that would offer a chance of success next year.

Moving across Ruth Glacier, they headed for the mountain's eastern approaches. One particular route had earlier looked impossible because it seemed to end atop a ridge like a knife blade; but when it was viewed from another height, there appeared to be "twenty-five to fifty feet of a flat space on top." After two days spent scaling the ridge of the glacier—the men, connected by a safety line around their waists, did no time-consuming "relay work or double-tripping" that larger climbing parties necessarily engaged in—they made it to the top of this "mighty cornice." They built an Eskimo-style igloo for protection from the wind, slept comfortably, and started out refreshed in the morning. Thereafter, Cook told the audience, all the bad luck of the past few months changed for the better as they kept finding one path after another that took them ever higher.

Cook said they passed twelve thousand feet and kept going; at fourteen thousand feet, they tried in vain to find a level surface on which to camp, and finally gave up. Hacking out a step on a nearly vertical ice slope with their axes, they sat down side by side. In this cramped position they spent the night, keeping each other from falling asleep for fear they would slip down the mountainside.

Too cold to make breakfast the next morning, they got an early start, Cook told the hushed mountaineering crowd. For a few hours, they cut steps up the mountain until coming to a narrow level area. They made camp, served out double rations of pemmican, lit the stove, melted ice, and prepared cups of hot tea, which Cook thought tasted better than any drink he'd had in his life. This respite was a "cheerful time" for the two exhausted climbers, who by then had made the decision to try for the top.

The next day, they continued cutting steps upward, aiming for a ridge between the mountain's two peaks. That night they reached their mark at eighteen thousand feet, Cook said; there they spent the coldest night of his two seasons of mountaineering. The thermometer showed eighteen degrees below zero, but at that altitude and with the wind blowing "almost a hurricane," Cook estimated it was equal to seventy degrees below zero. They could not sleep for the fierce cold and spent the night conversing between chattering teeth in trembling voices, surrounded by the roars of avalanches sweeping down McKinley that shook the ground around them. Whenever a leg or arm went numb, they kicked or pounded themselves until the circulation returned. In the morning, they could hardly move, and they jumped about some more, stamping their feet and waving their arms to bring back the lost circulation.

It was on that day, September 16, 1906, shortly before noon, Cook said, that they reached the summit. The sky above them was "as black as that of midnight," and the visibility unlimited; their view went two hundred miles to several simmering volcanoes and fifty miles farther to the rim of the Pacific.

Cook told his audience that during the twenty minutes they remained at the top, they left a record of their achievement. However, as there was "not a stone . . . nothing from which a cairn could be constructed," they could only leave a note in a case propped up against a granite cliff before heading back down.

That day's entry in Cook's diary, in penciled longhand that became more scrawled and illegible the higher the reported altitude, read,

Sun Sept 16 The Top
Exhausted—nearly frozen not in shape to enjoy the scene—
The slope, the snow, wind, clouds out of Pacific Japan current out
of the Arctic clouds both meeting & drifting northeasterly. 250 miles.
50,000 sq. miles
Alcohol stove inefficient.
The hand shaking 20 minutes tube with date etc. flag & names
Peculiar cloud effects No longer see mirages.

ON DECEMBER 15, 1906, Peary and Cook were both seated at the head table for the National Geographic Society's annual dinner in Washington, D.C. Among the four hundred guests at the black-tie affair were cabinet members, senators, congressmen, ambassadors, military leaders, and captains of industry.

On the program to speak first, Cook was introduced by inventor Alexander Graham Bell, the second president of the society and father-in-law of its new leader, Gilbert H. Grosvenor. "I have been asked to say a few words about a man who must be known by name, at least, to all of us—Dr. Frederick A. Cook," said Bell, who had been a teacher of the deaf in Boston before patenting the telephone and co-founding Bell Telephone Company thirty years earlier. "We have had with us, and are glad to welcome, Commander Peary of the

Arctic regions, but in Dr. Cook we have one of the few Americans, if not the only American, who has explored both extremes of the world, the Arctic and Antarctic regions. And now he has been to the top of the American continent, and therefore to the top of the world, and tonight I hope Dr. Cook will tell us something about Mount McKinley."

At the podium, Cook started by speaking not of his own accomplishments but of the "splendid achievement" of Peary, who had pushed "human endeavor to the utmost limit of endurance, all with the unselfish motive of carrying the honor and flag of his country to the farthest north."

About the McKinley expedition, Cook said their success was "mostly due to our use of the working equipment of polar explorers."

At the sound of the door of the banquet hall flying open, all heads turned. President Roosevelt rushed in and hurried to an empty seat at the head table.

Cook stepped aside as the president was announced, then seemed reluctant to take up time on his own expedition; indeed, the only award to be given out that night was to go to Peary. Cook promised the audience that he would tell the McKinley story another time, and returned to his seat.

Roosevelt delivered a short address commending Peary for "year in and year out" having to "face perils and overcome the greatest risks." He went on, "You did a great deed, a deed that counted for all mankind, a deed which reflected credit upon you and upon your country; and on behalf of those present, and speaking also for the millions of your countrymen, I take pleasure in handing you this Hubbard medal, and in welcoming you home from the great feat which you have performed."

The large gold medallion that Roosevelt presented Peary was named for the society's late founder, Gardiner Greene Hubbard. The inscription read, "Awarded by the National Geographic Society to Robert E. Peary, For Arctic Explorations, Farthest North 87°6', December 15th 1906."

Peary had a history with the Society, of which he was a longtime member. Appearing in the inaugural issue of *National Geographic Magazine,* in October 1888, was an article, "Across Nicaragua with Transit and Machete," written by a young naval engineer named Robert E. Peary. Seven years later, when Josephine Peary was soliciting contributions to pay for the 1895 relief operation to bring her husband home, the society organized a paid lecture to raise funds. Already this year the society had given a grant in the amount of $1,000 toward the cost of Peary's next assault on the North Pole.

In his acceptance speech, Peary thanked the society on behalf of the Peary Arctic Club and its president, Morris K. Jesup. He acknowledged his gratitude to Roosevelt for his "continued interest." The true explorer, Peary went on, "does his work not for any hopes of reward or honour, but because the thing he has set himself to do is a part of his being, and must be accomplished for the sake of the accomplishment. And he counts lightly hardships, risks, obstacles, if only they do not bar him from his goal.

"To me the final and complete solution of the Polar mystery which has engaged the best thought and interest of some of the best men of the most vigorous and enlightened nations of the world for more than three centuries, and today quickens the pulse of every man or woman whose veins hold red blood, is the thing which should be done for the honour and credit of this country, the thing which it is intended that I should do, and the thing that I must do."

For Mount McKinley, Cook received honors of his own. His descriptive report of attaining the peak was accepted by alpine climbers and other experts the world over. In the same month that Peary was honored by the National Geographic Society, the Explorers Club elected Cook its president—succeeding the well-known explorer General Adolphus Greely—and invited him to make a presentation at its annual dinner. He delivered an illustrated talk to the Association of American Geographers and was honored at the American Alpine Club annual dinner.

Settling into life at home, Cook soon felt the "confinement of prison" surrounding his routine, and "fretted and chafed" at being its captive for long. Marie and the girls, their cheerful home filled with souvenirs of his travels, his professional practice—though he cherished each of them, together they were somehow not enough. With no plans for his next exploration, he busied himself by seeing a steady stream of patients, finishing the article he owed *Harper's Monthly*, and working on a book about his McKinley expeditions.

In March 1907, a wealthy member of the Explorers Club made a proposal to Cook that would change his life. John R. Bradley, along with his brother, owned one of the world's most exclusive gambling clubs: the Beach Club in Palm Beach. Known as Gambler Jim, Bradley had been, at the age of twenty, a crackerjack faro dealer at a popular gambling house in New Orleans. He and his brother, Edward, went on to own their own casino in Texas before relocating to Florida. As their wealth grew and his brother indulged himself in the gentleman's sport of horse racing—his stable would win four Kentucky Derbies—Bradley found excitement in another gentlemanly pastime of the day: hunting wild animals in exotic locales. He had hunted in most regions of the world, and upon returning from a safari to Asia the same month Cook came back from Mount McKinley, Bradley began giving serious thought to bagging his first trophies in the Arctic.

Cook quickly accepted Bradley's offer to finance an Arctic excursion that Cook would organize and lead. Cook looked on it as a chance to further his ethnological studies of the Eskimos. "He was to photograph Eskimos," Bradley said later, "and I was to shoot walrus and polar bear."

Cook left for the commercial fishing harbor of Gloucester, Massachusetts, to find the right ship for the voyage. He ended up purchasing, with Bradley's money, a 110-ton, wooden-hulled schooner. Certain modifications were required for operating in icebound waters: sheathing the bow and stern with plates of steel; hardening the hull with a four-inch layer of white oak; adding a gasoline-powered auxiliary engine; and upgrading the interior to provide comfortable

accommodations. When the schooner emerged from dry dock, she
was christened *John R. Bradley*. Although the cruise was planned to
last only one season, enough supplies for two years were boarded in
the event the ship became trapped in the ice pack.

That May, *Harper's Monthly* published Cook's sixteen-page article
"The Conquest of Mount McKinley," along with drawings and photographs. The last picture was a long shot of a man atop a peak
holding an American flag. The caption read: "The Flag on the
Summit of Mt. McKinley, 20,300 Feet above Sea-Level." Near the
end of the article, Cook summed up his thoughts:

> . . . I shall always remember, with a mental focus sharpened by time,
> the warm friendship of my companion, Edward Barrille [*sic*], the
> curious low dark sky, the dazzling brightness of the sky-scraped
> granite blocks, the neutral gray-blue of space, the frosty dark blue of
> the shadows, and, above all, the final pictures which I took of
> Barrille with the flag lashed to his axe as an arctic air froze the
> impression into a relief which no words can tell.

In June, a month before they were to set sail, Cook and Bradley
met for lunch at the Holland House in Manhattan. Both were
excited about the upcoming Arctic voyage, although no doubt for
different reasons.

"Why not try for the Pole?" Cook blurted out.

Bradley, who made no secret of his desire to be counted among
the best big-game hunters in the world, was not easily surprised.
Well groomed in fashionable three-piece suits, he had a gambler's
watchful eye, always calculating what the man across the table from
him was up to. He judged Cook to be "seasoned and resourceful . . .
full of courage," which was why he had given him command. At the
same time, the two men had very different lives and goals. Bradley
would gladly have traded either Pole for a horse, a gun, and a dog.

"Not I," Bradley said, eyeing Cook. "Would you like to try for it?"

"There is nothing I would rather do. It is the ambition of my life."

While Cook had followed his ambitions to other parts of the

world—unlike Peary, who had long remained northbound—he found his thoughts increasingly returning to the Arctic. Should he ever find himself in a position to try for the Pole, Cook had some definite ideas on what he would do differently—in equipment, tactics, route—from what he saw Peary and others doing. Was it Peary's looming shadow of proprietary ownership over all things Arctic that had struck a nerve in the independent, free-spirited Cook? Peary had announced plans to depart in July 1907 for his last attempt to gain the Pole. So, for Cook, was it about competition? or personal ambition? Cook himself wasn't sure, but he did know that he had "a crazy hunger" he had to satisfy. Later he would try to explain his motivation: "The attaining of the North Pole meant at the time simply the accomplishing of a splendid, unprecedented feat—a feat of brain and muscle in which I should, if successful, signally surpass other men. . . . To reach it would mean, I knew, an exultation which nothing else in life could give."

Bradley asked what added costs would be involved to outfit the expedition for a possible attempt on the Pole. Cook estimated $8,000 to $10,000 and added that he would be willing to contribute some of his own funds.

There were no guarantees that such a venture could be undertaken, Cook cautioned. Once in northern Greenland, he would have to assess several variables, including the weather, ice conditions, and the availability of willing Eskimos and trained dogs. Cook reiterated that the hunt could take place in any case. Then, if he decided against trying for the Pole, he would "return quietly home" with Bradley, avoiding any publicity about an aborted polar effort.

Bradley thought they had a working plan; his bet was covered on the hunt, and he admired Cook's willingness to gamble. "We'll fit this expedition for the Pole," Bradley said, "and say nothing to anyone about it."

Cook stayed busy making final preparations. The speed with which he organized the trip was unprecedented; he went from having neither funds nor ship to being poised for departure within four months, and to ready a polar expedition in only *one month*. By day, he ordered supplies, and at night he pored over charts, laying out his route and making his plans.

After the girls went to bed, Marie often sat with him; over cups of tea, they looked at the maps and talked. Originally opposed to his leaving so soon after the McKinley expedition and hoping he would stay home at least a year, she came around to sharing his belief that this was an opportunity not to pass up.

He explained to her that his best chance for a successful dash to the Pole lay in thrusting aside the unsuccessful methods of previous expeditions. He intended to move fast with a small party, accompanied by only a few Eskimos and sledges. Marie at first was concerned. Wasn't there safety in numbers? No. In the Arctic, more numbers meant more mouths to feed, which involved the hauling and caching of supplies, from which they could be dangerously cut off anyway, as Peary had been in 1906. Also, Cook had decided to take an entirely new route to the Pole, one that he had arrived at after studying Otto Sverdrup's book *New Land,* which included the results of the several years the Norwegian had spent laboriously mapping previously uncharted areas in the Arctic. Sverdrup described a promising region that contained plenty of fresh game—with which to augment an expedition's supplies—and offered specific and useful information on ice conditions. To Cook, the new route promised "immunity from the highly disturbing effects of certain . . . currents," meaning the ice could be slower drifting, smoother, and altogether easier to travel across.

He and Marie agreed that she and the girls would sail with him as far as Nova Scotia, where they would summer in Baddeck, on Cape Breton Island, and await the return of *Bradley* in the fall. Whether he was aboard or had remained in the north to try for the Pole, she and the girls would at that time return home.

One of the last things Cook did was make arrangements to have the completed manuscript of his McKinley book, *To the Top of the Continent,* along with photographs, delivered to Doubleday, Page & Company, the publisher that had signed him to tell the story of his two climbing expeditions.

At dusk on July 3, 1907, *John R. Bradley* pulled away from the pier at Gloucester and turned her prow to sea. There was no ceremonial send-off, not a single politician or reporter aboard, and no tooting whistles or cannon fire. As far as anyone watching knew, the little ship was taking her rich owner to Greenland to collect trophies for his wall.

THREE MONTHS LATER, a letter was mailed from Nova Scotia by John Bradley, on the way back from his Arctic hunt on the schooner named for him. The missive was addressed to Herbert Bridgman, secretary of the Peary Arctic Club, and dated August 26, 1907, from Etah, in northern Greenland. An apparent gesture of professional courtesy, it read,

> I have hit upon a new route to the North Pole and will stay to try it. By way of Buchanan Bay and Ellesmere Land and northward through Nansen Strait over the Polar Sea seems to me to be a very good route. There will be game to the 82nd degree, and here are natives and dogs for the task. So here is for the Pole. . . .
>
> *Kind regards.*
> *Frederick Cook*

CHAPTER FOURTEEN

"I SHALL WIN THIS TIME"

AGAIN AT THE BEHEST of President Roosevelt, Peary was granted three years' paid leave beginning April 1907. And again his orders from the Navy Department were explicit: "to undertake expedition to North Pole." In a letter to Roosevelt thanking him for his continued support, Peary, who felt certain his next expedition would be his "last attempt," wrote, "I believe that I shall win this time, and I believe that this is the work for which God Almighty intended me."

Peary also received help of a less constructive nature: "a small flood of 'crank' letters" from people "oozing with inventions and schemes" that would "absolutely insure the discovery of the Pole." One fellow wanted to sell him a portable sawmill to set up on the polar sea, for use in making lumber with which to construct a wooden tunnel over the ice all the way to the Pole. Another proposal involved establishing a central soup station and running hose lines over the ice in order to invigorate the exploring party with hot soup. The "gem of the whole collection," however, was the inventor who proposed turning the explorer into a human cannonball. Although the man declined to offer many details for fear that his invention would be stolen, he claimed that at some point they could aim his cannon in the right direction and shoot Peary to the Pole. Left unexplained were any specifics about the landing, or how Peary might get back.

Other methods of reaching the Pole suggested to Peary involved "motor cars, guaranteed to run over any kind of ice," "flying machines," and a "submarine boat," although Peary noted it was not explained "how we were to get up through the ice after we had traveled to the Pole beneath it." These proposals struck him as a "contemporaneous drift of inventive thought." Indeed, some would prove to be not so much outlandish as ahead of their time.

Notwithstanding contracts promising the completion of $75,000 worth of repairs to *Roosevelt* by July 1, 1907, the work to replace the damaged boilers dragged on, forcing a crestfallen Peary to postpone his departure until the following summer. A crushing blow, it meant that Peary, who had turned fifty-one, would be a year older before he left. Already he had begun to recognize the "loss with each successive year, of the elan, the elasticity, the inexhaustible energy and vitality of youth, which this work demands."

Peary considered his inability to attain the Pole on his previous trip "the greatest disappointment of my life." Men, dogs and supplies had been stretched to the limit, he would explain, only to add wistfully: "Before me I could see a stretch of clear ice—200 miles to the Pole. Ten days more and we could have made it."

Peary knew the importance of delivering a success story. His book *Nearest the Pole,* about his farthest-north journey, flopped; only 2,230 copies sold in 1907, not enough to cover the $5,000 advance he received from Doubleday, Page. The segment of the reading public that regularly devoured Arctic adventure stories had seemingly had enough of *farthest* and *nearest.*

That fall, Peary received a visit from Vilhjalmur Stefansson, a twenty-eight-year-old Canadian-born Icelandic anthropologist just back from his first expedition (led by the Danish explorer Ejnar Mikkelsen), whose object was a mystery continent believed to be located north of Alaska. After their ship sank, they hadn't gotten far by sledge, only a hundred miles north of the Yukon before turning around. Stefansson told Peary of rumors he heard in Alaska among locals who were openly offended that an outsider had come in and claimed to have climbed *their* mountain; the word was that Cook might not have made it to the top. Peary dismissed the report as malicious gossip, explaining to Stefansson that he knew Cook well and believed him to be "an honorable man."

Not long afterward, Peary heard something about Cook that he *did* take seriously: the distressing news that his former expedition physician was in place to try for the Pole before *Roosevelt* could even get away from the dock.

When John Bradley had appeared in Nova Scotia at the conclusion of his hunt, the flamboyant gambler gave interviews to newspaper reporters about Cook's ambitious plans, which led to front-page headlines around the country similar to what appeared in the *Boston Herald* on October 2, 1907:

DASH TO POLE
TO FORESTALL
PEARY IS PLAN
OF DR. F.A. COOK

*Cook Landed at Etah with
Provisions, and Will in the
Spring Undertake Trip That
Has Baffled Many of the
World's Explorers*

Two days later, the *New York Times*, quoting Bradley that Cook's expedition was "provisioned for two years and fully equipped with dogs and sledges," published an editorial that read, in part, "That Cook has got the start on Peary does not count for so much. Peary will be in the race. . . . It is to men of this sort . . . that we must look for any further knowledge of the geography of the Far North. Dr. Cook knows his business, and he has started in the right way."

Even Peary's hometown paper, the *Portland (Maine) Press,* always an enthusiastic chronicler of his exploits, observed, "Peary would be chagrined if he should reach the Pole only to find Cook had been there before him."

Peary Arctic Club members were aghast at Cook's designs on the Pole after all the time, effort, and money that had been expended in support of Peary. An emergency meeting of club officers was held, with Peary in attendance. Heretofore, Cook had been considered a friend and Arctic colleague; the club had, after all, recruited him to lead the would-be rescue of Peary in 1901. But Cook was now seen in a completely different light: as a rival to be reckoned with, and a contender for the valuable prize sought by their own candidate. As a result of the meeting, a letter was sent to the International Bureau of Polar Research in Brussels, Belgium, complaining of Cook's tactics and charging that he was an insurgent who without permission had intruded upon Peary's sphere of influence and that, therefore, his future work should not be officially recognized. The letter was signed by Peary.

Peary seethed at what he considered a breach of polar etiquette, to wit, that Cook had gone north "sub rosa" to Etah, as he wrote in a letter to the *New York Times*, "which has been my rendezvous and depot for years," where Cook would be "appropriating to his own use" the services of Eskimos and dogs that had gained experience "under my lead and guidance," and whom Peary had intended to use for his own expedition to the Pole. All of this, Peary believed, was a conscious and unethical effort to "forestall me . . . of which no man possessing a sense of honor would be guilty." Suddenly, Peary no longer considered Cook so honorable.

More bad news came shortly after the holiday season that Peary would rather have spent on his ship high in the Arctic ice pack. On January 22, 1908, Morris Jesup, who had never gone to college but become rich in banking and manufacturing and was a generous benefactor to many charities, died in New York City at age seventy-eight.

To Peary, the loss of his most generous supporter—"financially a tower of strength" and the force behind the Peary Arctic Club—was incalculable. It seemed "an absolutely paralyzing defeat," and he had reason to doubt whether it would be possible to finance a new expedition. The shipyard work had depleted the club's treasury, and still more funds were required to buy equipment and supplies.

The reports of Cook's bold plans for the Pole increased the pressure on Peary to find the money to get *Roosevelt* underway by next summer, lest the race be over before he stepped onto the field. The country was mired in another financial crisis, and wherever Peary turned, hat in hand, "every one was poor." Only when he reached his "lowest ebb" did the tide start to turn.

An unexpected $5,000 donation arrived from Jesup's widow. Peary deemed the contribution "munificent," not only because of his desperate need for funds but also because the money was sent "in the midst of her . . . grief." (Although Jesup willed $1 million to the American Museum of Natural History, there was no provision in his $13 million estate to endow Peary's work.)*

Peary was further uplifted by the willingness of the wealthy, powerful New York attorney Thomas Hubbard to step in as president of the Peary Arctic Club, assuming the duties vacated by Jesup as main fund-raiser. As he took office, Hubbard made a large donation toward the upcoming journey, an action multiplied several times over by the club's old guard, most of whom, like Hubbard, had already contributed heavily toward the repairs to *Roosevelt*.

Money now came in from unforeseen sources: Zenas Crane, a Massachusetts paper manufacturer, wrote asking that Peary come for a visit. He did, and left with an unsolicited $10,000 check, along with the promise of more should it be required. Crane accepted the vice-presidency of the club.

Somehow, everything was coming together for a summer 1908 departure—an event, Peary began to feel, that was "too big to die." No sooner did new contributions come in than orders went out for more equipment and supplies.†

---

*The Peary family benefited one more time, however, from the largess of the Jesups. In February 1910, Josephine, who had been attempting to sell the three meteorites Dog, Woman, and Tent to the American Museum of Natural History for years, received a $40,000 check from Mrs. Morris Jesup, who then donated the meteorites to the museum, where they are still displayed. Josephine, who said that her husband gave her the meteorites so she could sell them and raise enough money to educate their two children, received the equivalent of more than $750,000 in today's dollars.

†Peary's purchases for his new expedition included 16,000 lbs. flour, 1,000 lbs. coffee, 800 lbs. tea, 10,000 lbs. sugar, 3,500 lbs. kerosene, 7,000 lbs. bacon, 10,000 lbs. biscuits, 30,000 lbs. pemmican, 3,000 lbs. dried fish, 1,000 lbs. tobacco, and 100 cases condensed milk.

Peary's blueprint for his final assault on the Pole was similar in respects to his 1906 trek, although he had modified some elements that had not worked. The route would be identical—one that he had labeled the "American Route to the Pole"—northward from the Strait of Belle Isle into the Davis Strait, through Baffin Bay, Smith Sound, and Kane Basin. He considered this the "best of all possible routes for a determined, aggressive attack upon the Pole," listing among its advantages the establishment of a land base (on Grant Land, at the northern end of Ellesmere Island) one hundred miles closer to the Pole than any other point on the periphery of the Arctic Ocean, and a long stretch of (northern Greenland) coast line along which to return. He had been relieved to learn of the new route Cook planned to take on the basis of Sverdrup's mapping. Peary rejected it out of hand, so convinced was he that his own route was the only practical way to reach the Pole.

As before, Peary intended for *Roosevelt* to winter on the north shore of Grant Land and for his sledge trip to begin in February. This time he would push farther west, to Cape Columbia, before turning north—an effort to compensate for the drift of the ice cap that had taken him so far east the last time. One difference would be "a more rigid massing of my sledge divisions en route" to prevent the separation of sledges and supplies "as happened on the last expedition." Also, Peary would locate his base camp north of the Big Lead, making the point of departure for his dash to the Pole some one hundred miles farther north than his previous jumping-off place. Anticipating the drift of the ice this time, Peary planned to return to the ship along the northern coast of Greenland, where one of his support parties would establish a supply depot.

To fill out his expedition ranks, Peary had chosen carefully from a field of volunteers, for he believed that in "those frozen spaces" a man came "face to face with himself and with his companions; if he is a man, the man comes out; and, if he is a cur, the cur shows as quickly."

Matthew Henson, "my negro assistant," would again be at Peary's side for reasons of "his adaptability and fitness for the work" and "his loyalty." Peary thought Henson could handle an Eskimo sledge better than "any other man living, except some of the best of the Eskimos hunters themselves." Peary also needed Henson for his Eskimo-language skills—after all these years, Peary still spoke only a few words of jargon—and to act as his go-between for any "disagreeable job" involving the natives, such as dismissing a hunter or "putting the undesirable ashore." Invaluable as Henson was, and though he had gone as far north in 1906 as Peary had, Peary had made no effort to have the National Geographic Society or any other group that had honored his farthest-north record recognize his loyal companion.

At forty years of age and after stints as a laborer, railroad porter, and holder of other jobs in which he had found little fulfilment, Henson would be making his seventh Arctic expedition. His 1891 marriage, victimized by his many long absences, had ended in 1897 when his wife, Eva, was granted a divorce. In 1902 in Greenland, Henson began an intimate relationship with Akatingwah, a feisty, independent young woman who had previously been given in marriage by her family to a hunter named Kitdlaq, often employed by Peary. Both natives were members of the Moriussaq (south of Etah) tribe, which numbered two hundred. Henson was revered by the northern Greenland Eskimos, who called him Mahri-Pahluk ("Matthew the Kind One"), and he had a special place in the tribe. It was customary for a wife to cohabit with other men of the tribe, and, in view of all the time Henson spent with them, he was considered something other than an outsider. In the summer of 1906, Akatingwah, who had been living off and on with Henson since his return the preceding fall, gave birth aboard *Roosevelt* to a dark-skinned baby with tight, curly hair, a genetic trait not found in Eskimos. No one doubted the lineage of the boy named Anaukaq.*

Other veterans of the 1905–06 expedition were, "first and most valuable of all," Robert Bartlett, serving again as *Roosevelt*'s master, and the Cornell-trained civil engineer Ross Marvin, a faculty mem-

---

*Another birth occurred that same summer aboard *Roosevelt*: Peary's longtime Eskimo mistress, Allakasingwah ("Ally"), delivered a second son, whom she named Kalipaluk. Like her firstborn, the new baby arrived with his father's pale skin and blue eyes.

ber at his alma mater, serving again as Peary's assistant and correspondence secretary. Expedition newcomers were the physician Dr.
John W. Goodsell of Pennsylvania, descendant of one of the oldest
families in America (his great-grandfather was a soldier in
Washington's army when Cornwallis surrendered); Donald
MacMillan, professor of mathematics and physical training at
Worcester Academy in Massachusetts, the son of a sea captain whose
ship had sailed from Boston thirty years earlier and was never heard
from again; George Borup, a graduate of Groton and Yale (class of
1907), where he had lettered in golf and wrestling but was best
known as a champion track runner. With the exception of the chief
engineer, George Wardwell, who had performed coolly in bringing
home the crippled *Roosevelt*, Peary left the selection of the ship's
other fourteen officers and crew to the seasoned Bartlett.

Shortly after 1 p.m. on July 6, 1908, *Roosevelt* backed away from
her berth at the foot of East Twenty-fourth Street into the East
River. On one of the hottest days recorded in New York City in
years—thirteen deaths attributed to the heat were reported that
day—this sturdy icebreaker and her crew were beginning their journey to one of the coldest places on Earth.

Aboard ship were about one hundred visitors, including Peary
Arctic Club officers Thomas Hubbard, Zenas Crane, and Herbert
Bridgman, most of them on deck peering over the rail as the ship
steamed upriver to the din of whistles from powerhouses and facto-
ries added to the tooting salutes of other ships. As the ship passed
Blackwell's Island, many of the inmates at the state prison waved
goodbye, no doubt to a man wishing to trade places with even the
lowliest seaman on the journey to a land without bars or guards.
Near Fort Totten, they passed President Roosevelt's naval yacht,
Mayflower, whose small deck gun barked a parting salute.

Not long afterward, the visitors were put ashore on the tug
Narkeeta. Peary and his family also disembarked, to spend the night
at a hotel, and *Roosevelt* went on to dock at the longtime home of her
namesake on Oyster Bay, Long Island, where the Pearys were to
lunch with the Roosevelts the next day.

During that luncheon at the sprawling estate known as Sagamore

Hill, Roosevelt spoke "earnestly and profoundly" of his interest in Peary's Arctic work and eagerly accepted an invitation to tour the Arctic-bound vessel. The president brought his wife, Edith, and three youngest sons aboard and spent an hour poking around every compartment, "allowing nothing to escape his inquiry and comment," and shaking hands with each member of the expedition party and ship's crew, exclaiming "Bully! Bully!" a number of times as he "blessed them with his confidence."

Peary, who considered Roosevelt "the most intensely vital man . . . America has ever produced," stepped forward as the president began to depart with his entourage. "Mr. President," he said in his loud and clear voice, "I shall put into this effort everything there is in me—physical, mental, and moral."

Roosevelt stopped at the rail and seemed to consider the tall, rangy man before him. They were both wearing white summer suits, starched shirts, ties, and nearly identical straw hats with black silk bands.

Peary's thick reddish hair was turning gray, as were his heavy eyebrows and walrus mustache. His steel gray eyes were alert, though, and with his wide chest and shoulders, long arms and slightly bowed legs, he still looked like a force to be reckoned with.

"I believe in you, Peary," Roosevelt said in his gruff, sincere manner. "And I believe in your success—if it is within the possibility of man."

CHAPTER FIFTEEN

POLAR QUEST

T HE SCHOONER *John R. Bradley*'s voyage to northern
Greenland in the summer of 1907 alternated between smooth sailing
and storm-whipped seas. After stopping along the way for its owner
to hunt, the yacht made Etah, then sailed a short distance farther
north to the tiny settlement of Annoatok, normally home to only a
few Eskimos but at the time populated with some of the region's best
hunters, their families, and sledge dogs gathered for the winter bear
hunt. Cook realized he would have no problem preparing and manning his expedition from here, trading such "rewards from civilization" as knives, guns, ammunition, needles, and matches for native
goods and services. Cook knew what he had to do, for "the expenditure of a million dollars could not have placed an expedition at a better advantage. The opportunity was too good to be lost."

At breakfast one morning, Cook told Bradley, "I'm going to stay."

"All right. You're past twenty-one years of age." Then, speaking
to a man he not only respected but had come genuinely to like over
the past months, Bradley added, "Think it over before you finally
decide."

The gambler in him would have wagered, however, that the doctor's course was set. Bradley had observed how Cook's every action
since their early summer lunch at the Holland House seemed in
preparation for the Pole. On the voyage, he had watched Cook brush

up on using his sextant by taking regular observations with Captain Moses Bartlett, an experienced ice navigator and ship's master (and cousin of *Roosevelt* skipper Robert Bartlett). The captain coveted Cook's fine sextant—an aluminum surveyor's model, made by Hurleman of France and purchased from Keuffler & Esser in New York, with a vernier (small calibrated scale) reading to ten inches, terrestrial, astronomical, and night telescopes, and double refracting prisms—a high-quality yet lightweight instrument that Bartlett used to shoot the ship's daily position when Cook was attending to other matters. Bradley admired Cook's patience, "how he plays along at a thing and won't give up," whether it was taking observations or working "twelve solid hours" to get a stalled motorboat engine started during a walrus hunt, not giving up until the "cheerful toot-toot" was at last heard. "He never complains, never swears . . . just keeps plodding along."

Cook's announcement to the crew that he was going to try for the Pole was greeted with much excitement. Everyone volunteered to join in the adventure, even Captain Bartlett, though he soon realized the imprudence of the schooner's not having her skipper for the voyage back. Rather, Bartlett offered Cook his entire crew, except for the cook and the chief engineer.

Cook wanted only one white man to winter with him in Greenland, since he intended to take a largely Eskimo party on the sledge journey, convinced as he was that no group of white men, regardless how rugged and determined, "could possibly match the Eskimos in their own element." He selected as his companion Rudolph Franke, twenty-nine, a husky German with a scientific education who was good-natured, strong, and an "Arctic enthusiast."

In addition to the supplies Cook had already gathered, Bradley ordered offloaded for Cook's benefit any food, fuel, and other surplus goods not needed for the return voyage. Bradley also offered to send the ship back the following summer—at his own expense—to retrieve Cook and Franke, but the doctor had other plans. Next summer, they would sledge to one of the Danish ports in southern Greenland, Cook explained, catch one of the sealers that regularly traveled to and from Copenhagen, and come home on a ship from Europe.

On the morning of September 3, farewells were exchanged, and *John R. Bradley* sailed south over the horizon, leaving Cook "alone with [his] destiny" seven hundred miles from the Pole.

By nightfall that first day, Cook and Franke had erected a 13-by-16-foot structure, made of packing boxes held together by strips of wood and the joints sealed with pasted paper, to serve as storehouse/work-shop/bunkhouse. For the framework of the roof they used long boards, and the covers of boxes as shingles. They cut out squares of turf, which they placed atop the shingles for insulation. That night, they slept comfortably inside their new home heated by a coal-burning stove. They soon had the supplies inside, safe from the ravages of winter, and had only to walk a few feet to find whatever they needed.

Cook's next priority was manufacturing and assembling his polar sledges; he sought to combine what he and Amundsen had learned in the Antarctic with the "durability of the Eskimo sledge and the lightness of the Yukon sledge of Alaska." The sledges he would take north were twelve feet long and two and a half feet wide, and weighed fifty-five pounds each. Peary's sledges weighed twice as much; the difference in dead weight, Cook calculated, was enough to carry food for one man to the Pole and back. Since a polar explorer's success and even survival was based primarily on his ability to transport enough food, Cook believed it crucial to "eliminate useless weight."

For the framework of the sledges, Cook had brought with him hickory from home. He had learned about Sullivan County hickory—strong and durable as well as lightweight and flexible—as a young boy building his first sleds for winter play.*

---

*Frederick was not the only member of his family who became skilled at such construction; his older brother, Theodore, was also an accomplished sledge builder, and he too used only Sullivan County hickory. Theodore had written to Peary more than once offering to build sledges for his expeditions. Peary was interested enough in 1905 to review the designs and ask for an estimate. Peary decided against the sledges when he found a source of cheaper wood, and also because he questioned the suitability of Theodore's eight-foot-long sledges, since he favored larger and heavier ones. Theodore's sledges were used by the Baldwin-Ziegler polar expedition (1901–02), and other Arctic explorers. In 1903, he shipped sixty-three of his handcrafted sledges. A mechanical genius by reputation, Theodore spent virtually his entire life in Sullivan County and never went to the Arctic. In 1923, he became trapped inside a walk-in ice cabinet and froze to death.

Instead of using solid beams for runners, as Peary and the Eskimos favored, Cook interlocked crossbars, struts, and posts to support lighter runners, which he found offered less friction and easier movement over the ice. For added strength, the runners were shod with strips of iron. Sledge parts were made interchangeable to fit not only other sledges but other parts of the same sledge, allowing for replacement pieces to be mixed and matched.

Eight to ten men, working at Cook's side and under his supervision, toiled daily at benches set up in the workshop, shaping and bending runners, fitting the interchangeable support struts, and riveting the iron strips to the runners. The streamlined sledges had a flexible framework that gave without breaking, and joints made elastic by seal-thong lashings.

Cook also redesigned the traditional Eskimo dog harness made of walrus hide, which he had observed the dogs would eat when they were hungry. He used canvas for shoulder straps and cut traces from heavy cotton line.

A key element of Cook's polar plan was to bring a boat with him. He knew that Nansen's life had been saved by his having an Eskimo kayak and that the lives of others had been lost for lack of a boat. Concerned that a kayak would take up space and be difficult to transport without damaging, Cook had selected a collapsible twelve-foot boat and loaded it onto *Bradley*. It would serve, he reasoned, to ferry men, dogs, and even a sledge across leads and could be useful for hunting excursions. He disassembled the boat and worked the parts into the design of a sledge, with its slats, spreaders, and floor pieces reinforcing sections of the sledge, and canvas cover serving as a floor cloth. The boat "never seemed needlessly cumbersome" on the journey; indeed, anyone looking at the sledge party would not have known it carried a boat with them.

To test his equipment and condition himself, Cook hunted with the Eskimos in the gloom of the approaching winter—caribou, reindeer, narwhal, bear, fox. On one trip, they traveled five hundred miles by sledge; to Cook's satisfaction, the polar equipment proved sound. They stockpiled meat, and native women made boots and garments with the skins and furs. He wanted each man on the polar journey to take two sets of fur clothing, so that a set could always be drying out from the constant perspiration that resulted from marching at one's physical limit. Cook thought that avoiding sweat-soaked furs in freezing temperatures was the "only safe way, if health is to be preserved."

On a hunt in early December in the area where he had spent his first winter in Greenland seventeen years earlier (close to where Red Cliff once stood), Cook happened upon a hunting party that included Knud Rasmussen, a Greenlander born to an Eskimo mother and a Danish father. The two men had first met when *Bradley* made a stop near Cape York; Cook learned that Rasmussen had been schooled in Denmark and had returned to his native land to study and write about Eskimo life. Rasmussen looked so Eskimo that when Cook invited him to dine aboard ship, Bradley barred him from the wardroom, and Cook had to ask Rasmussen to eat with the crew. Now hearing from Rasmussen that he was heading to the Danish settlement of Upernavik, where mail could be sent out on ships, Cook dashed out a letter to Marie:

> I have this opportunity to send a letter to Upernavik by Rasmussen during this moon and I must hasten to report our progress to the present. I have 100 dogs and as many more as I desire, with 15 of the best men of the tribe assembled here for the attack over the new route across Ellesmere Land out by way of Nansen Sound and back by Kennedy Channel, thus using to good advantage the drift and the musk oxen so abundant in Ellesmere Land. All of my equipment is ready and we hope to start for the goal late in January. With men and dogs well fed, and under normal conditions . . . I feel confident, as our equipment means perfection.*

*Cook's letter to Marie, dated December 6, 1907, reached her in Brooklyn seven months later, on July 11, 1908, only days after Peary left on his polar journey aboard *Roosevelt*. With no word from Cook for nearly a year, concern had been mounting for his well-being. A relieved Marie shared the letter with the press immediately, and news of Cook ran in newspapers throughout the country, with headlines such as "EXPLORER COOK IS PUSHING ON TO NORTH POLE: Friends Had Feared He Had Met Disaster" (*Boston Herald*, July 12, 1908).

In late January, an advance party made up of Franke and a number of Eskimos crossed ice-covered Smith Sound to set up a cache on Ellesmere Island. When they returned and reported that the ice was solid and offered good traveling, Cook saw it as a positive omen. An advance party of eight native sledges left the first week of February to take supplies farther north to Flagler Bay, then hunt game to feed the sledge teams as they moved inland.

Cook was eager to be on the move, but with the polar night upon them, "the light was still too uncertain to risk the fortunes of the entire force." So they waited for increased sunlight. The window for travel was a narrow one, since winter in these higher latitudes lasted nine or ten months, with the other three seasons compressed into the remaining calendar days of the year.

Before departing, Cook left a letter for Rasmussen, who had indicated he would be working his way back north after Upernavik. Cook explained he was departing for "the far north" and offered the Greenlander use of his house and provisions. Cook said he expected to be back at Annoatok by May or early June. However, there was a "chance of our being carried too far east" on the drifting ice pack, Cook wrote, and if that happened he would head down the east coast of Greenland—or, should they find "much land to westward of Crocker Land," they might follow it and walk to Alaska.

Dawn on February 19 brought the year's first sighting of the sun, and a line of sledges was quickly formed at the door of the storehouse. They were loaded with four thousand pounds of supplies and equipment, and a quantity of frozen walrus skin and fat to feed the dogs prior to securing the musk oxen that Cook was counting on finding in great numbers.

At eight o'clock that morning, the final lash had been tied and all was ready—eleven fully loaded sledges pulled by 103 dogs driven by Cook, Franke, and nine Eskimos, "the pick of the lot" from a sizable pool of native volunteers. Cook attributed his ability to "win the friendship and confidence" of the Eskimos to his speaking their language "well enough to hold ordinary conversations." It helped, too, that since his earliest days in the Arctic he had been interested in learning their ways and respectful of their traditions.

The Eskimo tribes of northern Greenland did not believe the Earth was round. Somewhere on the darkest edge of their flat world, a huge iron spike had been driven into the ice; hence, "Big Nail" was their name for the Pole. They believed this giant nail had somehow fallen over and become lost, and because iron was more valuable to them than gold, they understood its value. Through their oral histories, they knew that white men speaking many different tongues had been engaged in the search for centuries—providing further evidence of the nail's value—and they also understood that countless men who went looking for it had not returned. Eskimos on their own had never sought out the Big Nail, for they knew better than any race in the world the dangers of long journeys on the ice that covered the world's northernmost ocean. They preferred to stay on or near land, close to the hunting grounds that provided them with their food and clothing. Hunting was what they understood best, and when Cook told them of the new lands where musk oxen, whose meat they prized, roamed freely, they were enthralled. Together with the tools, weapons, and other implements Cook offered for their services, they were motivated to take part in the expedition for the chance to discover new hunting grounds.

As Cook surveyed the line of sledges awaiting his go-ahead, he felt that his "heart was high," knowing that his polar quest was about to begin. The hunters were excited to start on the journey, too, and the half-wild dogs picked up on the energy of the assembled men and barked madly, eager to start pulling. Whips snapped in the air, and yelping dog teams leaped forward.

Northwest they headed across Smith Sound, sledging across ice covered with a few inches of fresh snow. A gentle wind blew from the south, and the temperature was minus thirty-six degrees Fahrenheit. The sky was sufficiently dark for the men to see stars twinkling above wispy-thin clouds, but the glow from the orange rays of sunlight streaking across the sky provided good visibility for travel until late afternoon, when everything turned a darkish gray. They stopped, made igloos, and spent a cold, miserable night; "the first nights from camp always are," Cook knew.

Underway the second day, they circled wide around "a hopeless jungle of mountains and ridges of ice" until finding level ice, over which they made good time—about three miles per hour. At noon they stopped, and coffee was served from their "ever-hot coffee box," a luxury improvised by placing a can filled with hot coffee in a box protected by reindeer skins, which retained the heat for some twelve hours.

When they reached Cape Sabine in a few days, "a curious whim of fate" occurred to Cook. This camp of the ill-fated Greely expedition, one of such famine and death, was but a brief stop on his "modern effort to reach the Pole."

Heading north along the Ellesmere coast, they found the weather changing to a drier climate and lower temperatures, down to minus sixty-four degrees Fahrenheit. The intense cold made everything more difficult, from feeding the dogs—the frozen walrus skin had to be divided with an ax and thawed—to hunting, which resulted in painful burns when bare skin touched the metal of their guns.

Near Flagler Bay, they met up with the advance party that had been in the area hunting since bringing across supplies and establishing a cache. The natives had worked the entire valley, downing only a single musk ox and eleven hares, not enough to supply even their own needs. There was nothing for the hunting party to do but return to Annoatok; taking them along when fresh meat was scarce was out of the question. Cook also elected to send Franke back, deciding he would be of more value watching over their remaining supplies and possessions left behind—including Cook's sizable collection of blue-fox skins, narwhal horns, and walrus ivory acquired through hunting and trading. Franke was instructed to wait four months and, if Cook was not back by June 5, to leave the stores with a trusted Eskimo and head south to catch a departing ship. Before Franke and the others left, Cook selected the best dogs and sledges to keep with him, and only the fittest natives were chosen to continue north.

The head of Flagler Bay was reached late one night after an exhausting march of twenty-five miles, through a punishing cold that nearly "paralyzed the dogs" and that the men survived only because they ran nonstop alongside the dogs.

In the morning, Cook judged there was still much enthusiasm among his companions, rather like "soldiers on the eve of a longed-for battle." They struck out inland across the middle of Ellesmere, where the feeding grounds for the musk oxen were said to be found. After several days, there was still no sign of the burly creatures. The musk oxen were key to the entire effort; Cook knew if they were not found, his effort was doomed because they would have to start too soon using the supplies intended for the northern end of the journey.

The dogs were placed on reduced rations, and their hunger heightened their wolfish senses. During one rest stop, the dogs became excited, all their noses pointing toward some steep slopes, where several dark shapes were soon detected on a snowy hillside. The dogs jumped, and the men went for their weapons. For speed, fifty dogs were leashed to three empty sledges. The hunters stepped onto the upstanders and cracked their thirty-foot whips. Off the hunting party flew, sledges and men bouncing hard over the terrain—snowy or rocky, it mattered not. In an hour, after a coordinated attack by dogs and men, three fat carcasses were being sliced up, and fresh raw meat was served to canines and humans alike.

Once across Ellesmere, they headed north along the eastern coast of Axel Heiberg Island. Providence delivered the musk oxen here, too, and numerous successful hunts followed in the course of their travels. In one killing orgy, a herd of twenty went down, one by one, after forming a circle as the bulls tried in vain to defend their cows and calves against dogs, men, bullets, and lances. "Now even the Eskimo's savage thirst for blood was satisfied," Cook noted. "The pot was kept boiling, and the igloos rang with chants of primitive joys."

The meat meant a food supply to the shores of the Arctic Ocean. A weight was lifted from Cook, who in spite of his trust in Sverdrup's reports, had begun to doubt the "existence of game far enough north to count on fresh meat to the sea."

Tracks of bears and wolves intermingled with those of musk oxen; seal blowholes, which an Eskimo would stake out for as long as twenty-four hours to lance a seal rising from under the ice for air, were countless. The natives talked excitedly about returning to these fertile lands the following year to hunt.

They had, Cook realized, "advanced beyond the range of all primitive life. No human voice broke the frigid silence." Sverdrup had mapped the channels of the west coast, and an inlet had been named for an earlier visitor, Nansen, but inland there was "no trace of modern or aboriginal residence."

Camping in the lowlands just south of Svartevoeg, they found themselves surrounded by fields of grass and moss, surprised to find on the shores of the Arctic Ocean "a garden spot of plant . . . and animal delight." At Cape Svartevoeg, on the northernmost tip of Axel Heiberg Island, lay a great blackened cliff, its sheer walls dropping into the frozen sea. Here, at approximately 82 degrees north, they had reached land's end, and here the real journey to the Pole would begin.

Cook assessed his situation. They had weathered the worst storms and were benefiting from longer days as winter retreated. They had made it this far by subsisting on the land, with the supplies they had hauled from Annoatok practically untouched. He viewed for the first time the "rough and heavy ice of the untracked Polar sea," imagining before him the "fields of crushed ice, glimmering in the rising sunlight with shooting fires of sapphire and green; fields which have been slowly forced downward by strong currents from the north, and pounded and piled in jagged mountainous heaps for miles."

Sending out advance parties from this point would not work, Cook believed, owing mainly to the difficulty of having to follow one another on the ever-shifting ice cap. He also thought a large expedition of men and equipment to be imprudent, recognizing that increased numbers would not enable them to carry supplies for more days; rather, they would require them to haul that many more supplies to feed additional stomachs. Moreover, to accommodate the burden of taking extra supplies, the sledges would have to be loaded more heavily, which would hamper their progress.

Cook decided to reduce the party to the smallest possible number. Having watched and evaluated all the natives, he chose to take with him Etukishook and Ahwelah, both about twenty, certain that these young hunters could be "trusted to follow to the limit of [his] own endurance." For their effort, they were each promised a gun and a knife, which Cook knew would keep "a lively interest in them" during the long journey.

Two sledges would be taken, including the one with the disassembled canvas boat, to be pulled by the twenty-six strongest dogs. On the return trip, Cook planned to be down to one sledge and six dogs. The other twenty canines "were to be used one after the other, as food on the march, as soon as reduced loads and better ice permitted." That, he computed, would mean about one thousand pounds of fresh meat to feed the dogs (and men, if needed) over and above the pemmican supply they would carry.

They began loading the designated sledges.

Food for eighty days would be carried, with pemmican as their staple and the rest meant to be "mere palate satisfiers." They loaded 805 pounds of beef pemmican, 130 pounds of walrus pemmican, 50 pounds of musk ox tenderloin, 25 pounds of musk ox tallow, two pounds of tea, one pound of coffee, 25 pounds of sugar, 40 pounds of condensed milk, 60 pounds of biscuits, 10 pounds of powdered pea soup, 40 pounds of petroleum, two pounds of wood alcohol, three pounds of candles, and one pound of matches. They also packed a silk tent, two canvas sledge covers, floor furs, reindeer-skin sleeping bags, and extra wood, screws, nails, and rivets for sledge repairs.

The camp equipment was reduced to the bare minimum: a blow fire lamp, three aluminum pails, three aluminum cups, three aluminum teaspoons, a tablespoon, three tin plates, six pocket knives, two ten-inch butcher knives, one thirteen-inch saw knife, a fifteen-inch long knife, a single-shot Sharp's rifle (also known as the Buffalo Gun), a Winchester lever-action rifle, 110 cartridges, a hatchet, an alpine ax, extra line and lashings, and three personal bags. Inside their bags were four pairs of boots with fur stockings, a woolen shirt, three pairs of sealskin mittens, two pairs of fur mittens, a blanket, a sealskin coat, and a repair kit for mending. On the march, they were to wear snow goggles specially made by Cook from optical glass to eliminate the glare of the sun on the ice, blue-fox coats, bird-skin shirts, bearskin pants, sealskin boots, and hare-skin stockings.

Cook's instruments included his trusty Hurleman sextant; aluminum compass with azimuth attachment; a glass artificial horizon set in thin metal frame and adjusted by spirit levels and thumbscrews; an aluminum aneroid barometer; an aluminum case with maximum and minimum spirit thermometer; a field glass; three Howard pocket chronometers; three thermometers; a Tiffany watch; a pedometer; and mapmaking materials and implements. He brought a camera with packets of film, a notebook, and pencils. (He already knew the difficulty writing in low temperatures, when the paper was so cold that the pencil barely left a mark. He had learned to spend a few minutes warming over the flame of a candle the page he wished to write upon, as well as the pencil. Bare fingers also had to be warmed to hold the pencil.)

Since leaving Annoatok, Cook and his companions had traveled a circuitous four hundred miles to advance not quite two hundred miles north. From here on, Cook planned to make his "dash in as straight a route as . . . possible" for the Pole.

They were ready on the morning of March 18. Before departing, Cook grasped the right hand of each hunter and shook farewell. It was his custom, not theirs, and yet they shook firmly and smiled broadly. In their language, he thanked them for their faithful service. *"Tigishi ah yaung-uluk!"* each hunter exclaimed before releasing his grip. The Big Nail! they had said, as if ordaining its discovery by the man before them.

Into a drifting snowstorm the sledges, dogs, and three men disappeared.

Five hundred and twenty miles away lay the North Pole.

CHAPTER SIXTEEN

"FORWARD! MARCH!"

ROOSEVELT DROPPED ANCHOR at Etah the first week of August 1908.

Unable to begin his own ice cap journey until winter released its grip in the new year, Peary realized he was a full season behind Cook. Although he remained convinced that Cook's announced route to the Pole was inferior to his own "American Route," the Brooklyn doctor was a major topic of conversation during the voyage; Peary had spent one entire meal voicing his opinion of his competitor. In letters home to friends and family, some of Peary's men expressed their dismay at their leader's animosity toward Cook.

Erik, a steamer hired by the Peary Arctic Club, arrived at Etah a few days later, carrying three hundred tons of coal to replenish *Roosevelt* and another fifty tons to cache onshore for her expected journey home the following year. Fifty tons of walrus and whale meat were also transferred to *Roosevelt*.

Aboard *Erik* were several paying passengers, including Harry Whitney, a millionaire sportsman in his midthirties from Connecticut who had come north to hunt. A tall, wiry self-made man (ranching and copper), Whitney, who had spent time in northern Greenland and could converse with the natives in their own language, was invited by Peary to dine aboard *Roosevelt*. A fastidious eater, Whitney had removed the soft middle of a biscuit and pushed it to the side of his plate. A voice from the head of the table boomed forth; it was Peary, instructing his guest that *everything* served on a ship must be eaten, because no waste was allowed. Whitney meekly picked up the discarded biscuit and put it in his mouth.

Peary soon set off on a recruiting trip to surrounding Eskimo camps. His fears of Cook's raiding the supply of natives and dogs proved unjustified, for he obtained all he wished to take north: twenty-two experienced Eskimo drivers (including their families— seventeen women and ten children—who were to stay aboard ship), and 246 dogs, believed to be the greatest number of canines ever pressed into service by any polar expedition.

During Peary's absence, Rudolph Franke showed up at *Roosevelt*'s gangway. He was in terrible shape, with long, filth-matted hair, unkempt beard, and glassy, bloodshot eyes protruding from a sunken, yellow-tinged face. He had waited until June 5 as instructed and, in the absence of any sign of Cook, begun a long sledge trip south with several Annoatok Eskimos. Delayed by storms and ice conditions, they arrived after the whaling ships had already departed for the season. Working their way back through miserable traveling conditions, they reached Etah about the same time as *Roosevelt*.

Franke came out to the ship in a small boat, asking to see Peary, but was told the explorer was away. A *Roosevelt* sailor observed that Franke "could hardly walk." In spite of his obvious incapacities, the steward refused Franke "a drop of coffee or anything to eat," and he left. Learning of the incident the next morning, Captain Bartlett came ashore, found Franke and apologized, and took him back to the ship, where he was fed. When Bartlett mentioned that *Erik* would soon depart southward, Franke pleaded for passage home. Bartlett explained that only Peary had the authority to grant such a request.

That afternoon Peary returned to the ship with Henson, Dr. Goodsell, and the Eskimos. Franke pushed his way through to the explorer and seized his arm. "Please, dear God, take me away. I can't stand it." Holding out a folded paper, he cried, "Look! I can go away! I have permission from Dr. Cook."

At the mention of Cook's name, Peary's expression soured. He asked about Cook's whereabouts, and Franke explained that he had not been heard from since departing Axel Heiberg for the Pole five months earlier. Franke handed Peary a letter of instructions Cook had left him. Peary read it and announced tersely to the others, "This man is Rudolph Franke. Cook left him in charge of a cache of supplies, with permission to go home on the first boat."

Peary wanted more details about Cook and was interested to learn that the doctor had gone onto the ice cap with two Eskimos and three sledges. Franke, desperate to receive Peary's blessings for the trip home, covered his face with his shaking hands. The physician, Goodsell, stepped forward and led Franke away for an examination. Peary turned toward his assembled men. "That, gentlemen, is an example of what can happen to a white man in the Arctic."

When *Erik* departed for Newfoundland on August 21, Franke was aboard. Although Goodsell diagnosed Franke as suffering from "incipient scurvy" and being in a "serious mental state," Peary had not made it easy for him. Peary insisted that Franke relinquish Cook's collection of skins, furs, horns, and ivory. Peary also coveted Cook's supplies at Annoatok.

It had been a difficult decision for Franke because of his loyalty to Cook. He well knew that Cook was counting on having not only the supplies upon his return but also the collection for barter purposes. In a letter carried back in March by the last Eskimos returning from Axel Heiberg, Cook had explained to Franke that some of the blue-fox skins "must be our money on the return trip."

Franke later stated, "In a critical condition . . . and under duress, I was obligated to hand over all the property belonging to Dr. Cook. . . . Peary put the alternative to me, the furs, etc., or you stay here [and] that meant in my invalid condition to perish." When Franke relented, Peary demanded a signed release, in which Franke authorized him to "make the best use" of the five wooden boxes and one steamer trunk containing two hundred blue-fox skins, furs, horns, and ivory. Franke also provided for Peary's taking over "all the stuff laying at Etah and Annoatok," noting, "Your judgment and experience will know to make the best use of them." Franke was then granted passage on *Erik* to Newfoundland, with Peary advancing him fifty dollars for boat fare from there to New York.*

Peary assigned two *Roosevelt* crewmen to stay behind and guard the supplies at Etah and Annoatok and to keep the natives from pilfering. In a five-page letter of instructions to boatswain John Murphy, he noted, "Franke has now turned over all these supplies and equipment to me so that Dr. Cook has no longer any claim upon them." He directed them to use whatever they needed and to engage in trade with the natives for "skins, horns and hides," explaining how he wanted these items prepared by the natives and preserved for maximum value. In the event Cook appeared, Peary said, his two representatives were to "still remain absolutely in charge of the station and . . . not permit Dr. Cook to interfere with you or with your control of the natives." Should Cook need food or other supplies, they were to be given to him out of the stores in exchange for "his receipt"—Cook would, in that event, be charged for receiving his own goods.

Also staying behind at Annoatok was Whitney, who, disappointed with his luck in the field, had decided to winter over for "a year's big game hunting under the shadow of the Pole." He, too, was given permission by Peary to consume and otherwise utilize Cook's stores.

Before his departure, Peary prepared several letters to influential friends; his correspondence (to be dispatched on *Erik*) was handled by his assistant, Ross Marvin, who, as a trained civil engineer, had also assisted Peary in planning the details of the incremental

---

*Upon his return to New York in October 1908, Franke told an officer of the Arctic Club of America of being forced to surrender Cook's possessions "just as the enemy has to hand over their arms to the victorious party." He reported it was common knowledge on *Erik* that the skins, furs, and ivory were aboard for the voyage from Greenland. In November (1908), the *Brooklyn Eagle* unsuccessfully attempted to discover the whereabouts of Cook's collection, later valued at ten thousand dollars by Cook. Officials of the Peary Arctic Club confirmed only that "a consignment of goods was sent down by Peary, and that it passed through the Custom House," but refused to allow an examination of the bills of lading. Upon hearing Franke's story, Marie Cook sent a fifty-dollar check to the Peary Arctic Club to repay the money Peary advanced him. Subsequently, the Peary Arctic Club sent a bill to John Bradley for one hundred dollars, for expenses incurred in sending his crewman, Rudolph Franke, "home for humanity's sake."

advance across the ice cap, including the various assignments of the supporting divisions. In his missives, a worried Peary issued urgent warnings to his backers about Cook, saying that if the doctor reappeared from his northern journey, they should discount any claims he might make.

In his own letter home to a friend, Marvin expressed concern about "the Dr. Cook affair," which he described as having become "a tangle and a hard nut to crack." He went on,

> I am writing Peary's confidential letters concerning the matter, and so my lips must be closed. . . . I know more about it than anyone else, but I can say less . . . it would be a breach of trust. I imagine the [Franke] affair will create newspaper talk when *Erik* returns, so I want to keep out of it. . . . I would like to tell you all, but I know a duty to Com. Peary.

Shortly after 4 p.m. on August 18, *Roosevelt* hoisted anchor and steamed toward ice-packed Kane Basin for a return to Cape Sheridan, where Peary would again winter on the frozen shore of the Arctic Ocean in preparation for an assault on the Pole. Many of the ship's crew and expedition members, joined by a multitude of Eskimos, stood on deck waving and cheering as the vessel disappeared into the northern mists and faded from sight.

Before leaving, Peary posted a sign on Cook's storehouse for all to read:

THIS HOUSE BELONGS TO DR. F. A. COOK, BUT DR. COOK IS LONG AGO DEAD AND THERE IS NO USE TO SEARCH FOR HIM. THEREFORE, I, COMMANDER ROBERT E. PEARY, INSTALL MY BOATSWAIN IN THIS DESERTED HOUSE.

AFTER A WINTER of planning and preparing—as his expedition members hunted with the Eskimos, trained with sledges, and otherwise readied themselves in body and spirit for the task before them—Peary began, in early February 1909, dispatching his support parties from *Roosevelt* to Cape Columbia, ninety miles to the west. By February 22, all the expedition members were deployed except for Peary and his natives. When he got away at ten o'clock that morning, seven members of the expedition, nineteen Eskimos, and 140 dogs were in the field. The force was divided into six divisions to serve in support of Peary, the only member of the expedition who did not drive his own sledge. Each division was outfitted for independent travel, as was each sledge within a division, in the event one became separated from the others.

Each sledge was loaded with supplies for one man and dog team for fifty days, which could be extended ten days beyond by "sacrificing a few dogs and using them as food for the other dogs and the men." The daily ration for the dogs was one pound of pemmican; Peary believed "these descendants of arctic wolves" could work "a long time on very little to eat."

The daily ration for the men on the final push to the Pole, once all the support divisions had returned to base, would consist of one pound of pemmican, one pound of biscuits, four ounces of condensed milk, half an ounce of compressed tea, and six ounces of fuel for melting ice and making tea. On this ration, Peary believed, a man could "work hard and keep in good condition in the lowest temperatures for a very long time."

Peary intended to alternate the pioneer party between the divisions every five marches, thus spreading out among men and dogs the most grueling task. Designated as the first to lead the way was Bartlett, a capable man with a ship or a sledge, and a natural-born leader of men. As for which natives to assign to the divisions, Peary gave the division leaders their choice. That would change when he manned his own division for the Pole; for the final dash, he intended to take his "favorites among the most efficient of the Eskimos."

When Peary arrived at the Cape Columbia base camp that had been established during the winter with a store of supplies, equipment, and spare parts, he was displeased by what he considered inactivity. He immediately began shouting orders, and "by the time he had calmed down," Bartlett was loaded up and pushing forward on the ice cap, with Borup, the Yale runner, close behind; each was in command of a four-sledge division and three Eskimos.

Henson, who considered Peary's method of discipline "the iron hand ungloved," knew that more of the same awaited them "bound for the trophy" that their leader had long sought. Henson, MacMillan, Goodsell, Marvin, and fourteen Eskimos waited their turn to depart, because Peary wanted the pioneer party to have a sizable head start.

They awoke at daybreak the following morning, March 1, to a furious wind and blinding snowstorm. Peary was not to be deterred. One of his final acts was the folding and stowing of flags on his sledge—banners that he expected to fly at the top of the world. By 6 a.m. each driver was at the upstander of a sledge, dog teams readied, everyone poised to go on Peary's command, which never varied. As if leading a regimental charge, he always boomed at the start of each day of sledge travel, "Forward! March!"

Henson went first, followed in single file by the other teams, as Peary's Eskimo-driven sledges "brought up the rear." As he had on his farthest-north journey, Peary was like a general at the rear of his army—making decisions, giving orders, conserving his energy, and following a trail forged by his troops.

Henson's sledge broke down in the first mile, and he had to drop out of the caravan for repairs. All the other teams, Peary's included, passed Henson as he continued mending his sledge. No sooner had Henson's party started again than one of his natives crashed his sledge, and this time repairs were not possible. They had to unload everything onto the ice, and the Eskimo led his dogs back to Cape Columbia to get a spare sledge and catch up.

After proceeding twelve miles, with the temperature hovering in the minus fifties, the advancing teams were exhausted from battling the headwind that had turned into a full gale, and were ready to halt at the first camp that had been set up by Bartlett's crew. Just as they arrived, Bartlett's crew was off. In the long days of sunlight now upon them, Peary planned for the pioneer party to be traveling while the main party was sleeping, and vice versa, to ensure daily communication and facilitate the issuance of new orders. When

Peary reached camp, one of the igloos was his by default, with the occupancy of the other one alternating between divisions from camp to camp. Those left out in the cold built their own igloos (an hour's work for three Eskimos) or, if they were too tired to do so, slept on the sledges bundled up in furs.

The next morning the trail forged by the Bartlett and Borup teams was discernible in freshly fallen snow that made for slow going. They hit a region of pressure ridges—mounds of compressed ice as high as a house and a quarter mile wide—and it was necessary at times to chop away the ice rubble with pickaxes to clear the way for the sledges. Whenever they stopped to do so, the dogs took it as a signal to lie down and curl up, noses tucked under furry tails.

Peary counted pressure ridges as one of the most difficult aspects of polar travel. Broken off from the floes that cover nine-tenths of the Arctic Ocean, sheets of ice drift over the sea until crashing into more ice and coming to a halt—"impinging against one another, splitting in two from the violence of contact . . . crushing up the thinner ice between them, and having their edges shattered and piled into pressure ridges." (This permanent ice mass is not to be confused with the pack ice that covers the remainder of the polar sea and is formed by the freezing of seawater in the winter. Usually no more than six feet thick, pack ice melts in the summer, which causes the often impassable leads.)

Near the end of the second day, Peary spotted a "dark ominous cloud upon the northern horizon," which most often meant open water. Coming closer, he saw black spots against the snow; he knew them to be his sledges held up by a lead. They faced a lane of open water a quarter mile wide that stretched to either side as far as the eye could see. A sounding taken at the edge of the lead measured the depth at ninety-six fathoms, approximately six hundred feet. It was apparent the pack ice had opened since Bartlett's team passed the day before—the work of forceful winds and shifting ice floes. They had no choice but to make camp and wait for nature's forces to close the ice back up.

The men had already built Peary's igloo, to which the exhausted explorer, at age fifty-three the eldest in the group by ten years, soon retreated. In addition to his crippled feet, which prevented him from wearing snowshoes for any length of time, the leg he had broken in Greenland in 1891 was hurting for the first time in sixteen years, causing him "considerable trouble." Walking on the ice had become so difficult that he soon took to riding on a fur-lined sledge driven by an Eskimo and would do so for the greater part of the trip.*

By morning, the shifting ice had shut portions of the lead; in other places, young ice had formed over the water. Unwilling to wait any longer, Peary gave the signal to move out quickly. They were soon sledging across—rather like "crossing a river on a succession of gigantic shingles, one, two, or three deep and all afloat and moving." Such going was dangerous and unnerving; at any moment, a sledge and its haltered team, or a man on snowshoes, could break through a section of thin ice into the frigid waters.

There was no sign of Bartlett's trail on the other side, which Peary attributed to the lateral movement of the ice carrying the path with it. He sent out natives to find the trail, and within half an hour they had done so. Once on the trail again, they saw from the tracks of men and dogs that another party had passed going south. Peary knew that would be Borup, heading back to Cape Columbia as planned; his team was the first scheduled to return to base camp, reload its sledges, and ferry additional supplies northward.

Marvin's division, also shuttling supplies, soon caught up with an encamped Peary, who on the spot decided to dispatch Marvin and one Eskimo back to base camp to bring up more fuel. Some of the alcohol and petroleum tins had sprung leaks from faulty solders, and running short of fuel could not be chanced.

After two more days of marching, all the divisions were again held up by open water. The "white expanse of ice cut by a river of inky black water" was a "familiar unwelcome sight"—reminiscent

---

*In his own published accounts of his last Arctic expedition, Peary gave the impression that he walked and ran beside the sledges all the way up and back. However, Henson provided the public with a different description of Peary's method of travel. "Because of his crippled feet [Peary] had ridden on the sledges the greater part of the journey up, as he did on the return," Henson reported. "He was heavy for the dogs to haul. We knew he could walk but little on rough ice. . . . He was compelled to ride."

of the Big Lead, which had stalled their progress in 1905–06. Despite that experience, Peary was again traveling without a boat or any other means of crossing leads. They had no choice but to wait.

Days passed and Peary grew fretful. He knew that if the lead did not soon close, his final attempt to reach the Pole would fail after only a few days. Peary had long considered leads the "worst feature" of Arctic ice, "far more troublesome and dangerous" than pressure ridges. There was something else for him to consider: what if the lead closed, allowing them to pass, but then reopened and cut off their return to land? Peary considered that a distinct possibility and, of course, so did the Eskimos, who were always wary of traveling on the ice cap.

The natives began to grumble among themselves about their plight. Finally, two of the older natives—one of them, Panikpa,* had been with Peary on his farthest-north expedition—approached "pretending to be sick." Peary was unsympathetic. "I have had sufficient experience," he later wrote, "to know a sick Eskimo when I see one, and [their] excuses . . . did not convince me." Hoping to set an example for the others, Peary dismissed them on the spot, ordering their return to the ship. The loss of the expedition's two most experienced drivers had the opposite effect of what Peary desired, and the revolt soon threatened to spread, as more natives complained of "this and that imaginary ailment," hoping to be sent back. Peary knew the Eskimos were losing their nerve at being halted far removed from land, but he was "seriously puzzled" as to what to do. MacMillan, the college professor and physical training enthusiast, swung into action, organizing games such as wrestling and tug-of-war. The Eskimos gleefully engaged in the competitive contests, preferring the physical activity to waiting for the unknown.

By the sixth day, the lead began closing, and Peary issued orders to prepare to move out in the morning. He now had another concern: Marvin had not yet returned with the cans of fuel. Before leaving, Peary posted a note at the campsite telling Marvin they were running

---

*Panikpa, the father of Cook's companion Etukishook, served as hunter and guide for several later Arctic expeditions. In 1929, Panikpa and his second wife died together, when they fell through the sea ice and froze to death.

short of fuel, and ordering, "Push on with all possible speed to overtake us. . . . *Do not camp here*. CROSS THE LEAD. Feed full rations &
speed your dogs. It is *vital* you overtake us and give us fuel."

They crossed the lead without mishap and made four more
marches before Marvin's division, with its precious load of fuel,
caught up with them on the afternoon of March 14, the day after
Borup's division had arrived with more supplies. That night, his
burden eased, Peary "slept like a child."

In the morning, he tabbed Henson's division as the pioneer party,
and it took off immediately. Peary also ordered Goodsell to take his
division back, its work being done. He considered Goodsell's efforts
in the field "gratuitous," his true value to the expedition being his
medical skills. Rather than subject him to more dangers of the ice,
Peary thought the physician should assume his rightful place aboard
ship, where the greater number of people remained.

As he would each time a division left the expedition, Peary culled
through men and equipment, giving the returning party the poorest
dogs, the damaged sledges, and the most unfit or unmanageable
Eskimos to drive them. As final adjustments were made to the
sledges and loads redistributed, Peary received disappointing news
from MacMillan. The professor revealed a badly frostbitten heel,
which he had been enduring silently for several days. Although
Peary had hoped MacMillan would go to "a comparatively high latitude," the only thing to be done was to send him back, too.

Once underway again, the main expedition now consisted of sixteen men, twelve sledges, and one hundred dogs divided into three
support divisions, in addition to Peary's own. They had gone only a
few miles when they found themselves cut off by another lead. It
narrowed toward the west, so they headed in that direction, coming
to a place where large sections of floating ice—some a hundred feet
wide—formed "a sort of pontoon bridge."

Moving the dogs and sledges from one icy platform to another, they
progressed steadily until Borup's dogs slipped through an open crack
into the water. Leaping forward, the young athlete managed to stop
the sledge from following. Taking hold of the traces, he pulled the fastened dogs from the water. A man less agile and muscular, Peary

observed, could have lost the whole team as well as the sledge, filled
with five hundred pounds of supplies "worth more to us than their
weight in diamonds." Had the sledge gone into the water, its weight
would have carried everything tied to it, dogs included, to the bottom.

After another day's march, Peary decided it was again time to
thin out the party, designating Borup's division as the next to go.
Even though Borup had performed well, driving his team "with
almost the skill of an Eskimo," he was the least experienced of the
remaining members. Also, he had a painful patch of frostbite on the
bottom of one foot. The young man and his Eskimos turned their
sledges around and left; Borup's face "clouded with regret."

The expedition now consisted of twelve men, ten sledges, and
eighty dogs. Marvin joined Peary's division, with the remaining two
divisions headed by Henson and Bartlett, the latter again serving as
the pioneer party. Peary was pleased with the way the captain had
"responded like a thoroughbred to [his] urging," and he decided to
keep the Newfoundlander in the lead as long as possible.

On March 22, Peary asked Marvin to take an observation for latitude, the first of the trip. They had been proceeding by "dead reckoning," based on their "previous ice experience," although Peary
trusted only two other members of the expedition to estimate the
distance of a day's journey accurately: Marvin and Bartlett, also the
only ones (other than Peary) competent with a sextant.

Up to now, Peary judged the "altitude of the sun . . . so low as to
make observations unreliable." Even as the summer sun advanced
higher in the sky, however, they would take observations only when
"necessary to check [their] dead reckonings." Peary intended to have
Marvin take all the observations until it was time for him to turn
around, and then for Bartlett to take over. Peary had two reasons for
doing so: "partly to save my eyes, but principally to have independent observations with which to check our advance."

First, a semicircular wind shelter, with its opening to the south,
was built of snow blocks and a musk ox skin laid on the ground. As
the mercury of the artificial horizon was warmed over a flame in an
igloo, an instrument box was placed at the opening of the shelter.
Placed atop the box was an artificial horizon trough. When the mer-

cury was ready, it was poured into the trough until it was full, at which point the trough was covered with a glass horizon roof.

Lying on his stomach facing the opening, Marvin, resting on his elbows, held the sextant steady to get the contact of the sun's angle in the narrow strip of the artificial horizon. As he did, he jotted down numbers in a notebook—altitude figures that had to be corrected for refraction based on temperature.

Marvin calculated they were at 85 degrees, 48 minutes, north— 252 miles from the Pole and 161 miles north of Cape Columbia. In sixteen days of travel (not counting the days held up at leads), they had averaged ten miles northerly progress per day.

Directed by Peary to take another observation on March 25, Marvin determined a latitude of 86 degrees, 37 minutes—twenty-eight miles short of Peary's farthest north. It was the last observation Marvin was to make, because Peary designated his division the next to turn back, pointing out that his assistant had gone farther north than Nansen, an honor Peary expected Marvin to share with the faculty and alumni of Cornell University, a number of whom were "generous contributors to the Peary Arctic Club."

The next morning, after redistributing the sledges, dogs, and supplies, Marvin prepared a statement certifying the latitude at which he turned back. He verified that Peary was "advancing with nine men in the party, seven sledges with the standard loads, and sixty dogs. Men and dogs in first class condition."

Marvin and two Eskimos selected by Peary headed south with one sledge and seventeen dogs. The engineering professor's native companions were Kudlooktoo, nineteen, who had been in Peary's division since Cape Columbia, and Inukitsoq, a member of Bartlett's pioneer division. Peary's last words to his assistant were a caution: "Be careful of the leads, my boy!"

Marvin, the keeper of Peary's confidences, was never seen again.*

---

*Kudlooktoo and Inukitsoq, upon reaching *Roosevelt*, told of Marvin drowning at a large lead on the way back. They returned with some of Marvin's personal belongings, including a canvas pouch containing notes and letters later turned over to Peary, but claimed that it had been impossible to recover his body. When Bartlett heard the story upon his return to the ship, he refused to believe it and accused the Eskimos of having deliberately caused

Under dark, overcast skies, they proceeded for much of the next day over young ice no more than a foot thick. Peary and the others followed Bartlett's trail, without which "the march would have been even more difficult." As planned, Peary reached the next camp as the pioneer division was readying to leave. Peary and Bartlett agreed that they had made "a good fifteen miles" in spite of the rough going, and were pleased with their progress.

March 27 presented a brilliant display of Arctic sunshine. Notwithstanding the sunny skies, the march was one of the hardest yet, as they made their way over broken layers of ice so sharp and jagged that it cut their furs and boots. They then hit a stretch of heavy rubble ice covered with deep snow, through which they were forced "literally to plow [their] way, lifting and steadying the sledges until [their] muscles ached."

During the next march, after following Bartlett's trail for six hours, Peary came upon the pioneer division camped beside a wide, impassable lead stretching without end into a wall of heavy fog. So as not to disturb the sleeping men, Peary had his Eskimos build their igloos a hundred yards away, and they, too, turned in after their customary supper of pemmican, biscuit, and tea. As he was dropping off to sleep, Peary heard nearby "creaking and groaning," which he attributed to the pressure of the ice working to close the lead. He rolled over in his bed of deerskins, but before sleep came he heard excited shouts.

Leaping to his feet, Peary looked out the peephole of the igloo to see a large body of blackish water between his and Bartlett's igloos. He kicked out the block of snow in place at the entrance to his igloo and jumped outside.

The pack ice had split open between the two camps, and

Marvin's death. When Peary returned, he was "staggered" by the news, although he readily accepted the circumstances of Marvin's death as reported by the two Eskimos. In his book *The North Pole* (1910), Peary provided details of Marvin's drowning, such as that "he did not notice the gradual thinning of the ice toward the center of the lead until it was too late and he was in the water." This is surprising since Peary also wrote, "No human eye was upon him when he broke through the treacherous young ice that had but recently closed over a streak of open water."

Bartlett's natives were yelling as they were drifting away on an ice raft toward open water. Peary hollered for Bartlett to have his men load up, hitch the dogs, and be prepared to cross as soon as the opportunity presented itself.

Peary realized that another crack, several yards wide, had left his and Henson's igloos on their own little ice island. He fired off more orders, telling the men to grab pickaxes and level off the formations of ice around them, dropping the rubble into the crack to make a surface over which they could drive the sledges. That was done in rapid order, and everyone was soon across.

The section that had marooned Bartlett's division began drifting steadily toward where Peary and the others waited, until its edges crunched against the floe. At that instant, Bartlett's men rushed across with their sledges and dogs.

Some of the men had still not slept. Having lost their igloos, they had no choice but to build new ones, which they did and then turned in immediately. They awakened to the same large body of water before them obscured by heavy condensation. They could not see where the water ended, or even whether it did. The thought occurred to Peary that they could be encamped on the edge of the open polar sea that "myth-makers have imagined" since the Renaissance. Every bold plan for sailing to the North Pole had been thwarted by seemingly unending ice. Although Peary had never believed in the existence of an open polar sea route, here he sat with his expedition—at water's edge, unable to proceed.

After breakfast, they overhauled the sledges, mended rips in their garments, and laid out their wet things to dry over little oil lamps that they carried for that purpose. In the afternoon, Bartlett took a sounding at the edge of the lead, carefully letting out a weighted line for more than a mile, but found no bottom. After eating and when their watches told them it was bedtime—they were now in a period of perpetual sunlight—they returned to their igloos.

There was much groaning of the shifting ice during the night. Peary looked out once to see that the fog was lifting. By eight o'clock in the morning, it had disappeared and the grinding had ceased—and miraculously the lead had closed. Everyone hurried across before the ice had a chance to reopen.

That day all the sledges traveled together, strung out in single file—Bartlett's, Henson's, and, lastly, Peary's—constantly navigating around and over lakes of young ice, some of them miles long and so thin that, as the sledges crossed, the ice buckled underneath in a life-or-death race to the opposite side.

The region through which they were passing made Peary think of "unpleasant possibilities for the future," namely that their return could be cut off as suddenly and unpredictably as some of their forward marches. Also, they would be coming back much later in the summer season, when even more patches of open water were likely. If they found themselves returning low on food, sick, or seriously injured, long forced delays at leads could prove perilous.

In camp on the evening of March 30, Peary informed Bartlett he would be next to turn south after the following day's march. Peary explained that he had decided to take Henson with him to the Pole, along with the four best Eskimos.

For Bartlett, it was a "bitter disappointment." He felt strong physically and believed that his hard and effective work leading the pioneer division this far north had earned him a ticket to the Pole. In fact, he had convinced himself that he would not be sent back, since he had proven himself too valuable to Peary, not only to have his division in the lead for the final push but also because he could use a sextant and take observations, something Henson could not do.

Peary was immovable, however. Clearly, he had his reasons.

The next morning, Bartlett got up early while the rest were sleeping, and began walking north. He was very emotional and felt "a little crazy." The rugged man of the sea "cried a little"—tears of self-pity that froze on his cheeks. He had come thousands of miles to get this close and was now being ordered back. It seemed to Bartlett he could "make it alone" from this point without dogs or food or anything. He felt so strongly about it that he kept walking. After about five miles, however, he came to his senses and knew he "must go back."

The camp was stirring when Bartlett returned. He found Peary straightaway and said with conviction that if he was going to be a hindrance and contribute to a failed attempt, he would gladly turn around and go back.

An impassive Peary said only that Bartlett must go back.

Bartlett was again in disbelief. Although he did not wish to argue openly with his commander, he decided he would rather go out on the trail and die during a solo effort than "give it up." So he headed north again, following his own trail, and "kind of went on in a daze." Once again, however, he reached a point where he realized the right thing to do was obey orders.

Upon his return, having finally and begrudgingly accepted Peary's edict, Bartlett readied himself for the journey back. Before leaving, he took his last noontime observation, which placed their location at 87 degrees, 46 minutes, north. The captain prepared and signed two originals of a written statement to that effect—one for Peary and one for himself—and after heartfelt farewells to all, departed south with two Eskimos, one sledge, and eighteen dogs.

In a month, Peary and his party had advanced some 280 miles north. When adjusted for the days they were held up by leads and unable to travel, their average per march came to approximately 13 miles a day.

Peary was left with Henson and four Eskimos: Ootah, Egingwah, Seegloo, and Ooqueah. Ootah had been on the farthest-north expedition, and Egingwah and Seegloo were also experienced polar travelers. The fourth native, Ooqueah, was the youngest and had never served in an expedition, although Peary considered him "even more willing and eager than the others." Ooqueah's motivation was clear to Peary: "He was always thinking of the great treasures which I had promised each of the men who should go to the farthest point with me—whale-boat, rifle, shotgun, ammunition, knives, et cetera— wealth beyond the wildest dreams of Eskimos." With his riches, Ooqueah intended to win the daughter of a Cape York elder.

Peary believed his companions all had "a blind confidence" that he would "somehow get them back to land." He also thought that "all the impetus of the party centered" in him. Whatever pace he set, the "others would make good," but if he faltered in any way, "they would stop like a car with a punctured tire."

When the sledges were packed and the dogs in harness, everyone looked to Peary. He inhaled deeply the cold air "sweeping over the mighty ice, pure and straight from the Pole itself." Over the frozen horizon, 134 miles distant, his life's dream, if not his destiny, awaited him.

"Forward! March!"

CHAPTER SEVENTEEN

"I Have Reached
the Pole"

UPON HIS RETURN to Annoatok in April 1909, Cook felt he had aged twenty years in the fourteen months he had been gone. Along with his two Eskimo companions, he had survived the most arduous struggle of his exploring life.

Had the "desperate battle against famine and frost" been worth the price? he wondered. The best answer, he knew, was that at some point they had had little choice as they found themselves "suspended on the bridge between life and death." Many times they had been resigned to death, though without losing the will to live. An "unknown capacity in the spirit" kept them going long after they should have been finished. Each time they had wandered lost and afraid in the "shadow of death," they inexplicably emerged to see the morrow.

Cook understood that his companions, Etukishook and Ahwelah, considered the journey over the vast frozen sea a wasted trip because they had located no new hunting grounds after leaving land. Indeed, the two Eskimos had become so uneasy on the ice cap that Cook had "with good intentions encouraged an artificial belief in a nearness to land." The idea to help assuage the natives of their anxiety—"which every aboriginal involuntarily feels when land disappears on the horizon"—occurred to him when one of the Eskimos in the last support party pointed to a bank of low-lying clouds to the north over the polar sea and said approvingly, *"Noona"* (Land). The others had nodded. Once the journey to the Pole started, Cook pointed to similar "mirages" against the shimmering frozen seascape to further the "delusion" of nearby land to keep the natives from losing heart and turning back, for they knew better than anyone the threat of sea ice breaking up and carrying people away to their death.

In his first days back at Annoatok, as he ate his fill and rested, Cook found a willing confidant in Harry Whitney, who seemed to take it as his mission to attend to the explorer's recovery. From Whitney, Cook learned of Rudolph Franke's sad state of health and his return south on Peary's supply ship eight months earlier. He heard, too, of Whitney's coming to Greenland on *Erik* and subsequently staying over in the hope of winning musk oxen and bear trophies come spring and summer. To that end, Cook marked on a chart the locations on Ellesmere where he had encountered large herds of musk oxen.

Whitney told Cook about his difficulties over the winter with John Murphy, the boatswain Peary had left in charge. Cook shared his own complaints, appalled as he was with Peary's confiscation of his possessions, including his valuable blue-fox skins, furs, horns, and ivory tusks. Cook had more than one sharp exchange with the boatswain over the matter. "Now if Mr. Peary required my supplies for legitimate exploration," Cook later wrote, "I should have been glad to give him my last bread; but to use my things to satisfy his greed for commercial gain was . . . bitter medicine."

As he began to regain his strength, Cook told his story to Whitney, who was "honored . . . and thrilled" by what Cook soon revealed: that he and his two Eskimos had attained the North Pole on April 21, 1908.

"I have reached the Pole"—hearing himself make that statement in English for the first time, Cook wondered whether it sounded like a "remarkable thing." He noted that Whitney showed "no great surprise, and his quiet congratulation" reinforced what Cook had been pondering—that he had "accomplished no extraordinary or unbelievable thing." In his view, reaching the Pole the preceding spring had not been nearly as demanding as their yearlong fight for survival thereafter.

Cook told of the abundance of musk oxen on Ellesmere and Axel Heiberg, providing sustenance to the edge of the Arctic Ocean. Drawing his route on a chart and consulting a diary he had kept that contained the results of his sextant readings and calculations as well as variables such as temperature, wind direction, barometric readings, types of cloud formations, color of the sky, and other observations, Cook described being halted by a large lead after three days at the approximate latitude Peary had reported being stopped at the Big Lead in 1906. He decided to wait and see whether the lead—"a tremendous cut several miles wide"—closed before breaking out the canvas boat. The next day, they found ice thick enough to cross on foot. Six days into the journey, Cook took his first observation, which gave a latitude of 83 degrees, 31 minutes. Five days later, on March 30, he sighted to the west what appeared to be far-off land, at which he "gazed longingly and curiously." Although it was "never clearly seen" in a "low mist" that obscured the horizon, he estimated the mass rose to an elevation of one thousand feet and extended for fifty miles. Etukishook and Ahwelah were excited to see the promise of nearby land kept so soon. Cook decided against expending any effort to investigate the sighting, because to him "the Pole was the pivot of ambition." He took another observation, placing their position at 84 degrees, 50 minutes, and named the uncharted discovery Bradley Land in honor of his benefactor.*

After twenty-four days, they had advanced 360 miles from land, Cook said, an average of 15 miles per day. At that point, they had consumed not quite half of their food. As the sledge loads lightened, the dogs had been reduced in number, with the least fit killed and fed to the others, thereby conserving dog rations. Cook figured if they maintained their rate of progress, they would have enough food

---

*Cook reported taking seven sextant readings on the way to the Pole, on March 24, March 30, April 8, April 11, April 14, April 19, and April 21. Due to thick fog almost daily during his journey back to land, he reported taking only three observations: on April 30, May 24, and June 13.

to make the remaining 160 miles to the Pole, and back safely. Any long delays, however, jeopardized their attainment of the Pole—and possibly their lives.

On April 13, having traveled five days through a violent, freezing wind that made every breath painful, Ahwelah and Etukishook refused to go any farther. The "equality of the length of shadows for night and day puzzled them," as did the unchanging position of the sun, which remained at the same height in the sky, low on the horizon, regardless of the hour—phenomena of a very high (or low) latitude never before attained by them. "Lost in a landless, spiritless world, in which the sky, the weather, the sun and all was a mystery," Cook wrote emphatically of their fears. They told him they wanted to go home. Cook understood their desire to return to their families, sweethearts, and hunting grounds, but he judged that "the Pole was only one hundred miles beyond," and its "attainment seemed almost certain." He worked to soothe their concerns; "never did I speak so vehemently." He said, *"Tigishu-conti"* (The Pole is near). He promised, *"Sinipa tedliman dossa-ooahtonie tomongma ah youngulok tigilay toy hoy"* (At the end of five sleeps it is finished, beyond all is well, we return thereafter quickly). *"Ashuka-alningahna-matluk,"* he said, predicting their return to Eskimo lands with open waters and fresh meat in two moons. As they listened intently, he added, *"Kabishuckto-emongwah"* (Come walk a little farther). The two natives, pathetically thin and half-starved figures as a result of a diet of pemmican and tea, went to their sledges, lifted their whips, and commanded their dogs forward with *"Huk, Huk, Huk."* Northward they pushed for "that last hundred miles."

Cook told Whitney about having determined at local noon on April 21 that they were "at a spot which was as near as possible" to the North Pole. They remained for two days, during which Cook took observations and measurements to confirm their latitude. Before leaving, he deposited a note in a brass tube, which he buried in an icy crevasse. Then the race to return alive was fully on.

The weather turned abominable almost immediately, and the ice began to crack apart into drifting floes. Without the collapsible boat, Cook explained, they would have been hopelessly cut off and trapped any number of times that spring and summer. Facing the breakup of the ice pack, they took a single sledge and remaining supplies, loaded them into the boat, and forded one open lead after another—even a large bay as they closed on land. Fogbound most of the way back, Cook told how, when he was able to take a sextant reading on June 13, he was shocked to learn they had drifted not to the southeast, as he had expected, but to the southwest. His sextant observation of 79 degrees, 32 minutes, north, and 101 degrees, 22 minutes, west, placed them in the Crown Prince Gustav Sea, fifty miles west of Axel Heiberg Island and far southwest of their destination, Cape Svartevoeg. They were far removed, too, from their caches, set up on Ellesmere in anticipation of the known southeasterly drift. The ice cap's drift in the opposite direction in this region—then unknown and wholly unexpected—had nearly cost them their lives. They made several "hard-fought efforts" to cross in the boat to the east toward Axel Heiberg, but were repulsed by fields of "crushed ice." There was a real danger that the canvas boat would be crushed in the unstable pack ice, throwing them and everything they carried into deep, frigid waters. Also, even if they reached Axel Heiberg, there would still be an unknown course of eighty miles across the desolate island to the nearest cache on its eastern coast. Land to the south was nearer, so they headed in that direction. The next day, they reached a small island at the entrance to Hassel Sound, near the northwestern coast of Amund Ringnes Island. After eighty-six days on the polar pack, they reveled in the relief of finally stepping onto terra firma, with the knowledge that their perilous journey over the sea ice had come to an end.

Their joy was short-lived, however. Their supplies were nearly exhausted (with reduced rations, they had about twenty days worth of food), their dogs were gone (rather than kill them, they had let loose the handful of survivors in the hope they would join up with their relatives, the Arctic wolves), and they had no ammunition except for the four cartridges Cook had "secreted for use in a last emergency." Hoping to reach a native settlement, they continued south, by boat and by foot, eating off the land whenever possible. By

September, they had reached Cape Sparbo, on the northern shore of Devon Island. With winter approaching, Cook knew they must find shelter and prepare an ample food supply if they were to survive the Arctic night. They dug out the ruins of an old ice cave that had once served as someone's home—complete with a raised sleeping platform, fire pit, and room for supplies. They came across a "hollow-eyed human skull," and although the "omen was not good," they had no time to dwell on another's misfortune. For added insulation, they cut sod for the roof before permanent frost hampered such work. They hunted through October by means of stone-age weapons made from wood and metal stripped off the sledge and boat, devising an efficient, if death-defying, method with rope and lances for downing musk oxen, by nature "a peace-loving animal" that when forced to fight is "one of the most desperate and dangerous of all the fighters of the wilderness." Finding abundant game, they stored the meat in their cave, where it quickly froze. In those cramped quarters, they lived from November until February, when weather and ice conditions allowed them to begin their grueling two-month march to Annoatok.

Eager now to return to civilization, Cook prepared himself for travel. He explained his plan to Whitney to sledge seven hundred miles south to the Danish trading post of Upernavik and catch a ship to Denmark. The sledge trip would involve climbing mountains and glaciers, crossing open leads of water late in the season when the ice was in motion and snow was falling, and dragging the sledges through "slush and water." Cook had no false illusions about the trek, considering it "nearly as difficult as the journey to the North Pole."

Whitney tried to dissuade Cook from going, offering him free passage on a chartered vessel expected at Etah by the end of summer to take Whitney home—arrangements his two hunting friends, who had gone back on *Erik*, set in motion upon their return. Cook felt, however, that he could be home months sooner if he caught a ship to Copenhagen and from there continued on to New York.

As Ahwelah and Etukishook had returned to their village south of Annoatok, Cook found two new Eskimos to accompany him. He thought he might see Ahwelah and Etukishook, and since Whitney was short of natives and dogs for his planned hunt on Ellesmere, Cook said he would try to arrange for them to return to Annoatok and serve as Whitney's guides.

The day before Cook was to leave, one of the Eskimos he was to travel with fell sick, which meant Cook would be taking one fewer sledge. Whitney suggested that he leave any possessions he would not need right away. Whitney, who expected to reach New York via Hudson Bay in October, promised to bring them with him and personally return them to Cook in Brooklyn.

Cook thought it was a good idea. In addition to meteorological data, ethnological collections, geological specimens, and some furs and other clothing, Cook boxed up his instruments and left them with Whitney. These included his French sextant, compass with azimuth attachment, glass artificial horizon, aluminum aneroid barometer, maximum and minimum spirit thermometer, and a liquid compass—all of which had aided him in measuring key variables, including his position, during his polar trek. They would be unnecessary on this trip because he would be following the coast of Greenland, and he did not want them to be lost or damaged on the sledge trip. He also decided to divide up the original record of his journey, keeping in his possession his manuscript, diary, and some original field papers containing astronomical calculations for some of the sextant readings made during the journey north. He packed the remainder of his original record of the journey—"old, rubbed, oily, and torn field papers," as well as notebooks and loose papers containing "instrumental corrections and the direct [sextant] readings." Whitney asked about the flag that Cook had flown at the Pole, suggesting it would be safer kept with him. Cook agreed and placed it, carefully folded, with his instruments. In all, he left three boxes with Whitney.

Cook knew that his instruments, especially the sextant, and original field reports would be "important for future recalculation," and as proof of his polar claim in the event that something went wrong and he failed to make Upernavik.

Before departing, he wrote out instructions for Whitney that directed the hunter, upon his departure in the summer, to give possession of the house and remaining supplies to Etukishook and Ahwelah for their loyal service. Furthermore, Cook allowed that the two *Roosevelt* sailors, boatswain Murphy and cabin boy William "Billy" Pritchard, "may remain as tenant(s) of the house until [they] leave with the understanding that the rental is to be regarded as full pay for Franke's return passage . . . and all expenses incurred thereby."

Other than Whitney, the only person who had heard Cook speak of his North Pole discovery was Pritchard, a likable young man whom Whitney had come to trust over the winter. Cook asked Whitney and Pritchard not to reveal to Peary or any of *Roosevelt's* crew anything about his having reached the North Pole until an announcement could be made to a bona fide news organization. It was agreed that whenever Peary reappeared, they would simply say that Cook claimed to have exceeded Peary's farthest north.

Cook departed Annoatok the third week of April. Crossing over a glacier to reach Sonntag Bay, Cook and his native companion were caught in a violent gale that buried them in snow drifts on the highlands. Descending toward the sea, they found much improved conditions and soon came across Etukishook and Ahwelah in the native village of Nuerke, which was in the midst of the spring walrus hunt. The hunters were in a "gluttonous stupor from continued overfeeding," and Cook and his companion soon "succumbed to similar pleasures." He found here that the "principal pastime was native gossip about the North Pole," as Etukishook and Ahwelah recounted their long journey to a place of strange shadows, where the sun never rose or dipped and where there was no game or other life. Cook had instructed Etukishook and Ahwelah to say nothing to Peary or his men about having been to the Big Nail, although he well knew they would tell their own people. Seldom was there big news among the natives other than births and deaths, and young and old alike gathered around to hear the tales that would become tribal oral histories. The nature of the hardships and unique methods of hunting during the sparse winter seemed to interest their listeners the most, Cook observed, and they sat mesmerized by stories of hunts involving slingshots, string traps, and arrows.

As they continued on toward Cape York, Cook began to consider for the first time the "public aspect" of his homecoming. He thought that the newspapers would give his announcement "a three days' breath of attention, and that that would be all." His chief thought as he headed south was that after hundreds of lives and millions of dollars had been sacrificed in seeking the Pole, he had proven the feat could be "done by simpler methods."

On May 21, Cook reached Upernavik. He went to the house of the Danish governor, who put him up in guest quarters until transportation could be arranged. It turned into a longer wait than Cook had hoped. Not until August did a Copenhagen-bound ship show up: *Hans Egede*, a Danish government vessel carrying dignitaries and scientists on an official tour of Greenland. The ship anchored off Egedesminde, at the mouth of Disko Bay, three hundred miles south of Upernavik—a trip Cook made on a coastal trawler.

To a few local officials who had treated him with kindness, Cook told of his North Pole conquest. The night before *Hans Egede* was to depart, a dinner was held in Cook's honor at the King's Guest House, the only hotel in all of Greenland. About twenty Danish officials and scientists were present, as well as a familiar face from the Far North, Greenlander Knud Rasmussen. For forty-five minutes, Cook spoke of his springtime polar journey and winter ordeal.

Next to rise was Rasmussen, who began by saying that the natives he had talked with not only confirmed Cook's story but also provided additional details. He had spent the summer at Cape York, Rasmussen explained, where he had heard about the North Pole trip from the natives. Taking a keen interest in the story, he had interviewed scores of Eskimos—research for an article he hoped to publish. Although by then Ahwelah and Etukishook were on Ellesmere hunting with Whitney, Rasmussen had spoken to thirty-five natives, many of whom claimed to have heard the story directly from the two young hunters, including how Cook had "jumped and danced like an *angacock*" (witch doctor) when he looked at his "sun glass" and realized they were only a day's march from the Big Nail. Rasmussen heard how Etukishook and Ahwelah feared on the long march that they would never return to their homes, and how disappointed they were to find no open water or game, only more ice.

Rasmussen congratulated Cook, believing he had "won the victory
. . . the greatest in Arctic history." The Greenlander offered a note of
warning about Peary, a man he knew by reputation from the
natives—a man who had for years dominated the profitable blue-fox
and ivory market in northern Greenland, prohibiting natives he
employed or traded with from doing business with other white men;
a man known to have taken away essential items other explorers gave
the natives so they would be obligated to trade with him; a man who
had long treated the natives as a stern colonial governor overseeing
an unruly province; a man who abided no Arctic competition.
Rasmussen did not think that such a man would be in a congratulatory mood when he came out of the north and heard news of Cook's
claim to the Pole. That evening, Rasmussen "foretold the return of
Peary and prophesied discord."

Hans Egede departed for Copenhagen on August 9 with Cook
aboard. For the next three weeks, during the North Atlantic crossing, he entertained passengers and crew alike with spellbinding
accounts of polar discovery and survival. At the captain's behest, he
gave a formal lecture to a group of Danish officials, correspondents,
and scientists, all of whom were won over by his knowledge of the
Arctic and its people, coupled with his humble demeanor.

The enthusiastic reaction from the journalists, in particular, got
Cook to thinking that his story might have "considerable financial
value." He could sorely use the money. As usual, he was short of
funds. His expenses at the hotel in Egedesminde and on *Hans Egede*
were unpaid; he had only fifty dollars and needed to buy new attire
to make himself more presentable, as well as purchase passage from
Copenhagen to New York. He spent time in his cabin polishing a
2,000-word narrative that he had drafted at Upernavik and which
he intended to offer for publication to an American newspaper. In
this short account, condensed from his other writings and from his
diary and observation papers, he provided the first descriptions of
natural conditions at the North Pole, as well as other regions
through which he had traveled. The captain, who appreciated the
news value of Cook's story, suggested it be sent by wireless from the
nearest port, and offered to put in at the Shetland Islands, a group of

a hundred sparsely populated islands that constituted the most northerly British territory.

On September 1, *Hans Egede* steamed into the Shetland Islands' main harbor of Lerwick, anchored close-in, and launched a skiff. Only two men were allowed ashore at this unscheduled stopover: a ship's officer and Cook.

At the town's one-room telegraph station, Cook sent a wire to Marie at their Brooklyn home, telling her he was "successful and well," and another to Harry Whitney's mother, letting her know that her son was safe and sound.

Next he wired the *New York Herald*, the most powerful paper in America's largest metropolis. Although Cook had never before had any dealings with the *Herald*, the paper had a long history of covering explorers, having sent its star reporter Henry M. Stanley to Africa in 1871 in pursuit of Dr. David Livingstone, of whom little had been heard since his departure five years earlier on his ultimately unsuccessful quest to find the source of the Nile.

Cook informed the editors of the *Herald*,

> REACHED NORTH POLE APRIL 21, 1908.
> DISCOVERED LAND FAR NORTH.
> HAVE LEFT SEALED EXCLUSIVE CABLE OF 2,000 WORDS FOR YOU
> WITH DANISH CONSUL AT LERWICK. EXPECT $3,000 FOR IT.
> I GO STEAMER HANS EGEDE TO COPENHAGEN.
> FREDERICK A. COOK*

The ship's officer sent a wire to Copenhagen on behalf of Jens Daugaard-Jensen, Denmark's highest-ranking official for Greenland, who happened to be aboard *Hans Egede*. Addressed to Maurice Francis Egan, the U.S. minister to Denmark, it told of Cook's attainment of

---

*Cook's wire was forwarded to the *Herald*'s Paris bureau, from where the second-generation owner and publisher, James Gordon Bennett Jr., ran the paper. Bennett considered Cook's price a bargain for the North Pole story and immediately wired Lerwick for Cook's narrative, which was published under a banner front-page headline the next day (September 2, 1909).

the Pole and added, "The Eskimos of Cape York confirm to Knud Rasmussen Dr. Cook's story of his journey."

Hans Egede was met two days later off Skagens Gren, the north-ernmost tip of the European continent, by a Royal Danish Navy torpedo boat, whose skipper came aboard bearing a congratulatory telegram from the Danish prime minister, along with news that dinners and receptions awaited Cook in Copenhagen. He also brought Cook a copy of a Danish newspaper that had reprinted his story from the *New York Herald*, which was the first Cook knew that his polar narrative had sold. Taking one look at the explorer—in Eskimo boots and a soiled, bagged-at-the-knees suit—the military officer, under orders to speed his vessel ahead and report back as to when *Hans Egede* could be expected at Copenhagen, quickly had Cook's measurements taken so that proper attire could be readied for his participation in the upcoming festivities.

A few visitors had been allowed on the torpedo boat. One was a young *London Daily Chronicle* reporter, Philip Gibbs, who later admitted that he knew nothing about Arctic exploration, had not had time to read up on the subject, and had difficulty even remembering Cook's name, making a point to repeat it to himself on the way to the at-sea rendezvous. Upon meeting Cook, Gibbs emulated Stanley's greeting to Livingstone, beginning with "Dr. Cook, I believe." Without further ado, he asked to see Cook's diary and all his papers and records. It was a cheeky request that ignored the possibility that Cook had sold his exclusive story or might be interested in doing so. Cook deflected Gibbs by explaining how he had left his instruments and many of his original reports at his Greenland base with a sportsman friend who was returning them to the United States.

Gibbs was incredulous. "What evidence can you bring to show that you actually reached the North Pole?" he demanded.

Cook eyed the impetuous reporter who seemed so full of himself. In the history of Arctic exploration, men had long been taken at their word. Did this reporter not know that? Nansen, Amundsen, and Sverdrup were believed, Cook said. "They had only their story to tell. Why don't you believe me?"*

As *Hans Egede* steamed into Copenhagen's harbor on the morning of September 4, smaller craft of all types swarmed—flags waving, horns blowing, cheering people from tugs, motorboats, sailboats, and rowboats, many of them decorated. The flags of nations flew in the breeze, including more than a few Stars and Stripes. For centuries, the Danes had sent intrepid sailors to the Arctic, and news of its conquest brought out thousands lining the waterfront to greet the man who had succeeded in winning the prize. Cook stood on deck, "dazed, simply dazed" at the "clamor of Copenhagen's ovation," and noted crews of "moving-picture-machine operators at work . . . their heads hooded in black."

A welcoming committee soon boarded. It included Prince Christian, the crown prince, King Frederick's brother, Prince Waldemar, U.S. Minister Egan, and other distinguished officials. Through a crush of spectators, Cook was whisked to the Phoenix Hotel, where an apartment filled with bouquets of fresh flowers had been reserved for him. A wire from home awaited him: "THANK GOD ALL WELL = MARIE." A barber arrived, followed by a manicurist, then by tailors, bringing suits of stylish clothes that needed only slight alterations.

Faultlessly groomed and attired and looking nothing at all like the ragged figure of the morning, Cook was picked up by the U.S. legation and taken by horse-drawn carriage to the royal palace, where he was received by King Frederick. Left alone for what turned into a two-hour visit, the elderly king and the soft-spoken explorer were soon engrossed in the subject of the North Pole.

One of the first reporters to greet Cook in Copenhagen had been the well-known English editor William T. Stead, Hearst's lead cor-

---

*Amundsen, Cook's shipmate from *Belgica*, had become the first to navigate the Northwest Passage (1903–06), finding a sailing route connecting the Atlantic and Pacific Oceans along the northern coast of North America. His success in avoiding the hardships—scurvy, starvation, exhaustion—suffered by other explorers trying the same feat was universally credited to his great preparation. Amundsen had learned some lessons from that long entrapment in the Antarctic ice.

respondent in Europe. Stead helped Cook through the exuberant crowd dockside and later wrote that the explorer seemed a "naive, inexperienced child, who sorely needed someone to look after him." As they struggled through the crowd, Stead told Cook he could arrange a press conference for him to face at one time all the reporters who would be clamoring for interviews. Cook asked whether it could be put off a day. Stead later wrote, "'Why this hurry?' he was always asking, with the absent air of a man who has lived in the timeless solitude of the arctic night. . . . As if the ravenous maw of the world's press with its teeming special editions could wait complacently for 24 hours before hearing what he had to say!"

After his visit with King Frederick, Cook went back to the Phoenix, where fifty reporters representing the great dailies and magazines of the world had gathered in a cavernous banquet room. Cook entered without being recognized by the reporters except for Stead, who made the introduction.

Stead seized the opportunity to ask the first questions. Was Cook certain—"down deep in your own heart"—that he had discovered the North Pole?

"I think so," replied Cook, blushing like a schoolboy.

"You have set your foot right on it?" asked Stead.

"Oh, I couldn't say that. I got to where there wasn't any longitude."

There was the first colorful quote—*I got to where there wasn't any longitude*—and every reporter in the room scratched away in his notepad. Stead went on, asking for assurance from Cook that his records were authentic and that he considered himself competent to keep such records.

Cook said that he was capable of taking observations and keeping records and that he had "carried certain instruments" for that purpose, including a sextant, chronometer, and barometer—all of which he knew how to use.

"But you did not set your foot upon the exact point of the Pole?" Stead persisted.

"I doubt if anybody could do that," replied Cook, neglecting to explain for the benefit of any Arctic neophytes in the group that the ice pack at the Pole is constantly adrift. "I got within the circle, I think. I went around it for two days making observations."

"What does it look like?" asked another reporter.

"Ice."

"Some details as to your journey up there, Doctor?"

"It was simply . . . a dash. We did not try to carry all the heavy instruments. . . . There is nothing so very scientific about the achievement. We traveled as lightly as possible, and made fifteen miles a day."

"Impossible," someone murmured.

"You say 'we,' " Stead said.

"Myself and the two Eskimos."

"Can you get these two men to testify that you have been to the Pole?" another reporter asked.

"They can testify in a general way to the number of days' travel they made from a certain point of departure. . . . They have no knowledge of latitude and longitude."

Cook understood it was the job of the press to be skeptical, and at this point he felt the need to explain to the "circle of glittering eyes" that he had no reason to hoodwink the world as to his achievement, but that they would have to take his word for it until the complete record of his trip and his polar instruments could be examined by a proper board of experts. "I am in this work for the love of the work, gentlemen," he said. "And I have brought back just exactly the sort of records and proofs that every Arctic explorer brings back."

Except that he did not yet have the instruments and a complete record with him, he explained, since they were in transit from Greenland with a trusted companion, Harry Whitney, who would be bringing them to New York.

At that point, the members of press of the world seemed to let down their guard and push back their professional skepticism, and started warming to the American discoverer. They signaled their acceptance by asking silly questions.

"Do you like to eat fox?"

"I want to know, are you a Christian?"

After an hour, the explorer was thanked and given his release.

Reporters on deadline rushed off to file their stories, with the initial wave of reportage capturing Cook's demeanor as much as his words.

"Calm and imperturbable though wincing under the cruelty of the thrusts," wrote the United Press correspondent. "Dr. Cook modestly met every inquiry with a directness and frankness that quickly won all his hearers."

"He entirely satisfied me as to his good faith," reported the *Times* of London representative. "The sincere manner in which he answered awkward questions produced in all present a profound impression."

Cook turned down the three biggest offers for his story—including one from Stead's boss, William Randolph Hearst, to double the best offer of any other newspaper or syndicate—and sold his lengthy narrative of polar conquest to the *New York Herald* for $25,000.* About Cook's decision, Stead wrote:

> It is enough to make one weep! But as he used to say plaintively, "I am not out for money." He certainly is about the last man whom any business firm would send out for money. . . . Everything a clever rogue would do instinctively, if he wished to hoax the public, Dr. Cook did not do. . . . Some believed in Dr. Cook at first; all believe in him now.

Stead's statement was not quite correct, because *Daily Chronicle* reporter Philip Gibbs was on the warpath. From the moment Cook declined to produce any records aboard *Hans Egede*, Gibbs, by "intuition rather than evidence," was convinced that the American had not gone to the North Pole. Gibbs soon became so unobjective in his reporting as to be removed from the assignment by his editors. However, his reassignment did not come before he wrote several articles bashing Cook, including one on the day of Cook's news con-

---

*Cook, grateful to the *Herald* for printing his first, skeletal account of attaining the North Pole, accepted publisher Bennett's latest offer without quibbling, believing it was important to publish his "narrative story as an honest and sincere proof of [his] claim as soon as possible." Cook sent the *Herald* a 25,000-word narrative, "The Conquest of the Pole," typewritten by secretaries from the original manuscript he had begun writing during the winter at Cape Sparbo. A twelve-part series began in the *Herald* on September 15, 1909.

ference—an event Gibbs did not attend but included in his story as if he had been a participant, observing that Cook's "answers to Mr. Stead's examination have caused a great deal of uneasiness," which clearly they had not, least of all to the man who had asked the questions. Gibbs was roundly criticized by his contemporaries; the Copenhagen *Politiken* observed, "[Gibbs] statements are full of lies." One Danish newspaperman was so upset by Gibbs's treatment of Cook that he challenged the brash young Englishman to a duel.*

That night Cook dined with the royal family at King Frederick's summer palace. When pressed by the younger members of the family, he told of the wild animals that inhabited the Far North and exciting big-game hunts in the Arctic.

Upon his return to the hotel around ten o'clock that evening, an exhausted Cook found two officials of the Royal Danish Geographical Society waiting to see to him. For several hours, he answered questions put to him by Royal Danish Navy Commander Hovgaard, a member of the Nordenskiöld expedition (an attempted Greenland crossing in 1883), and Professor Olafsen, secretary of the society, regarding his astronomical observations. The focus was on questions of navigation and the determination of location on the drifting pack ice of the Arctic Ocean. Certain of the "verity" of his claim and believing he had been "as accurate in [his] scientific work as anyone could be," Cook explained in detail his methods.

On the basis of the technical discussion its experts had with Cook, the society awarded the discoverer of the North Pole its prestigious gold medal at the Palace Concert Hall before the king and queen, the royal family, and the elite of Copenhagen society. With a long pointer in hand, the tuxedo-clad Cook lectured from a stage before a large map that showed the American flag at the top of the

---

*Gibbs's articles were reprinted in the *New York Times,* beginning September 5, 1909—the day after its bitter crosstown competitor, the *New York Herald,* printed its exclusive of Cook's discovery of the North Pole. The *Times* had advanced Peary, before his departure, $4,000 against syndication earnings for his expedition story, with the proviso that should he fail to reach the Pole and his story have lesser value, the money would be subject to reimbursement. The newspaper battle lines were indelibly drawn; the *Herald* had Cook, and the *Times* had Peary.

world. "This northward dash occupied the minds of different men for more than three hundred years," Cook said. "Slowly but surely the ladder of latitude has been climbed, and as degrees of increased experience have been gained each expedition has profited from the misfortunes of its predecessors. The failure of one expedition led to the success of subsequent efforts. This is the art of Polar travel. . . . All honor, therefore, to pioneer pathfinders of the Pole. We are particularly indebted to Nansen, Sverdrup, Peary."

Over lunch the next day with a delegation from the University of Copenhagen sent to determine his worthiness for an honorary degree, Cook was again examined on celestial navigation, as well as on "an exhaustive series of mathematical questions" posed by a professor of mathematics. The university's rector, Dr. Carl Torp, who took part in the session, reported, "Dr. Cook answered all [our questions] to our full satisfaction. He showed no nervousness or excitement at any time. I dare say that there is no justification for anybody to throw the slightest doubt on his claim to have reached the North Pole."

Back at his hotel, Cook was swamped with hundreds of telegrams, many containing "tremendous offers of money." From *Outing Magazine:* "YOUR OWN PRICE NARRATIVE FINDING POLE." From a Pennsylvania promoter: "WILL YOU ACCEPT TWENTY FIVE THOUSAND DOLLARS BASED UPON POLE FOUND. SIX MONTHS EXCLUSIVE TOUR. OPENING CARNEGIE HALL." From Major Pond: "MAY WE BOOK LECTURE TOUR YOUR OWN TERMS." Cook read the messages "just as a man looks at his watch and puts it in his pocket without noting the time," since he had little opportunity to respond, given the excitement "by day . . . by night" and even in his "dreams." He longed to return to America and partake in the "joys of a family reunion," and was delighted to be able to book passage home on the steamship *Oscar II* of the Scandinavian-American Line, readying to depart Copenhagen for a ten-day crossing to New York.

In a final ceremony, this one before twelve hundred spectators who applauded nonstop for five minutes before he could speak, Cook received an honorary doctorate in philosophy from the University of Copenhagen, one of Europe's oldest institutions of higher learning and the alma mater of most educated Danes. This recognition had received the blessing of King Frederick, the titular president of the university. In appreciation for the university's recognition, as well as the grand welcome and hospitality he had been accorded by the Danes, Cook had already volunteered to submit for evaluation to a faculty committee the entire original record of his journey, along with his instruments, as soon as he had everything back. University officials were delighted and surprised by the offer, considering that Cook, as an American, might well have been expected to entrust an institution in his own country with such a responsibility and honor. At the end of his speech in the university's great hall, Cook reaffirmed his intention to submit to the Danes his North Pole data and instruments. "I can say no more," he added, holding his hands out before him. "I can do no more." The applause was spontaneous and thunderous.

By September 6, from the perspective of the assembled reporters in Copenhagen, the breaking story had been covered, and most packed their bags and prepared to leave. As a farewell, the owner of the *Politiken* hosted a dinner that night for the foreign press at the Tivoli restaurant, and Cook was invited. "Tired to death and exhausted with want of sleep," he declined. However, some of the reporters he had gotten to know best came to his hotel and lobbied him to be a good sport and appear even for only a short while. After all, he was the reason they had all come to Denmark.

As Cook entered the dining room a garland of fresh flowers was wrapped over his shoulders, and he received a warm greeting. The evening was planned for frivolity, not work—drinking, eating, smoking cigars, and engaging in collegial repartee. Shortly after the first speaker began—a Frenchman with *Le Matin*—a messenger tiptoed in and handed the host an envelope. The Danish publisher opened it, expressed surprise, and passed the message to Stead, sitting next to him.

Stead was quickly on his feet, holding up a hand. As a hush fell over the room, he announced, "In a wire to the Associated Press from Indian Harbor, Labrador, dated September 6, 1909: 'Stars and Stripes nailed to North Pole. Peary.'"

Given the environment of the evening, some thought the message might be a hoax sent by a jokester. Asked what he thought, Cook said he thought it was genuine. He recognized Peary's characteristically patriotic phrasing.

In that case, one of the reporters asked, did he have a comment?

Suddenly, notebooks appeared, and the roomful of newsmen waited.

"I am proud that a fellow American has reached the Pole," Cook said. "As Rear Admiral Schley said at Santiago, 'There is glory enough for us all.'" Cook called Peary "a brave man" and added that he was confident that if the reports were true "his observations will confirm mine."

Cook would later describe his initial feelings as "not of envy or chagrin," for he knew "no rivalry about the Pole." Rather, he thought of Peary's "hard, long years of effort," and believed that his trip "might be of great scientific value." Perhaps Peary had "discovered new lands and mapped new seas of ice."

Some of the guests made a run for hotel phones and telegraph offices.

Cook that evening sent a wire to the *New York Herald*:

KINDLY CONVEY TO MR. PEARY MY HEARTY
CONGRATULATIONS UPON HIS SUCCESS. THE VICTORY IS
SURELY ALL AMERICAN. I AM GLAD HE HAS WON, AS TWO
RECORDS ARE BETTER THAN ONE. . . .

The *Herald* relayed Cook's telegram to Labrador.

Later that day, Peary wired the Associated Press from Labrador:

COOK'S STORY SHOULD NOT BE TAKEN TOO SERIOUSLY.
THE TWO ESKIMOS WHO ACCOMPANIED HIM SAY HE WENT
NO DISTANCE NORTH AND NOT OUT OF SIGHT OF LAND.
OTHER MEMBERS OF THE TRIBE CORROBORATE THEIR STORY.

CHAPTER EIGHTEEN

"NAILED TO THE POLE"

By THE TIME Peary came out of the north in August 1909, Cook was already crossing the North Atlantic aboard *Hans Egede* bound for Copenhagen.

Roosevelt's first anchorage in Greenland, after a leisurely trip from Cape Sheridan that included a walrus hunt in Smith Sound, was off Nuerke, the native village where Cook had stopped four months earlier on his way to Upernavik and feasted with Ahwelah, Etukishook, and the locals. A boat crew went ashore to land natives, leaving with them a quantity of fresh meat for the winter. At both Nuerke and Etah, which *Roosevelt* reached on August 17, Peary's men heard reports of Cook and his Eskimos having gone to the Big Nail a year earlier.

Fearing such a scenario ever since Cook's letter from Etah in summer, 1907—"I have hit upon a new route to the North Pole and will stay to try it"—Peary regarded the situation with the utmost seriousness. He first questioned Whitney about what Cook had told him. Whitney said Cook had a "successful trip and accomplished all that he had hoped to," and reported besting Peary's farthest-north record. In Peary's widening investigation, the boatswain and cabin boy were questioned next; the former had no knowledge of Cook's travels, and Pritchard related hearing talk of Cook having gone "way, way north." Pritchard and Whitney both kept their promise to Cook.

That same day, Ahwelah and Etukishook were rounded up and brought to the ship. Since Peary was still unable to converse at length with natives in their own language, he prepared a list of questions and delegated the interviews to a committee composed of Bartlett, MacMillan, Borup, and Henson. Although Henson had familiarity with the language, he spoke a mixed jargon with a limited vocabulary. The Arctic newcomer Borup was picking up the dialect, but the group as a whole, Bartlett reported, "couldn't talk Eskimo." Dr. Goodsell, who spoke the native language fluently, asked to take part in the questioning of the natives, but his request was denied by Peary.

The two Eskimos were questioned separately in Henson's cabin. The method of interrogation was later described by Borup: "We pretended to know they had been far north and tried to make them admit they'd been [only] ten or fifteen marches out to sea." The natives were asked to trace their route on a Sverdrup chart. Neither had consulted a map before or even used a pencil.

Etukishook had gone into the cabin first. When he emerged and Ahwelah was ushered in, Whitney happened to be nearby on the bridge. Whitney, who had come to like the two young natives during their long hunting trip on Ellesmere, spoke Eskimo as fluently as Goodsell. Whitney's presence had also not been requested in Henson's cabin. Noticing that Etukishook looked "rather excited," Whitney went over and asked whether anything was wrong. "No sabe," an agitated Etukishook said. "No sabe." The young Eskimo explained he had been shown papers and maps he did not understand and asked confusing questions.

Whitney had been impressed with Ahwelah and Etukishook during the time he spent with them; with their assistance, he had bagged some impressive trophies to take home. He found them to be the "best dog drivers and sledge handlers" he had ever been around, able to get their sledges over the ice "faster than any other drivers, pushing, lifting and jumping them." He had heard from them details of their journey north and long winter ordeal. On the basis not only of what Cook had told him but also of what he learned that summer from Ahwelah and Etukishook, Whitney had "no doubt" that Cook and his capable companions had reached the Pole.

Believing he had the ammunition to counter any preemptive claim by Cook, Peary had the results of the interrogations transcribed, and he directed Bartlett, MacMillan, Borup, and Henson to sign the eight-page statement. The "testimony" provided by Cook's two Eskimo companions was declared to be "unshaken by cross-examination . . . corroborated by other men in the tribe [and] elicited neither by threats nor promises." Both Eskimos were quoted as saying they had not gone far with Cook, venturing no more than a few days from land. The statement concluded with this claim: Ahwelah and Etukishook were purported to have said Cook had "threatened them if they should tell anything."

As *Roosevelt* prepared to steam for home, there was still no sign of the vessel Whitney was expecting to take him back. Peary pointed out there may have been a shipwreck or some other mishap, and warned it would be unwise for Whitney to wait; with the season for Arctic sea travel coming to a close, he could be iced in for a second winter unless he took passage on *Roosevelt*.

Whitney accepted Peary's offer to leave Greenland, and went to gather his things. He returned with a line of natives toting assorted trunks, boxes, and even a sledge, and brought everything aboard under Peary's watchful gaze.

"Have you anything belonging to Dr. Cook?" Peary asked.

Whitney pointed to the three boxes containing Cook's instruments, notebooks, and other personal items, explaining he was going to be delivering it all to Cook in New York. He also had Cook's polar sledge—at least what was left of it—which the doctor had given him as a souvenir.

Peary came over and looked down at the beat-up sledge.

In Whitney's view, the sledge's sorry state confirmed Cook's story of a long and difficult journey on the ice. It was badly cut up; some of the wooden strips slivered for firewood. The base of the frame had been cut down to make lances and harpoons to kill game, and the iron runners removed to make blades. Whitney considered the sledge a prized possession.

"Well, I don't want any of them aboard this ship," Peary said.

It was not open to discussion; Peary turned and strode away.

Whitney recognized that he was confronted with a dilemma similar to that faced by Rudolph Franke. If he passed up returning on Peary's ship, he probably would not get home for another year, but if he capitulated to Peary's demand, he would be forsaking Cook's possessions.

Whitney sought the advice of a member of Peary's inner circle whom he "knew well," explaining how much he disliked leaving Cook's things behind. "I would not do it if I were you," said the expedition member. "The commander won't think any more about it and it would be a shame to leave them here."*

Whitney had Cook's sledge taken ashore and did some repacking, taking enough out of his personal trunks to make room for Cook's possessions. No sooner had everything been stowed aboard ship than, two hours before *Roosevelt* was due to sail, Whitney was summoned to Peary's cabin.

"When I said I did not want anything belonging to Dr. Cook aboard this ship," Peary said, "I meant I did not want a single thing he had. Now I am not going to say any more about this. I am going to place you on your word of honor as a gentleman not to take a thing belonging to Dr. Cook aboard this ship."

Disarmed by Peary's ultimatum, Whitney believed there was nothing for him to do but remove all of Cook's possessions from the ship. With Bartlett's help, he placed the contents of Cook's boxes in an empty gun chest and nailed the lid shut. The box was taken ashore, where it was hidden among large rocks in the hope of preventing native looting. Whitney's intention at that point was to return one day and retrieve everything.

Roosevelt sailed south on August 20 with Whitney aboard.

Three days later at 76 degrees, 40 minutes, north, they came upon *Jeanie*, a schooner dispatched to pick up Whitney, and also consigned by the Peary Arctic Club to deliver sixty tons of coal to *Roosevelt*. In addition to Whitney and the Peary Arctic Club, the

---

*Whitney never revealed the identity of the Peary expedition member to whom he spoke, although it might well have been Bartlett, who subsequently helped Whitney with Cook's things.

Arctic Club of America paid a portion of the charter to provide transportation home for Cook if he was still alive—this at the behest of Marie Cook, who had been unable to raise $30,000 to hire a ship to retrieve her husband, about whom she had heard nothing in more than a year.

Jeanie had been slowed by auxiliary engine trouble and had no engineer aboard to fix the problem. The ships came alongside in the quiet waters of North Star Bay so *Roosevelt* could be coaled. Aboard the schooner was *New York Herald* reporter Royal K. Fuller, who requested an interview with Peary.

Peary and the reporter spoke at length on August 24. In the course of their conversation, Peary had no dramatic news to tell the reporter, although he did remark that Cook had returned from his latest expedition in April. Peary said he did not believe his farthest-north record had been broken by Cook, but made no mention of the interrogation of Cook's two Eskimos. Fuller later wrote that in opining as to how far north he thought Cook had gone, Peary "intimated at the time that he was depending on the condition of [Cook's] sledge."

Whitney also spoke to the reporter, declaring, "No more Arctic winters for me." He described meeting Cook, who they "had come to believe had long since perished in the North," as he stepped off the pack ice at Annoatok in April "half starved and very thin." Whitney, still keeping his word not to mention the Pole until Cook had the opportunity to make his own announcement, assured the correspondent that the explorer had "gone beyond the [farthest north] record made by Peary."

After transferring to *Jeanie*, Whitney faced a decision. Should he have the schooner take him back to Etah so he could pick up Cook's possessions? or should they head for home? The skipper of *Jeanie* was another of the Bartlett family of sailors: Samuel Bartlett, an old Arctic hand and the uncle of *Roosevelt*'s Captain Bartlett. When he learned about Cook's possessions being ordered off *Roosevelt* and left on the rocks, Sam Bartlett was all for sailing north to retrieve them, even sans an auxiliary motor and knowing that at this time of year new ice could quickly choke off Smith Sound and trap a small sailing vessel like *Jeanie*. Whitney wavered—he had promised Ahwelah and

Etukishook Winchester rifles and anticipated that extra guns would be on *Jeanie*, but there were none. Whitney was mortified at the prospect of going back to Etah empty-handed. He rationalized that Cook's most valuable possessions were the navigational instruments and decided he could replace them when he got to New York. Surely the explorer would be happy with new instruments? As for the papers and the rest of Cook's belongings, Whitney figured some-one—he or even Cook—could go back next summer and get them. Also, not having to double back with winter approaching would allow more time for hunting. So they headed west, and once across Baffin Bay, Whitney had the schooner stop along the coast of Ellesmere for him to take in one last hunt. The sportsman, it seemed, had not yet shot a polar bear.

Roosevelt steamed the short distance to Cape York on August 26 to drop off one last Eskimo, Minik, who had come north on *Jeanie*. One of the Greenland natives Peary brought home with him in 1897 and handed over to the American Museum of Natural History, Minik had lived the intervening years in New York, where he had been adopted by a museum employee, William Wallace, and his wife. (The other young survivor of the six museum Eskimos, Uisaakassak, had returned to Greenland in 1898.) A few years after the death of his father, Qisuk, and the mock funeral staged for the boy's benefit, Minik had learned the terrible truth when he discovered his father's remains in a display case at the museum. From then on, Minik wanted only to return to his homeland with the remains of his father. Frustrated at every turn in his public campaign, he was quoted in the press as saying he would like to shoot Peary. Finally, after Herbert Bridgman, on behalf of the Peary Arctic Club, negoti-ated a contract in which Minik agreed to absolve the museum, Peary, and his supporters of "all claims of every kind," the teenage Eskimo was provided passage north. Before boarding *Jeanie*, Minik had a parting blast for reporters: "You're a race of scientific crimi-nals. I know I'll never get my father's bones out of the American Museum of Natural History. I am glad enough to get away before they grab my brains and stuff them into a jar!" *Herald* reporter Fuller, who had shipped on *Jeanie* also to cover the story of Minik's repatriation, reported that after being given furs, food, traps, guns, and ammunition, Minik was left ashore at Cape York, where he was "again among his tribesmen of the Far North" and would have to relearn his native language and hunting skills to survive. As Minik predicted, his father's bones remained on display at the New York museum.*

During *Roosevelt*'s long absence, the crew's mail from home had been cached at Cape York. Peary also found waiting for him a note from the skipper of an American whaler, *Morning Star*, which had recently headed home. Peary was advised that Cook claimed to have discovered the North Pole on April 21, 1908, and was on his way to Copenhagen to make the official announcement.

Idle native rumor in northern Greenland was one thing, but for Cook to tell the world *he* had discovered the North Pole! Peary ordered Bartlett to fire up the boilers of *Roosevelt* for maximum power and make full speed for the nearest wireless station—fifteen hundred miles away at Indian Harbor, Labrador.

Suddenly, Peary had his own urgent announcement to make to the world.

PEARY, WHO HAD never been known for modesty when it came to claiming an exploration record, had told none of the crew of *Roosevelt* that he had attained the Pole, nor did he say anything to expedition members Borup, MacMillan, or Goodsell. Bartlett had surmised it and rushed onto the ice to greet Peary when he returned to the ship on April 27, 1909, from his ice cap journey, with a hearty "I congratulate you, sir, on the discovery of the Pole!"

A weary Peary had countered, "How did you guess it?"

And that was the end of the discussion about the Pole.

---

*Unable to adjust to Eskimo life, Minik returned to New York in 1916; bitter and frail, he died two years later in his late twenties. In the summer of 1995, the bones of Minik's father, Qisuk, and the other long-deceased museum Eskimos were returned to northern Greenland for burial.

Henson believed they had made it, but of course he could not take observations and relied on Peary to document their position with his instruments. Henson would long remember those final marches north after Bartlett turned back at 87 degrees, 47 minutes, filled as they were with "toil, fatigue, and exhaustion." Usually at the beginning of a new march, as Henson and the four Eskimos were harnessing the dogs and breaking camp, Peary shuffled out of camp on snowshoes, breaking trail until they caught up with him in less than an hour. From then on, Peary rode wrapped in furs in Egingwah's sledge, with the sledges driven by Henson, Ootah, Seegloo, and Ooqueah hauling the bulk of the supplies and equipment. Henson judged their advance forward as "in practically a straight line," although they fell down in their "tracks repeatedly."

Peary took an observation on April 5 and computed 89 degrees, 25 minutes—thirty-five miles to the Pole. Henson "witnessed the disappointment" on the leader's "long and serious" face. The next morning, Peary was slow to rise. Henson, after awakening the Eskimos, harnessed his team and "dashed out of camp." He continued on until certain he had "more than covered the necessary distance to insure [their] arrival at the top of the world," although he found the surroundings "not different from any other section of the Polar Sea ice."

Henson stopped and, with Ootah, went to work building two igloos.

Forty-five minutes later, Egingwah's sledge pulled in with its passenger.

Hurrying to meet Peary, Henson said, "We are now at the Pole, are we not?"

Henson had a "feeling" that they had covered the 132 miles since Bartlett turned back, "if they had traveled in the right direction."

"I do not suppose that we can swear that we are exactly at the Pole," Peary answered evasively.

Peary unpacked several bundles from the sledge. He pulled out from his outer garment a small folded package, and Henson knew what was inside: the silk flag sewn by Josephine Peary years before and carried by Peary on all his Arctic trips. Small squares of the U.S.

flag had been cut out and left with records in other cairns at each of Peary's northernmost attainments.

Peary silently fastened the flag to a staff and planted it at the top of his igloo. It hung "limp and lifeless" until a breeze caused some of the folds to straighten out "in sparkling color." The Stars and Stripes had been "nailed to the Pole." On Peary's orders, Henson led the Eskimos in three cheers, then everyone turned in. Peary was "utterly exhausted, body and brain," and at that moment there was "not a thing in the world" he wanted "but sleep."

The next morning Peary took an observation, making notes "with sun-blinded eyes . . . on a piece of tissue-paper." Because of the "res-olute squaring of [Peary's] jaws," Henson believed that the leader was "satisfied" with what he computed. Feeling "confident that the jour-ney had ended," Henson ungloved his right hand and went forward to the man he had served for so many years. Peary quickly turned away before the handshake—forced to do so, Henson later speculated, by perhaps "a gust of wind [that] blew something into his eye, or else the burning pain caused by his prolonged look at . . . the sun."

A diagonal strip of the flag, together with a note, was placed in an empty tin and buried in the ice. The other flags Peary had brought were flown—the colors of his fraternity, Delta Kappa Epsilon, the Navy League flag, the Red Cross flag. Then they snapped pictures, ate a meal, and slept. The next day, Peary ordered their return south over their old trail. From the moment Peary gave the command "in a qua-vering voice," Henson observed him to be "in a continual daze" and "practically a dead weight" the entire way back to land.

For three weeks after they returned to *Roosevelt*, a morose Peary avoided Henson, who recalled, "Not once in all of that time did he speak a word to me." And when Peary did start acknowledging Henson again, it was only "in the most ordinary, matter-of-fact way. . . . Not a word about the North Pole or anything connected with it." Back among his cohorts who had persevered at great personal risk to assist him in realizing his "life's purpose," Peary stayed sequestered in his cabin, seeing no one. There were no toasts, and no cheers.

Unable to make sense of it all, Henson would long harbor questions about Peary's actions after that climatic moment when they flew the flags and took pictures on April 7, 1909. Why hadn't the commander felt like celebrating?

AFTER URGENTLY DISEMBARKING Cape York on August 26, *Roosevelt* dropped anchor at Indian Harbor on September 5 at 10 p.m. The trip had not been a pleasant one; upon the news of Cook's pending announcement, Peary's mood had shifted from depression to fury. To Peary, it was a terrible affront that Cook was about to lay claim to what he considered rightfully his own. To anyone who would listen, Peary vented his rage, promising to tell the world a story that would puncture Cook's bubble.

The next morning, Bartlett rowed Peary ashore in a dory. At the wireless station, Peary wrote out in longhand the first of a sheaf of dispatches he would send. "Have made good at last," he wired Josephine. "I have the old pole. Am well. Love, Bert." Peary next wired Herbert Bridgman in a code they had established, advising that he had reached the Pole and *Roosevelt* was safe. He then sent the "Stars and Stripes nailed to North Pole" wire to the Associated Press and a similar one to the *New York Times*, advising he would soon have a "big story" to send. The wireless operator was kept busy that morning; in all, Peary sent seventeen telegrams, including separate ones to his key supporters Thomas Hubbard, George Crocker, Zenas Crane, and others. He also wired Henry Romeike, owner of a national newspaper clipping service in New York, directing him to clip "all editorials, illustrations, cartoons, and jokes" about the North Pole. Peary did not want to miss any of the news coverage.

Peary need not have worried, because the coverage came to him, with reporters unwilling to await his return. It was, after all, an amazing story: following three centuries of courageous and costly effort, the North Pole had been claimed by two American discoverers just five days apart.

From Indian Harbor, *Roosevelt* steamed down the Labrador coastline to Battle Harbour, at the mouth of the Strait of Belle Isle, arriving September 8. It was here that Peary received Cook's congratulations, forwarded to him by the *New York Herald*, and where Peary in turn fired off his first disparaging comments about Cook, asserting that his former expedition physician "should not be taken too seriously" and that Cook's natives reported not being "out of sight of land."

Peary wired the *New York Times*: "DON'T LET COOK STORY WORRY YOU. HAVE HIM NAILED." He also sent the *Times* a 200-word "brief summary," published on September 9, providing the dates and latitudes of his journey sans geographical or physical descriptions of any kind, adding in conclusion, "All members of expedition returning in good health except for Prof. Ross G. Marvin who drowned April 10."*

The following day, Peary sent a long telegram to the *New York Herald*, which, he had been informed, had a week earlier published Cook's first narrative of his polar journey. While Cook, possessing a claim of polar attainment that preceded Peary's by a full year, could afford to be magnanimous, Peary had no such luxury. If Cook prevailed, then Peary's bid to be the discoverer of the North Pole was at an end. After days to brood on the matter, Peary had decided to launch a frontal assault against his nemesis, and he sent the following telegram to the editor of the *Herald*:

---

*In 1926, after his conversion to Christianity, Kudlooktoo, one of Marvin's Eskimo companions on his fatal journey, told of having shot the white man in the head on the third day after leaving Peary, some 165 miles from Cape Columbia. Questioned following Kudlooktoo's confession, Inukitsoq, Marvin's other native companion, admitted to having told a false story under duress from Kudlooktoo, who threatened to kill him if he revealed the truth about the drowning. Both Eskimos belatedly claimed that the motive for the murder was Marvin's threat to leave Inukitsoq on his own. Other details provided by the two natives varied; Marvin was angry at Inukitsoq for not going "ahead of the sledge" (Kudlooktoo) or because Inukitsoq had not quickly followed in Marvin's tracks (Inukitsoq). The observations of those who best knew Marvin under the stress of Arctic travel belied the charge that Marvin would angrily threaten to leave any man behind. Henson: "[Marvin] was a very quiet young man, but one of great . . . strength of character. He was a cool-headed, quiet and just man." And Bartlett, who correctly had suspicions of foul play from the start: "There wasn't a better man ever went north. He was always good natured, even tempered, and wonderful at getting along with the Eskimos."

BATTLE HARBOR, VIA CAPE RAY, N.F. SEPT. 10, 1909
DO NOT IMAGINE HERALD LIKELY TO BE IMPOSED UPON BY
COOK STORY, BUT FOR YOUR INFORMATION COOK HAS
SIMPLY HANDED THE PUBLIC A GOLD BRICK. HE'S NOT BEEN
AT THE POLE APRIL 21, 1908, OR AT ANY OTHER TIME. THE
ABOVE STATEMENT IS MADE ADVISEDLY AND AT THE PROPER
TIME WILL BE BACKED BY PROOF.
PEARY

Peary now took a curious course of action: with the world primed to hear more from him—and the *Times* eager to counter the *Herald*'s North Pole exclusive with one of its own—he lingered at Battle Harbour, not even wiring the *Times* his promised major narrative, for which it had already advanced him $4,000. There were no reported seaworthiness problems with *Roosevelt* or any lack of desire on the part of the crew to be homeward bound; indeed, the homesick sailors became increasingly disgruntled at the delay.

An oceangoing tug, *Douglas H. Thomas*, chartered out of Sydney, Nova Scotia, arrived at Battle Harbour on September 13. A rain squall swept over the little whaling and mission settlement as the tug chugged slowly in. Associated Press correspondent John Regan had endured a stormy passage of nearly five hundred miles to be the first reporter on the scene. Peary was duly impressed with the reporter's fortitude. "This is a new record in newspaper enterprise, and I appreciate your compliment."

After his long journey to reach Peary, Regan skipped the niceties and went to the heart of the matter: "Was Dr. Cook at the Pole?"

"Cook was not at the Pole on April 21, 1908, or at any other time," Peary said. "I have already stated publicly that Cook has not been to the Pole. This I reaffirm, and I will stand by it, but I decline to discuss the details of the matter."

News from Copenhagen of Cook's claiming to have told Harry Whitney of his success in reaching the Pole had reached the United States.

"Did Harry Whitney make any important statements to you about another Polar expedition?" Regan asked.

"He made no statement," Peary said. "He is on the relief schooner *Jeanie* now and is probably shooting bear on the western coast."

The next question concerned the reports that he had taken supplies belonging to Cook at Etah, but Peary declined to discuss the matter. Asked about some of the descriptions of hummocks and crevices near the Pole that Cook had provided in his published narrative and interviews, Peary said, "That is a range of information that I do not care to impart now."

Peary said he would wait for Cook to "issue a complete authorized version of his journey" before making "public the information" he had. In doing otherwise, he explained, he would "be giving out much information of which other uses could be made." Peary had touched on a possible motive for his delay in Labrador—was he stalling? There had long been intense speculation as to what exactly would be found at the North Pole—for starters, land or an open sea? Peary had addressed and harbored such questions himself, but now he seemed determined to give Cook ample time to go on record first regarding such descriptions and information. Peary's comment to the reporter made it clear he did not intend to provide details of the Pole that could be used in any way by Cook.

"Why did you not have a white witness at the Pole?"

"Because after a lifetime of effort I dearly wanted the honor for myself," Peary explained. "I am the only white man who has ever reached the North Pole, and I am prepared to prove it at the proper time."

Roosevelt was still at Battle Harbour three days later when a Canadian government steamer, *Tyrian*, arrived, carrying twenty-three correspondents.

Once the reporters had boarded *Roosevelt*, milling about on the main deck, Peary stepped from his cabin, "every ounce of him as hard as Bessemer steel," according to a *New York World* reporter. As Peary faced the "muzzles of a dozen cameras," the reporters sent up three rousing cheers. Peary bowed, and smiled "from ear to ear."

"Gentlemen, I thank you for coming to see me," Peary said. "It is an honor and I want to meet every one of you." He then worked the crowd like a Tammany Hall politician, shaking every hand thrust in front of him. Before a question could be asked, however, Peary excused himself to read the New York newspapers and letters brought to him on *Tyrian*, promising he would grant an interview thereafter. An hour later, he did so, in a barren fish storage loft; Peary settled on a pile of nets, and reporters stood or squatted on the floor.

Peary again refused to discuss physical descriptions and details of his journey, even though he knew, from reading the newspapers, that Cook was already going public with his own details.

"Was there more than one observation taken at the Pole, and by whom?"

"There were several observations, and I took them all myself," Peary said. "They all agreed. You must understand that the Pole is a theoretical point, without length, breadth or thickness. Its actual location depends on the accuracy of the instruments employed and the conditions under which the observations are taken."

Asked about his message that described Cook as having handed the world "a gold brick," Peary allowed that he should have used a more "elegant expression," but said he was willing to let those words stand. He avoided making any additional charges against Cook to the assembled press corps.

In reply to the question whether it would have been possible for a "rival expedition" to reach the Pole without his knowledge, even though they had been in the region at the same time, Peary said, "It would be quite possible for Dr. Cook's party or any expedition to arrive at the North Pole by any one of a hundred routes and for one to find no trace of it if our paths lay far apart."

When the session was over, the newsmen began wandering through the ship, questioning members of the crew and expedition party until Peary ordered his men not to speak directly to the reporters. A number had already said some interesting things, however, and from the wireless station at Battle Harbour stories flew back to home offices for publication.

"Peary's men are quoted as saying," read one September 16 news story, "that when the *Roosevelt* came down to Etah, Cook's Eskimos were found there. They gave the information that Cook had reached the Pole, and Peary at once became eagerly desirous of reaching wires so as to get his story in ahead of Cook. The men say that Peary was bitterly disappointed when he found that Cook had got his story out first. The men themselves appear to entertain no doubt that Cook had reached the Pole, but they were all unwilling to speak definitely or be quoted on the subject, as Peary had positively forbidden them to give any information on any subject connected with the trip."

One crew member Peary did give permission to speak to reporters was William Pritchard, convinced as Peary was that the cabin boy would deny reports out of Copenhagen that quoted Cook as claiming he had told Pritchard, along with Whitney, of his attainment of the North Pole. Prior to his interview, Pritchard was shown a wire from Cook giving both him and Whitney permission to speak freely, thereby releasing them of their promise.

To everyone's surprise—most of all Peary's—Pritchard confirmed Cook's story. Pritchard said he heard Cook describe how he went to the Pole and stayed two days. He said the doctor used a map to illustrate his route.

"Why didn't you mention this before?" a reporter asked.

"Because Dr. Cook asked me to say nothing," answered Pritchard, adding that he felt it was right to keep his promise to Cook and give the doctor the opportunity to make his own announcement about the Pole.

The next day, after the reporters had left, Pritchard was hustled into Peary's cabin and put through what the cabin boy later described as "the third degree" concerning everything he knew about Cook and his journey.

After a stay of thirteen days in Labrador, Peary finally gave orders to get underway, and *Roosevelt* left on the morning of September 18. Three days later, she reached Sydney, Nova Scotia, pulling into the harbor flying an American flag that had a band of white running diagonally through its field of stars with the black-lettered words NORTH POLE.

Among the three thousand spectators lining the waterfront to greet Peary were Josephine and their two children, who had been in Sydney a week awaiting *Roosevelt*'s arrival. Schools and businesses were closed, and the prime minister headed the official welcoming committee. Encouraged to make a statement, Peary offered his thanks. "If a man devotes himself to the accomplishment of one thing and sticks to it long enough, makes it the object of his whole life, he is bound to win."

It was the end of Peary's long seaward journey, for he would the next day board a train for home with his family, while Bartlett and his crew would return *Roosevelt*, and the other expedition members, to New York.

When a reporter advised Peary that Cook had landed in New York the day before to ten thousand cheering people at dockside, Peary "snapped his great jaws and glared fiercely from under his bushy eyebrows."

Peary received a telegram prior to his departure. Immediately after reading it, he sought out the correspondents and read a prepared statement:

Acting on the advice of General Hubbard and Mr. Bridgman, the president and secretary of the Peary Arctic Club, I wish to express my thanks to all my friends for their kind offers and invitations, and also to beg to say that I prefer to accept no invitations to a public reception or ovation until the present controversy has been settled by competent authority.

On the train ride home, Peary was met by Hubbard, heading north to intercept Peary. A strategy began to take shape, and Bridgman, who rode the rest of the way to Maine with Peary, soon had his own statement for the press:

Concerning Dr. Cook . . . let him submit his records and data to some competent authority, and let that authority draw its own conclusions from the notes and records. . . . Competent authority will determine from them where Dr. Cook has been. . . . All that is wanted is the data and records made in the Arctic.

Taken at face value, Peary's public challenge seemed fair enough.

Only a few people yet knew about Cook's boxes of instruments and records "made in the Arctic" that Peary refused to bring back on *Roosevelt* and that now lay hidden in the rocks on the rugged northern Greenland coast.

CHAPTER NINETEEN

SEIZED BY A
"HEARTSICKNESS"

SHORTLY AFTER MIDNIGHT on September 21, 1909, *Oscar II* arrived off Fire Island, where she waited to enter quarantine.

With the lights of New York glittering in the distance, Cook spoke with several newspaper reporters who had boarded. His absence of two and a half years seemed like a decade, he noted. Although "anxious to get ashore," he admitted he did not look forward to "the ordeal of landing tomorrow." Cook said he preferred landing "quickly and quietly without a repetition of the scenes at Copenhagen. I hope that I shall be left in peace with my family."

The reporters brought aboard the New York newspapers, and Cook read of Peary's polar claim, as well as his stinging accusations. Asked for his reaction to the latter, Cook said, "When I land I will examine the charges and reply when the proper time comes. . . . I have already expressed my readiness to place my observations before a committee . . . and the verdict of that committee will justify my story." He estimated that within "two months at the outside" his records and instruments would be ready for the "official tests." He explained how they would then be sent to Copenhagen University "as it was the first to officially recognize [his] work in the discovery of the Pole."

Early the next morning, ten days after he had stepped onto *Oscar II* a stranger to everyone aboard, Cook disembarked a friend to passen-

gers, officers, and crew alike, many of whom had sought to have their
picture with him, requests he had tirelessly accommodated. To the
cheers of hundreds of passengers and crew, the explorer descended the
companionway to a tug where Marie and their daughters awaited
him. Husband and wife embraced and kissed like long-lost lovers, in
a scene reminiscent, one newspaper gushed, of "the romance of the
wandering Ulysses and his faithful Penelope retold." Cook picked up
the girls, Ruth and Helen, in turn, bestowing kisses on them.

The Cooks soon transferred to the steamer *Grand Republic*, which
carried an official reception committee that included a beaming
John Bradley. A triumphant excursion to Brooklyn followed, complete with a serenade of "great tooting whistles in honor of the
explorer" and a full band that alternated playing the "Star Spangled
Banner" and "Hail to the Chief." Waiting at the South Fifth Street
dock was a sea of enthusiastic well-wishers, including hundreds of
children let out of school for the occasion, waving white handkerchiefs and American flags.

Upon arriving in his hometown, Cook issued a statement that
began, "I have come from the Pole." He promised to tell his story
and share his data "not to enter into arguments . . . but to present a
clear record of a piece of work over which [he had] a right to display
a certain amount of pride." He and his family were then taken on an
automobile parade through Brooklyn.

After they checked into the Waldorf-Astoria in midtown
Manhattan to escape the celebrating throngs and hordes of
reporters, Marie broke the news that they had been wiped out financially (during the nationwide Panic of 1907) by the failure of the
respected Knickerbocker Trust, where their money had been
deposited. Marie's own net worth had evaporated, too, and their
Bushwick Avenue home had been lost in foreclosure. In his long
absence, she had been borrowing to support herself and the children
while they stayed with various friends in Brooklyn and Maine. Cook
assured her things would be different now that he was back. He told
her of his plans for lecturing and publishing, which he thought
would keep him so busy for several years that he had no immediate
plans to resume his practice of medicine.

After spending most of the following day "seeking rest and seclusion," Cook that evening faced a group of newspaper representatives for two hours, submitting "cheerfully to one of the severest cross-examinations" to which he had been subjected. The Associated Press reported that Cook "did not depart greatly from his original story under the cross-fire of his forty inquisitors."

"Why did you not want Commander Peary to know of your exploit?"

Cook straightened himself in his chair, and replied "in the same steady tone" that he had used since entering the room. "Why should I inform Peary sooner than the rest of the world? He wouldn't have done so."

"Do you look upon Commander Peary as a friend or as an enemy?"

Showing what was described as a "rather rueful smile," Cook answered, "I must say I do not know. I have treated Mr. Peary as a friend, and until I know more about the situation, I shall continue to do the same."

When a question was asked—motivated perhaps by either trickery or ignorance—whether Cook's observations at the Pole were made with the aid of the North Star, he sat back in his chair and chuckled.

"How can the North Star be seen when the sun is shining all the time?"

His observations at the Pole, Cook explained patiently, all had to be made by means of measuring the sun's altitude in the sky.*

He was asked about the importance of producing the sextant used to take the measurements—what if something happened to Whitney and he failed to return? Cook's expression turned serious. He said his observations might be doubted if his instruments were lost and unable to be examined by experts.

---

*At the Poles, the height of the sun in the sky varies little and casts shadows close to uniform length. On April 22, 1908, Cook reported measuring with his sextant the height of the sun in the sky at intervals for twenty-four consecutive hours—ranging from 12 degrees, 9 minutes, 30 seconds, at 6 a.m. to 12 degrees, 18 minutes, 40 seconds, at 6 p.m. At the same time, he measured the length of the shadow cast by Etukishook standing at the center of a marked circle.

"Did you know Mr. Whitney when you had met him on your return?"

"No, I did not."

"What caused you to have such confidence in Mr. Whitney that you entrusted your instruments to him?"

"Circumstances arose while I was with him that justified my confidence. I gave him the instruments to bring back because I thought they would be less liable to injury on board his vessel than if I took them across glaciers and rough ice-covered country."

Asked whether he objected to showing his diary, Cook produced "a small octavo notebook which he showed freely." It was described by the press as a book of 176 pages, each "filled with fifty or sixty lines of pencilled writing in the most minute characters," totaling some 100,000 words.

That night, Cook was honored with a gala black-tie dinner at the Waldorf-Astoria hosted by the Arctic Club of America, a group composed of men who had explored the world's frigid seas or backed expeditions that had. Seated at tables elegantly set with white tablecloths and centerpieces of fresh-cut flowers, more than a thousand well-heeled men and a sprinkling of wives and daughters applauded and toasted the explorer, then listened attentively to his recital of polar attainment. Cook concluded by naming a number of intrepid explorers, Peary included, who had risked everything in pursuit of the Pole.

Four days later, Cook received a wire from Indian Harbour, Labrador—the first word he had heard from Whitney since they parted five months earlier in northern Greenland.

STARTED FOR HOME *ROOSEVELT*. NOTHING ARRIVED FOR ME. PEARY WOULD ALLOW NOTHING BELONGING TO YOU ON BOARD. SAID TO LEAVE EVERYTHING IN CACHE ETAH. MET CAPTAIN SAM [AT] NORTH STAR. DID NOT GO BACK. AFTER GOING SCHOONER ST. JOHN'S, TAKE STEAMER HOME. HOPE YOU WELL. SEE YOU SOON. EXPLAIN ALL. GOOD SHOOTING.

Cook was seized by a "heartsickness" at the news that Whitney had been forced by Peary to not bring home the "very material with which [he] might have dispelled suspicion and quelled the storm of unmerited abuse." Had he foreseen anything of the kind, Cook would have taken his instruments with him to Upernavik and supplied his "observations and notes at once." In retrospect, he said about his leaving them behind, "that was my folly—for which fate made me pay." It would be impossible, he knew, to show in his report to Copenhagen a "continuous line of observations." He also had no corrections for the instruments or any way for them to be checked for accuracy. Beyond that: "I had some copies of [my] original data, but they were not complete. I should have to rest my whole case on a report with reduced observations," rather like providing the answers on a mathematics test, not the equations used to reach those solutions—unacceptable in any prep school classroom.

As correspondents descended upon Whitney in Labrador, news that Cook's instruments and records had been booted off Peary's ship quickly spread. Trailed by reporters as he tried to take a quiet stroll through the park with his family, Cook was asked whether this would "complicate matters" for him.

"Well, I don't know," he replied haltingly.

"But you have said that without the instruments which you left with Mr. Whitney for safekeeping you would be unable to conclusively corroborate all of the proofs which you now have in your possession."

The explorer was noticeably "slow in answering." He seemed to stare into "blank space" before finally speaking. "I had counted on his bringing the instruments and everything with him. Naturally, I am disappointed."

What was to stop him, Cook was pressed, from sending a ship at once to Etah to retrieve the missing items?

"Nothing much," Cook replied with a wan smile, "except the ice and darkness, but that is enough."

Any effort to return the instruments and data would have to await summer. Cook also knew that unless responsible Eskimos had been given "strong explicit instructions" about protecting the cache of instruments and papers, "all would be lost" within a year through curiosity and pilferage.

As Americans learned of the loss of Cook's property, few missed Peary's double-dealing. "Mr. Peary insists that Dr. Cook prove his story," editorialized the *Philadelphia Inquirer*, "but it would seem as if Peary has been doing everything possible to hinder Cook." The *New York Evening Journal* expressed similarly strong sentiments on September 27: "The *Evening Journal* doesn't know who discovered the Pole. . . . It looks very much, however, as though Peary believed that Cook made the discovery. If not, why refuse to bring Cook's instruments and records? Those instruments and records surely could have been made to prove the falseness of Cook's claim, if it be false." That same day, the *New York Herald* published an editorial chastising Peary. "Dr. Cook's flag and sledge and records buried in the rocks at Etah are more damaging to Mr. Peary's case than they could possibly be if brought back on *Roosevelt*."

The only major newspaper to come to Peary's defense on the subject of Cook's belongings was the *New York Times*, which had finally begun publishing Peary's own account of reaching the North Pole.* "Suppose Commander Peary had allowed the boxes to remain on board *Roosevelt*, had brought them here and caused them to be delivered to the Doctor? What defense would he have had against a possible charge that records had been abstracted or instruments tampered with?"

Cook was the early public favorite. In a *Pittsburgh Press* poll of its readers, 73,238 were found to believe Cook had discovered the North Pole; only 2,814 believed Peary had done so. Some 18,000 thought Peary arrived at the Pole a year after Cook's discovery, while 58,009 believed that Peary had not reached the North Pole at all. Other newspaper polls showed similar pro-Cook results; the *Watertown (New York) Times* had it 3 to 1 for Cook, and the *Toledo (Ohio) Blade* found 550 to 10 in favor of Cook.

Cook's polar claim had been initially attacked by Peary Arctic Club officials for reporting an average speed across the ice of some

---

*As explorers and geographers had the first opportunity to compare the two polar narratives, they found Peary's "decidedly confirming Cook's story in several significant particulars and raising no points of disagreement," reported the *New York Daily Tribune*.

fifteen miles a day. They pointed out that the great ice traveler
Nansen could do no better than fourteen miles a day and often averaged much less, and the Abruzzi expedition, in setting its farthest-
north record in 1898, averaged less than seven miles daily. Then
came Peary's own reports: during his last three hundred miles to the
Pole (after Bartlett left) and back, he would have had to average in
excess of *thirty miles per day* to make the distances he claimed. Up to
that time, Peary's best daily average had been twelve miles. Peary
Arctic Club members ceased commenting on Cook's speed on the
polar ice, although their campaign against the explorer who claimed
to be the first at the Pole was ceaseless, involving press releases,
interviews, and much more. "I want this conducted like a presidential election campaign," Peary had written Hubbard, the club's
president, and the old explorer's strategy for a total mobilization to
win the day was being carried out. The names of Thomas Hubbard
and Herbert Bridgman, as surrogates for Peary, appeared nearly
daily in newspapers—clamoring for Cook's proof of his polar attainment (while Peary offered none of his own), attacking Cook's narratives, comments, and character. Their intent was clear: "to aid Peary
in destroying Cook," reported the *Lincoln (Nebraska) Evening News*.
Only by the annihilation of Cook's reputation, personally and pro-
fessionally, would Peary gain the Pole.

In mid-October, the Peary Arctic Club released an affidavit signed
by Edward Barrill, the Montana blacksmith who had accompanied
Cook on the 1906 McKinley expedition. After years of claiming to
friends, neighbors, and even his hometown newspaper in Darby,
Montana, that he had gone to the summit with Cook—proudly dis-
playing a complimentary copy of Cook's McKinley book, *To the Top of
the Continent,* which he had received upon its publication in 1908—
Barrill now changed his story. At no time did he and Cook get to the
top of Mount McKinley—in fact, they went no higher than about
eight thousand feet. Barrill had kept an expedition diary, filled with
his characteristic misspellings and ungrammatical phrasing, that he
had long shown to anyone remotely interested in his historic
McKinley climb. He now stated that Cook had at some point dictated false entries to him—presumably with the ungrammatical

phrasing and all, even though Cook always spoke and wrote like the learned man that he was. The conquest of McKinley was all a big hoax, Barrill claimed. The affidavit was published verbatim in a newspaper owned by Hubbard, the *New York Globe*, and thereafter reprinted in papers across the country.

"The Barrill affidavit was paid for, I am sure," Cook told reporters the day after its release. "It is a lie, made from whole cloth."

It was an astoundingly sudden reversal from Barrill, given that only a month earlier, upon the exciting news of Cook having discovered the North Pole, he proudly told a correspondent in Montana that he and Cook "were the only ones who climbed McKinley." Two weeks later, the attorney J. M. Ashton, retained by the Peary Arctic Club, had summoned Barrill to his Tacoma office and opened negotiations with Barrill regarding compensation for his signing the affidavit alleging that Cook had lied about their ascent of McKinley.*

Following the release of the Barrill affidavit, Hubbard declared the McKinley matter of vital importance in terms of resolving the North Pole dispute, quoting a Latin maxim to the effect that a man who was once a liar is always a liar. He meant, of course, Cook. But it could well have been said about Barrill, a curious choice of witnesses to parade forth to disprove another man's veracity. The

---

*Rumors persisted of a payoff to Barrill, although they were denied at the time by Hubbard, who insisted the blacksmith had received no more than $200 in travel expenses. In the *New York Herald* (October 24, 1909), Barrill's business partner, C. G. Bridgeford, reported that Barrill told him he had to go to Tacoma to see a representative of the Peary Arctic Club and "this means from $5,000 to $10,000 to me." An affidavit signed by a local attorney quoted a Tacoma bank bookkeeper, J. D. Burke, who claimed to have observed Barrill receiving, in an off-the-books transaction one day, $1,500 in $100 bills, which he secreted in his money belt. A financial transaction was eventually documented in 1989, when a copy of a bank draft for $5,000—worth more than $250,000 in today's buying power—was found at the National Archives in a section of the Peary Collection recently opened to the public. The draft was written by Ashton, payable to "myself" and charged to Hubbard's Fidelity Trust account—dated October 1, the day after Ashton wired Hubbard "will run over amount stated—many . . . wild demands." The Barrill affidavit was notarized on October 4. Whatever Barrill received, whether a lump sum or series of payments, the blacksmith and mountain guide was able to purchase a five-bedroom home and orchard and become the first resident of Darby, Montana—deep in the Bitter Root Mountains—to own an automobile.

Nation considered Barrill's affidavit "not conclusive evidence of the falsity of the Doctor's story; for, certainly, a man who signs a sworn statement that he had been a voluntary participant in the concoction of an elaborate and swindling falsehood cannot be accepted as an unimpeachable witness when he swears that he had lied." Perhaps that is why, after being whisked east by the Peary Arctic Club to testify against Cook at an Explorers Club hearing into the McKinley matter, Barrill was kept out of sight and put on a train back to Montana.

Barely a week after the Barrill affidavit, Peary released to the press, from his home in Maine, a fourteen-point, 2,500-word indictment of Cook listing all the reasons why his competitor's polar claim should not be accepted. Peary offered up as proof the testimony Ahwelah and Etukishook gave aboard *Roosevelt*, in which the two natives were said to have mapped their route, showing they traveled with Cook only a few marches north after leaving land at Axel Heiberg. One unanswered question, posed by more than a few pundits, was why, if Cook went only a few days north before turning around and heading south, did he avoid his own caches and force upon himself a year of near starvation? Peary also claimed to have carefully inspected Cook's sledge at Etah and determined it would not stand up to Arctic service—a strange charge since Cook had, without question, been in the Arctic more than a year with that very sledge. Also left unanswered was the question why Peary, if convinced that the sledge served as compelling evidence against a future claim by Cook that he had traveled any distance north of land, had not brought it home on *Roosevelt* as proof.

Beginning with an appearance at Carnegie Hall, Cook had launched a national lecture tour in late September. In all, he made nearly seventy appearances in twenty-four days and gave press interviews in every city and town he visited. Increasingly, he found himself on the defensive, if not about what his Eskimos purportedly told Peary's men, then about Barrill or McKinley or any number of outlandish and untrue stories that surfaced, including a silly one that made him the brunt of editorial cartoons for reportedly having hauled to the Pole a barrel of gumdrops with which to bribe the Eskimos.

For Cook, the loss of his instruments and data remained always near the surface, and with it the "growing uncertainty" of proving his claim. Unable to sleep, he fought despair and a "mental depression" that resulted in "desperate premonitions." He contracted a severe case of laryngitis in Washington, D.C., and took it to Baltimore and Pittsburgh. In St. Louis, where he was reportedly guaranteed $10,000 for his appearance before his biggest audience—more than twelve thousand people—he could not speak above a whisper and felt "feverish and mentally dazed" the entire lecture.

Along with the "physical anguish," Cook sensed growing "hostility" and began to feel "persecuted." The sight of crowds that he had once embraced now filled him with a "growing sort of terror." The pursuit by reporters, and even "good-natured demonstrations of friendliness," irritated him. His medical training allowed him to recognize he had passed from occasional depression into "dangerous periods of nervous tension." Cook abruptly ended his lecture tour in late October, canceling dozens of booked appearances, and went into seclusion to recover his health and work on his report for Copenhagen.

Since many of his field papers had been left in Greenland with his instruments and other possessions, he decided against sending to the university those portions of his original record that he still retained. Since they would not form a complete record, which would have been expected of him, he decided instead to ask Copenhagen to accept a reconstruction of his expedition from his original diary and other papers he had kept with him. Cook completed his reconstruction in late November and had it dispatched by personal courier to Copenhagen. He requested that the university consider the report an interim one and render a neutral judgment until an attempt could be made to retrieve his lost records the following year.

The committee of the University of Copenhagen formed to examine Cook's polar records received his report on December 8, 1909. The typewritten reconstruction was, of course, not at all what they expected, and the members were gravely disappointed. Two weeks later, the committee announced that Cook's report did not constitute proof that he reached the North Pole. Their official verdict was

"Not Proven," which many U.S. newspapers and readers interpreted to mean that Denmark, which had first honored Cook for his discovery, had determined that he had not reached the North Pole.

Cook was nowhere to be located by the horde of reporters seeking comment from him. Upon handing his final report to his secretary at the Waldorf-Astoria, he had said, "Now I'll be able to get some sleep," and took a cab for Penn Station. Cook later admitted to having been as confused by the advice he received from friends as by the attacks of his "foes." Many friends thought he should attack Peary in the same manner Peary was attacking him. Others counseled him to form his own organization to counter the attacks of the Peary Arctic Club. "Such a course," Cook wrote, "was distasteful to me . . . the selfish, envious origin of all of Mr. Peary's charges seemed evident."

A few days later, Marie received a letter from Canada, telling her when and where to meet him in Europe. "My life is more important than the Polar matter," he wrote, "which can wait if necessary."

The Copenhagen verdict, the well-financed campaign against him, and his self-imposed exile ensured that the man who had returned a hero two months earlier still had a long way to fall.

Not that Cook didn't still have his champions. Maurice Egan, the American minister to Denmark who had been among the first to greet him in Copenhagen, told the press he still believed Cook had reached the North Pole. "The decision of the Danish University is, of course, final," Egan said. "Unless the matter should be reopened by the presentation of the material belonging to Cook, which Harry Whitney was compelled to leave at Etah."

Those polar instruments and records of Cook's would never be found.

AFTERMATH

ROBERT PEARY found his acceptance as the discoverer of the North Pole to be neither immediate nor unanimous, a terrible disappointment that he believed tarnished his prize and which would rankle him for the rest of his days.

His claim of having reached the Pole did, however, receive a rapid endorsement from his allies at the National Geographic Society (NGS). As a private, for-profit publishing venture, the NGS was not the U.S. equivalent of the Royal Geographical Society of London or any of the other established and independent geographical organizations in the world. Nonetheless, the NGS anointed itself the arbitrator of the conflicting claims of the two Americans, inviting Peary and Cook in early October 1909 to submit their polar records for review. It was an unprecedented role for the NGS, which had never before concerned itself with reviewing records of explorers, not even Peary's evidence of attaining his farthest north before awarding him a medal in 1906. The NGS wired Copenhagen requesting that the Danish university waive its first claim to Cook's records, which the school declined to do. Given Peary's close association with the society, which had a history of supporting his work (including $1,000 donated toward his last polar expedition), Peary had every reason to expect favorable treatment, and he quickly accepted the offer.

A three-man committee was formed from the NGS's membership

rolls to examine Peary's claim; one member, Henry Gannett, a geographer, was a personal friend of Peary's; another member, O. H. Tittman, was the superintendent of the U.S. Coast and Geodetic Survey, to which Peary had been officially assigned (at his full naval pay) for his last expedition; the third member, Colby M. Chester, a retired Navy admiral, had already been quoted as "a skeptic on the question of the discovery of the Pole by Cook." Peary first turned over to the committee only the data up to the point when Bartlett turned back—that portion for which Peary claimed ordinary speeds over the ice and had with him credible witnesses who took their own observations. After reviewing these records for ten days, the subcommittee asked for the data pertaining to the remainder of the trip to and from the Pole. Peary brought these records to Washington, D.C., arriving on November 1, 1909. The examination, Peary later testified, took place that evening in the baggage room of the train station; Peary opened his trunk and the men peered inside, neither reading the records nor determining the accuracy of the instruments. They then adjourned to the home of Admiral Chester for dinner. Two days later, the National Geographic Society announced that Peary proved he had reached the North Pole on April 6, 1909.

A bill pushed by Peary's well-connected supporters to have him recognized as the discoverer of the North Pole, retired as a rear admiral, and receive an annual pension was referred to the House Committee on Naval Affairs in early 1910. The Naval Affairs' Subcommittee on Private Bills took testimony from the three members of the National Geographic Society's investigating committee, leading one congressman to label the examination of Peary's North Pole data at the railway station "perfunctory and hasty." The subcommittee requested Peary's records, but he declined, claiming he was unable to present his proofs because of publishing contracts. The subcommittee, noting that Peary had thrown up a "veil of secrecy . . . about his proofs and records," postponed further hearings until Peary was willing to comply with its request.

In spite of his standoff with Congress, the endorsement of the NGS—together with Cook's own difficulties over the verdict of the University of Copenhagen and the McKinley issue—swung the polar debate in Peary's favor. One by one, most institutions and reference book publishers came to accept Peary's North Pole claim. He spent the summer of 1910 in Europe, collecting honors awarded to him by foreign societies and universities in a dozen countries, not on the basis of any independent verification of his data but solely on the recognition of the National Geographic Society.

With controversy still brewing over his unprecedented speeds across the pack ice after Bartlett left—Peary flatly denied having spent any significant time riding on a sledge—that winter he submitted to a walking test. Required to walk a total of fifty miles in no more than twenty hours over three consecutive days—a considerably slower pace than he reported for the week prior to reaching the Pole and the return trip—Peary managed to do so on his crippled feet, although the test had limited application to one's ability to snowshoe over ice and snow across rough terrain.

After publication of his exclusive narrative for a national periodical, *Hampton's Magazine,* and the release of his book *The North Pole,* Peary agreed to appear before Congress in January 1911, and he did so for three consecutive days. In anticipation of his appearance, his supporters had done their homework, including the hiring of a lobbyist to count and influence votes and the printing of a pamphlet, *How Peary Reached the North Pole,* distributed to every member of Congress. Peary also paid for a recomputation of his observations, hiring two employees of the U.S. Coast and Geodetic Survey to carefully rework his polar observations. So organized was the effort to facilitate passage of the Peary bill that one member of the Private Bills Subcommittee, Representative R. B. Macon, called it "a paid lobby of the Peary Arctic Club and the National Geographic Society."

Asked by a congressman whether the observations he reported at the Pole could have been done by someone who wasn't there, Peary said some experts believed so and others did not. When it was pointed out that two witnesses—the two Coast and Geodetic surveyors he had hired to assist him—had testified that it *was* possible for someone with sufficient knowledge of mathematics to construct a phony observation, Peary shrugged it off as personal opinion.

Asked to leave his North Pole diary and data he had brought with him for further examination by subcommittee members and staff, Peary declined.

A cursory review of the handwritten diary led one congressman to note that it "shows no finger marks or rough usage; a very clean kept book." Beyond that, the diary offered no record of the thirty hours Peary spent in the vicinity of the Pole, and several pages were blank. The entry for April 6, when he supposedly reached the Pole, made no mention of the historic feat. Rather, a loose-leaf page had been inserted, declaring, "The Pole at last!!! The prize of 3 centuries, my dream & ambition for 28 years. *Mine* at last."

The diary's pristine condition caused Henry T. Helgesen of North Dakota considerable consternation. "Pemmican is the staple article of food," he said. "Its great value lies in its greasy quality. How was it possible to handle this greasy food and without washing write in a diary daily and at the end of two months have that same diary show no finger marks or rough usage?"

With Peary offering no suitable answers to such vexing questions, Representative Ernest W. Roberts labeled portions of his testimony "vague and uncertain." The chairman of the subcommittee, Thomas S. Butler of Pennsylvania, otherwise sympathetic to Peary's cause, was exasperated by the time Peary had concluded his testimony. "We have your word for it, and we have these observations to show you were at the North Pole," Butler told Peary. "Your word and your proofs. To me, as a member of this committee, I accept your word; but your proofs, I know nothing at all about."

The subcommittee voted 4 to 3 to move an amended version of the bill. The minority placed on the record "deep-seated doubts" about the accuracy of Peary's observations. The issue was finally decided on Peary's recomputed observations, although there were still doubts. "Assuming the observations were made as [Peary] states they were made . . . [Peary] was within a very short distance of the Pole; sufficiently near to warrant the claim." Rather than declaring him to be the discoverer of the North Pole, however, the bill approved by Congress credited Peary for "Arctic exploration result-

ing in [his] reaching the North Pole." The bill was signed into law
by President Taft on March 4, 1911; Peary was placed on the retired
list of the Navy's Corps of Civil Engineers with the rank of rear
admiral and given a $6,000 annual pension for life.

Embittered by what he perceived to be the antagonistic examination of his work and the personal grilling he had been subjected to
by Congress, Peary never again showed his polar diary, field papers,
or other data.

In 1913, Donald MacMillan, a member of Peary's last polar expedition who for the remainder of his long life remained a loyal Peary
supporter, went in search of Peary's Crocker Land. MacMillan did
so, in part, to repudiate Cook, who had reported passing that location on his return from the Pole and finding only ice where Peary
had charted the new land in 1906. A disappointed MacMillan, however, found nothing but pack ice where Peary had reported the new
land, thereby giving credence to Cook's report.

Additional discoveries of Peary's, such as "Peary Channel,"
"Peary Land," and "East Greenland Sea," were also proven nonexistent by other explorers, one of whom, Mylius Erichsen, misled
by a Peary map of northern Greenland, died when he was unable
to get through to an area where game was plentiful. Other Peary
discoveries, including "Jesup Land" and "Cape Thomas Hubbard,"
were disallowed because they had previously been found and
named by others. By 1916, the U.S. Navy Hydrographic Office
had removed most of Peary's discoveries from government maps
and charts.

In the years following his congressional testimony, Peary rarely
spoke publicly of the North Pole. He turned to other interests—
spending time with his family on Eagle Island, learning how to fly
and becoming an early advocate for air power, and briefly considering a run for the U.S. Senate. When America entered the world war,
Peary offered his services and organized the National Aerial Coast
Patrol Commission, which established land-based patrol units on
the eastern seaboard and helped train hundreds of pilots.

Following the armistice in 1918, Peary's health failed because of
pernicious anemia, the blood disease diagnosed in 1901 by Cook,

who had warned Peary to learn dietary lessons from the Eskimos, who never contracted scurvy or anemia—advice Peary had rejected. Peary's last public appearance was at a National Geographic Society program in 1919. Several hospitalizations and thirty-five blood transfusions later, Peary died on February 20, 1920, at the age of sixty-three, the victim of an Arctic malady.

Peary was buried an American hero at Arlington National Cemetery. A monument was dedicated at his grave site two years later. Inscribed on a granite spheroid representing Earth were words Peary had voiced many years earlier when trapped in an Arctic storm and unable to advance northward: *"I shall find a way or make one."*

Through thirty-two years of marriage and seven Arctic expeditions, Josephine continued to support and encourage her husband, in spite of the heartache of his absence and even abandonment. Though she outlived her beloved by thirty-five years, her family and friends observed that something inside her went with him. Josephine died in 1955 at age ninety-three and was buried not far from the grave of her husband. The Navy chaplain officiating at the graveside ceremonies said it was fitting that Josephine should rest in Arlington, too, because "her courage and devotion have achieved an honored place in our nation."

In 1988, the *National Geographic*, shortly after Peary's long-suppressed North Pole diary and data had been released by his heirs, published an article strongly suggesting that Peary, knowing he had failed in his final attempt, faked his 1909 claim to have reached the North Pole.

"Through 75 years the sole records upon which Peary based his claim have kept their silence, locked away from public scrutiny," wrote editor Wilbur E. Garrett, who described the magazine as "devoted to a once-in-a-century bit of introspection . . . holding up a mirror to ourselves for a change."

National Geographic concluded that Peary had missed the North Pole, ending up as far as eighty miles to the left.

FREDERICK COOK returned to America in late 1910 a vanquished hero. Having realized his "error in so long remaining silent," he settled into the Palatine Hotel in Newburgh, New York, sixty miles up the Hudson River from Manhattan, to write the story of his North Pole discovery for *Hampton's Magazine*, which had already published Peary's story, "The Conquest of the North Pole." The notion of "addressing the same public, through the same medium" as Peary had "strongly influenced" Cook to accept the magazine's offer.

The article, "Dr. Cook's Own Story," was printed in January 1911, the same month Peary went before the congressional subcommittee with his data. Weeks earlier, Cook had okayed the proofs and signed each galley page, then rejoined his family in London in anticipation of moving back to the United States, hopeful that the *Hampton's* piece would be the beginning of his public rehabilitation. Thereafter, the magazine's editors "made insertions and eliminations," according to a *Hampton's* editorial stenographer, Lilian Kiel, who later testified to the magazine's editors' "cutting through the galley proofs and inserting . . . Dr. Cook's confession." (While Peary's contract with *Hampton's* had expressly forbidden any editorial changes without his approval, Cook had signed a contract with no such provision.) Those changes resulted in a newly cast article billed on the cover as "Dr. Cook's Confession," in which Cook claimed "mental unbalancement" when he first told of having reached the North Pole. "After mature thought," Cook allegedly wrote, "I confess that I do not know absolutely whether I reached the Pole or not. . . . I have never questioned Commander Peary's claim to the discovery of the North Pole. I do not now. I did not consciously try to filch an honour which belongs alone to Commander Peary." To boost newsstand sales, *Hampton's* sent out a widely distributed press release concerning Cook's confession and "insanity plea." In many respects, the false confession was the worst and most bitter blow yet to Cook. *Hampton's* release and story were quoted in hundreds of newspapers, with the public assuming that Cook had finally come clean. Cook announced his "amazed indignation" at the magazine running "a sensation-provoking lie"—"I had made no confession," he said—but his denial was buried by most papers.

Later in 1911, following a year's work done mostly while he lived under an assumed name in hotels throughout Europe, Cook's book *My Attainment of the Pole* was published. In its dedication—believed to have been the first one in which a polar explorer dedicated a book to the Arctic natives—he wrote,

> To the Indian who invented pemmican and snowshoes;
> To the Eskimo who gave the art of sled traveling;
> To this twin family of wild folk who have no flag
> Goes the first credit.

The dedication seemed fitting, for Cook's book was filled with rich details about the aboriginal residents of the Arctic; clearly, he had not only sought the athletic feat of discovering new territories but also striven to learn about the culture of the natives he met along the way. As for the discovery of the North Pole, Cook wrote that he was prepared for history to render the final judgment. "History demonstrates that the book which gives the final authoritative narrative is the test of an explorer's claims. . . . Figures must inevitably be inadequate and any convincing proof that can exist is to be found only in the narrative account of such a quest." In the book's final paragraph, Cook wrote, "I have stated my case, presented my proofs. As to the relative merits of my claim, and Mr. Peary's, place the two records side by side. Compare them. I shall be satisfied with your decision."

While Cook acknowledged being "uncertain as to having reached the exact mathematical Pole," he believed he had gotten as close as any man of his day could intelligently claim. Given the ever-drifting ice pack, placing the toe of one's boot on the exact spot was rather like hitting a constantly moving target with a dart. Just how close did one have to come in order to claim the Pole? within a hundred feet? a mile? More than simply reaching that pinpoint spot on the ice at 90 degrees north for a moment in time before it drifted away, Cook yearned to be judged on the accuracy of his polar descriptions, while at the same time being recognized for having been the first to offer such details to the world—days, even weeks, ahead of Peary, who had the opportunity to read Cook's narrative before releasing his own, an advantage Peary had purposely withheld from Cook.

The points supporting Cook's claim to have reached the Pole in 1908 include the following:

• *Experience and Readiness for the Journey.* Cook had adopted many Eskimo methods of travel and designed his own sledges and other equipment. He believed in the importance of a smaller party that traveled as light as possible and lived off the land whenever possible. Experienced in Arctic travel, Cook was forty-three and in excellent shape, and he had in his company for the trek to the Pole two of the most capable native hunters and sledge drivers in the region.

• *Proven Ice Traveler.* For Cook to have traveled to and from the Pole, he would have gone approximately 2,680 miles. The uncontested part of the journey—that which Peary contended Cook's natives confirmed—amounted to 1,640 miles. Since Cook's capacity for making a long, sustained journey in the Arctic cannot be in doubt, it could be concluded that he had the ability to travel the additional 1,040 miles to reach the Pole and return.

• *Original Descriptions.* With the passage of time, Cook's original polar descriptions have held up. At the time of his journey, no one had seen the region between 87 degrees and 90 degrees north, and there was much speculation as to what would be found at the Pole, ranging from an open polar sea to land, even a new race of people. Upon his return, Cook described what he had seen: no land, a continuation of the polar ice pack, a frozen ocean in a state of continuous motion and upheaval. Subsequent accounts, including Peary's narratives, agreed with Cook's original descriptions.

• *Unknown Westerly Drift.* Caught in heavy fog on his return from the Pole, Cook navigated by dead reckoning, allowing for what he anticipated would be a slight eastward drift of the ice (previously reported in pack ice north of Ellesmere). It was not then known that the drift in the area he was passing through was westerly. As a

result, Cook and his companions were carried one hundred miles
west of their planned landfall near their caches, and the resultant
delay meant they were trapped by winter. This westward drift first
reported by Cook—between the Pole and 80 degrees north roughly
along 100 degrees longitude—was confirmed by later explorers.

• *Ice Islands.* Cook reported seeing at 88 degrees north an unusual ice
structure he described as flat-topped, and higher and thicker than sea
ice, with an upper surface marked by undulations or waves. What
Cook probably observed was an ice island, an Arctic feature never
before reported. At ten or more miles long, ice islands are "tabular
bergs" that at a distance can easily be mistaken for an island, since
most of their mass is above water, unlike that of smaller and more
common icebergs with only 10 percent exposed above the surface of
the sea. It was later discovered that ice islands originate from the ice
shelves that rim parts of the north coast of Ellesmere; when they break
off, they drift into the Arctic Ocean between Alaska and the North
Pole in a slow clockwise motion. Cook's description of the "flat-
topped" mass was largely forgotten until forty years later when several
large ice islands of the same description—named T-1, T-2, and T-3 by
oceanographers—were discovered during an aerial reconnaissance.

• *Credible and Consistent Narrative.* Cook's descriptions of his polar
trip have never been refuted, other than his reported sighting of
Bradley Land. Some modern Arctic experts believed that in reporting Bradley Land and Crocker Land (about 150 miles apart), Cook
and Peary, respectively, perhaps saw drifting ice islands. "Neither
investigated their find at close range," reported Rear Admiral C. W.
Thomas, a veteran of scientific work in the Arctic, some fifty years
after the reported sightings in 1908 and 1909. Thomas thought it
possible Cook and Peary had spotted the same ice island—"it is significant," Thomas went on, "that no one has since seen an island at
either location." Apart from that exception, no other original Arctic
description provided by Cook has ever been disproved.

Likewise, Cook stood by his descriptions of McKinley in *To the
Top of the Continent,* although because he was in the Far North and

unable to see the proofs before publication, he acknowledged that the book "contained some mistakes" in text and captions. He never indicated, however, that a photograph in the book captioned "The Top of Our Continent" was anything other than the summit, yet some fifty years later it would be proved that the peak shown in the book was a lower summit. Had the picture been miscaptioned or had Cook, without a viable picture of the summit to illustrate his book, substituted another image? During his lifetime, Cook remained confident that the written record of his descriptions would one day be verified, proving his claim to have reached the top of McKinley.

Among Cook's 1906 findings that have survived the test of time are these:

• *Elevation.* Cook reported an elevation of 20,391 feet. Readings that benefited from modern-day instruments have set the height at 20,320 feet. This would have to be categorized as a near-miss, yet an uncannily close one.

• *Twin Peaks.* In 1906, it was not known there were two peaks, one on the north and another on the south, or that the distance between the peaks was two miles or that the south peak was higher—until Cook reported same.

• *Upper Slopes.* The slopes above 18,400 feet were reported by Cook as surprisingly easy to climb compared with the lower slopes, allowing for the unexpected speed with which he reported making the climb. Every climbing party that has reached the summit since 1906 has confirmed this phenomenon.

• *View from Summit.* Cook's detailed descriptions of the summit and of the view of the surrounding panorama have been verified numerous times.

Cook's speedy climb to the summit of a mountain as high as McKinley was revolutionary in 1906, because most climbing expeditions of the day spent weeks relaying heavy loads toward the top.

Modern-day climbers favor Cook's approach of small parties, light equipment, and rapid ascents. In 1910, two miners, Peter Anderson and William Taylor, with limited mountaineering experience, set out to climb McKinley's northern peak, lower than the southern one by several hundred feet. Like Cook, they found the final ascent a relatively easy one and reported climbing from a camp at 4,500 feet below the summit to the peak, planting a fourteen-foot flagpole, and returning to camp in the course of one day. They were called liars and their claim considered a fake until three years later when another climbing party saw their flagpole sticking out of a pile of rocks on the north summit.

Cook never returned to the Arctic, although Harry Whitney and Robert Bartlett together went to northern Greenland in 1910, stopping at Etah. There were conflicting reports as to how carefully they searched for Cook's missing data and instruments, which in any case have never been recovered.

As for Etukishook and Ahwelah, Cook never saw or spoke to them again.

In 1914, U.S. Senator Miles Poindexter, who publicly favored new hearings concerning the discovery of the North Pole, received a letter from Edwin S. Brooke Jr., a member of MacMillan's 1913 expedition:

March 9, 1914

Dear Sir:

It will perhaps be a matter of interest to you to know that during the summer of 1913, as photographer of the Crocker Land Expedition, I had the opportunity of meeting and talking to the two Eskimo boys who accompanied Dr. Cook on his Polar trip.

During a good portion of my stay at Etah, I was with these two boys, and although I was unable to get a connected story from them, they told me that when they went with Dr. Cook, they went far from land for a long time.

Their statement is contrary to the one given out by members of the Peary expedition upon their return from the Arctic.

These boys are still loyal to Dr. Cook and asked about him.

I trust that this will aid you in furthering Dr. Cook's fight for Justice.

Poindexter, a former county prosecuting attorney and superior court judge from Walla Walla, Washington, introduced a resolution in April 1914, calling for new congressional hearings. In his remarks from the floor of the Senate, he said, "I have observed very closely the so-called 'Polar controversy,' and am firmly convinced that a grievous wrong has been done to Dr. Frederick A. Cook by the failure of his country to reward or officially recognize his great services in this connection." The Republican senator noted one of the more peculiar aspects of the controversy: that prior to claiming the North Pole first and incurring the wrath of Peary and his supporters, "everyone who had ever been associated with Cook in exploring expeditions spoke well of his character and ability." Only when the polar controversy arose and "grew bitter," Poindexter said, was "an attempt made to discredit Cook by attacking his account of the ascent of Mount McKinley."

As for McKinley, Poindexter observed that Hudson Stuck, credited in 1913 with reaching the mountain's summit, "corroborated in every material feature Cook's previously published account," including the "sharp backbone of the northeast ridge, the great granite rocks at the entrance to the Grand Basin, the Median Glacier, the north and south peaks, and that the south peak is higher." Poindexter found it "difficult to explain Doctor Cook's previously published accurate descriptions of these things, the first ever given, except by admitting his actual ascent of the mountain's summit."

Because Congress had previously "investigated the proofs of Robert E. Peary," Poindexter said, "it is right [we] should also investigate those of Frederick A. Cook—and if injustice has been done and merited honor has been withheld, we should now bestow it." That belated honor would involve Cook's receiving the thanks of Congress for "his discovery of the North Pole on April 21, 1909," and a gold medal of "suitable design."

Poindexter's resolution was assigned to a committee, where it died.

On January 21, 1915, a similar resolution to reopen hearings into the discovery of the North Pole was introduced in the House of Representatives, and testimony was heard a week later before the House Education Committee. Among the documents put before the committee was a list of testimonials from thirty-two Arctic explorers supporting Cook. Several witnesses sympathetic to Cook testified, including an engineer, Clark Brown, who confirmed that Cook's polar data proved that he had reached the Pole, and Lilian Kiel, the former *Hampton's* stenographer, who told how the magazine had distorted Cook's polar narrative into a sensational false confession.

Before more testimony could be heard, however, the final legislative effort to reconsider the North Pole's discovery was "squelched" in the committee, the *New York Times* reported, "which voted to proceed no further with resolutions for that purpose." The vote had been a tie, 6 to 6—hearings could not go on without the support of a majority—and had resulted from behind-the-scenes pressure applied by influential Peary supporters, who lobbied key members that Cook was a liar and yet were unwilling to take the chance that an investigation might show otherwise.

Amid the ongoing debate about America's role in the growing hostilities in Europe, Cook's chances for further congressional attention diminished, as did the public's interest in the North Pole. When an old friend, Dr. Frank Thompson of Chicago, asked Cook to utilize his exploring and geological background and investigate the potential of a Wyoming oil exploration company, Cook did so—and found a new calling, ending up in charge of field operations for New York Oil Company in Casper, Wyoming, then being named president of Cook Oil Company (although he was only a minority owner), which developed a number of successful tracks and prospered.

In 1918, when oil was discovered in Texas, Cook sold his Wyoming interests and moved his family to Fort Worth. After working for four years as a prospector and geologist in Texas and Arkansas, he founded the Petroleum Producers Association (PPA) in 1922. Many of the smaller oil companies in Texas, unable to afford the costs of locating and developing oil fields, had gone out of business or otherwise fallen on hard times. Cook's plan was to merge small companies that had weak financial backing but owned potentially valuable leases into a larger, better-financed operation. Stock in the new company was offered for sale to shareholders of the smaller companies—their choice was either to lose what they had invested in the smaller company or to risk additional dollars in the new umbrella company. If PPA succeeded, the shareholders would turn out winners; if it didn't, they stood to lose even more money. Cook, confident of results, invested most of his own net worth in PPA. Spending the majority of his time in the field managing the exploration and drilling operations, he delegated to others the marketing of PPA stock.

Although Cook had gone years without raising the subject of the North Pole, an old nemesis now reared its head: the Peary Arctic Club, as embodied by its former member Herbert Houston, then chairman of a national group soon to be known as the Better Business Bureau. In a major speech before the Associated Advertising Clubs of the World in January 1923, Houston decried what he called a "gigantic stock-reloading scheme" taking place in the Texas oil fields, which "led to the discovery of our old friend Dr. Cook. He did not discover the North Pole, but we certainly have discovered him. . . ."

Regulators were coming down hard on oil speculators as a result of the preceding year's Teapot Dome scandal, in which several members of President Harding's administration improperly leased the nation's oil reserves in Wyoming and California to private companies in exchange for cash gifts and no-interest loans.

Federal investigators quickly showed up in the PPA's offices, asking to see Cook and searching for any illegal activities. Cook cooperated, turning over the company's accounts to a government bank examiner. An order for Cook's arrest followed, and he surrendered to federal authorities on April 3, 1923. He was charged with using the mails to defraud—sending out mailers signed by him as president that overstated the oil-discovery prospects of PPA for the purpose of selling stock in the new company. A receiver was appointed to run PPA, effectively ending its operations. The assets of PPA, mainly its leases on land, were sold at bargain prices (some to Standard Oil), and PPA stockholders received only pennies back on the dollar. Among the work halted by the government takeover was Cook's test well in a Corsicana field that returned 245,000 barrels in 1922— the following year, under its new owners and as a result of deep drilling, the field produced 32,000,000 barrels of oil. Within a few years, some of the land PPA had held leases on would be part of what became known as the Yates Pool, which was the largest continental oil find in North America in the twentieth century and which created countless millionaires.

Cook's five-week trial began in October 1923, and before it was over 283 witnesses had testified. Although a bank examiner testified that PPA's books were in order—meaning there were no signs of embezzlement—the prosecution was able to convince jurors that PPA had misrepresented the company's position to potential stockholders. Sentencing was imposed immediately by the judge—U.S. District Court Judge John Killits, brought in from Ohio to hear the case because the local bench was too busy to try such a lengthy case. Before doing so, Killits unleashed a venomous tirade against Cook: "This is one of those times when your peculiar and persuasive hypnotic personality fails you, isn't it? You have at last got to the point where you can't bunco anybody. You have come to the mountain and can't reach the latitude; it's beyond you."*

Cook was sentenced to fourteen years and nine months in prison.

Months before the trial, Marie and Frederick had divorced to spare the children and protect what limited assets Marie could earn from operating a café in town. She was nonetheless in court every day, sitting close behind her former husband, and each evening she brought his dinner to the county jail for the sixteen months he awaited the outcome of an appeal, financed by $10,000 she raised from other Texas oilmen and friends.

When his appeal was exhausted, Cook entered the federal penitentiary at Leavenworth, Kansas, on April 6, 1925—a day that others were celebrating the sixteenth anniversary of Peary's discovery of the North Pole.

Cook adapted well to prison life, working the night shift in the

---

*Unknown at the time was the fact that Judge Killits was a friend to members of the Peary family. In an exchange of letters about the case with Peary's daughter, Marie Peary Stafford, Killits later wrote, "I agree with you that if [Cook] got everything that was coming to him for all the things he has done, he ought to stay in the penitentiary for life."

prison hospital and by day editing the prison newspaper, *The New Era,* in the process becoming popular with prisoners, guards, and administrators. Although he refused to see any visitors, even family—specifically asking Marie not to bring the girls to the prison— Cook did have a special guest in January 1926: Roald Amundsen, on a speaking tour of the United States.

Amundsen had in 1909 been making plans of his own to reach the North Pole, but upon hearing news of Cook and Peary, he looked southward instead. He departed in summer 1910 aboard Nansen's old ship, *Fram*, and by the following fall was in position to make an overland push for the South Pole. After careful preparations, he set out with four men, fifty-two dogs, and four sledges— like Cook, favoring a smaller party—and reached the Pole in December 1911, beating the Englishman Robert Scott by a month. Returning to Norway a hero, Amundsen had established a successful shipping business.

After his visit with Cook, during which the two old explorers talked about organizing another expedition, Amundsen stepped outside the prison to face a group of reporters. Amundsen described Cook as "the finest traveler" he had ever seen, adding that Cook was "practical, and would never say quit." Asked about the North Pole, Amundsen said Cook's claim was "as good as Peary's." His comments were widely circulated, and Amundsen was soon informed that his invitation to deliver a paid lecture to the National Geographic Society in Washington, D.C., had been withdrawn.

Cook applied for executive clemency in late 1928 and found support where he could have least expected it. The district attorney of Fort Worth wrote to President Coolidge, pointing out that there had been a large number of prosecutions of oilmen in the area, "yet no person received a sentence as severe as that given Dr. Cook." The judge who would have handled the trial, had it not been for his busy caseload, U.S. District Court Judge James Wilson of Northern District of Texas, even wrote the president in support of Cook's clemency request, declaring "the sentence in the case was excessive."

Judge Killits vehemently opposed clemency, and it was denied.

Cook, sixty-five, was paroled in March 1930. He stepped outside the walls of the prison wearing an ill-fitting suit and carrying a small suitcase. "I am tired and I am going to rest," he told the assembled reporters.

After residing in Chicago for a time with his doctor friend Frank Thompson, to whom he was paroled, Cook alternated living with the growing families of his married daughters, Ruth Hamilton and Helene Cook Vetter (who had changed the spelling of her first name).

He was in touch with Marie, living alone in southern California, and occasionally they crossed paths at the homes of their daughters. They clearly still had feelings for each other, but it was as if time had passed them by. "When you sign off with 'resigned love' I'm at a loss to know just what you mean by that word 'resigned,' " Marie wrote on May 11, 1931. "So I'm in a quandary whether to bawl you out or make love to you. I think I'll make love to you." At the bottom of the letter, he wrote a note to himself, *"Resigned to life as is,"* apparently a reminder to explain to her exactly what he meant.

The following month, Marie wrote,

> It's about midnite, and I'm a bit drunky. You have always drilled me into this idea that "it's a pleasure to be alone" but I can't agree with you there. . . . Why in heck do you always talk about "our autumn days"? There are no autumn days, why not feel that you are in the spring of life. . . . Now I must tell you something, and don't be sentimental, but the organ which is playing on my radio is playing the "Traumerie" which I think is the most beautiful thing that has ever been written, and is the same piece that Lotta Davidson played the first time I ever met you and it has always stayed in my consciousness. It is so beautiful, and I'm just going to enjoy it and wish you could hear it also. . . . I wish you lots of happiness. As ever, Marie.

Cook made a final attempt to have his North Pole case reconsidered. In February 1936, he wrote to R. Roland Redmond, president of the American Geographical Society (AGS),

> Twenty-eight years ago today I left Annoatok, Greenland, on a sledge journey which resulted in the attainment of the North Pole

on April 21, 1908. When I reached civilization eighteen months later and announced my success, I was immediately attacked by a jealous rival, and in the months and years that followed I was the target of the most vicious campaign of calumny and vituperation in history. . . . The time has come [for] a full and impartial investigation of my story. Because of its reputation for fairness and accuracy, I respectfully request that such an investigation be conducted by the American Geographic Society.

Cook's request was turned down by the AGS board, which decided such an investigation would be prohibitively expensive. Besides, there were still hard feelings among American geographers. "Dr. Cook had an opportunity to present his case 28 years ago," said an AGS spokesman. "At that time the Society expressed its willingness to investigate his case. Instead, however, he sent his material to Denmark."

On May 3, 1940, while a guest at the home of Ralph Shainwald von Ahlefeldt, a member of his 1903 McKinley expedition, and after three days and nights attending at home to his friend's dying wife, Cook suffered a stroke. As he lingered at the hospital in critical condition, Shainwald and other friends petitioned for a presidential pardon of his felony conviction. The act of mercy was granted by President Franklin Roosevelt on May 16. Photographed by a news photographer as Shainwald held the presidential pardon in front of him, Cook said feebly, "Thanks. Happy."

His spirits seemingly lifted, Cook recovered enough to leave the hospital in early June and return to the Shainwald residence to recuperate. Marie came to be with him and assist with the nursing duties. In what was in all likelihood his last letter to Marie, Cook had written three months earlier that he was "wishing for you all that is best in life," and signed, "Lovingly yours, Fred."

On July 24, Cook suffered a relapse and was again hospitalized.

One of his last visitors was another old friend: Rudolph Franke, who held Cook's hand and spoke of their winter together long ago in northern Greenland.

After lapsing into a coma, Cook died on August 5, at the age of seventy-five. He was interred in a ceremony at Forest Lawn Cemetery in Buffalo, New York, attended by sixty family members and friends. The Reverend William G. Woodward told of the man who had "literally gone to the ends of the earth" during his years of exploration, and he recalled the doctor as a "man of intrepid courage and fortitude and humility, who forgave his detractors and suffered the indignities of outrageous misfortune."

No monument marked Cook's resting place.

Marie Cook died in 1943 without ever remarrying.

Thirty-seven years after the explorer's death, in an effort spearheaded by the Frederick A. Cook Society—a group of 138 diehard members who meet annually and publish a yearly journal chronicling Cook's achievements—a simple bronze marker was dedicated at Forest Lawn. It reads,

> DR. COOK WAS THE FIRST CLAIMANT TO
> THE DISCOVERY OF THE NORTH POLE IN
> 1908. THE FIRST TO CLIMB ALASKA'S
> MOUNT McKINLEY IN 1906 AND THE
> FIRST AMERICAN TO EXPLORE BOTH
> POLAR REGIONS. HE WAS KNIGHTED BY
> THE KING OF THE BELGIANS AND BECAME
> A GOLD MEDALIST OF SEVERAL
> GEOGRAPHICAL SOCIETIES.

MORE PEOPLE have gone into space or climbed Mount Everest than have sledged to the North Pole. The vast expanse of pack ice that Peary and Cook traversed is rapidly vanishing, according to a NASA satellite study. Melting at a rate of 9 percent per decade as the world's climate grows warmer, the Arctic ice cap will disappear before the end of this century.

Peary and Cook each reported leaving at the North Pole a cairn containing a record of their attainment. Neither has ever been found.

"I shall not be satisfied until my name is known from one end of the world to the other . . . I *must* have fame."

ROBERT E. PEARY

"I reached the Pole. I climbed Mount McKinley. The controversy from my angle is at an end."

FREDERICK A. COOK

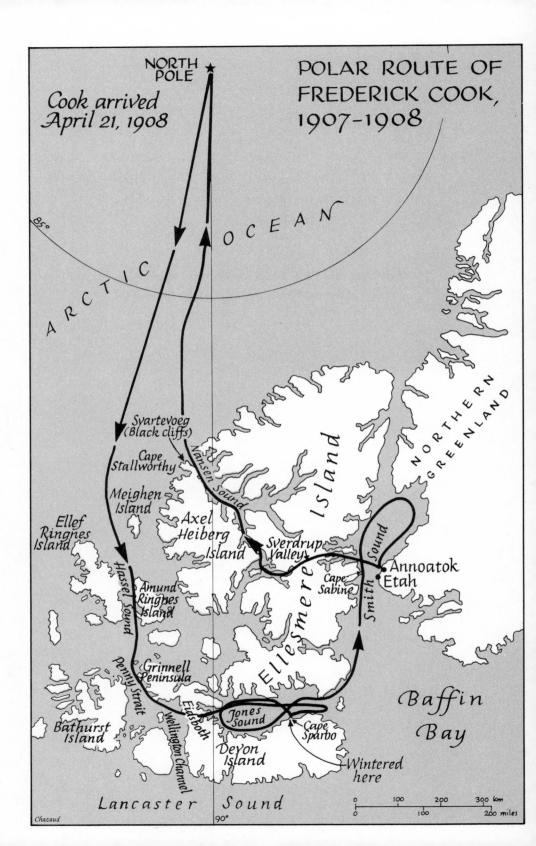

NORTH POLE

Cook arrived
April 21, 1908

POLAR ROUTE OF
FREDERICK COOK,
1907–1908

85°

A R C T I C   O C E A N

Svartevoeg
(Black cliffs)

Cape
Stallworthy

Nansen Sound

Meighen
Island

Axel
Heiberg
Island

Sverdrup
Valley

Sound

NORTHERN
GREENLAND

Ellesmere Island

Annoatok
Etah

Ellef
Ringnes
Island

Hassel Sound

Amund
Ringnes
Island

Cape
Sabine

Smith Sound

Baffin
Bay

Penny Strait

Grinnell
Peninsula

Wellington Channel

Eidsboth

Jones
Sound

Cape
Sparbo

Wintered
here

Bathurst
Island

Devon
Island

Lancaster   Sound

90°

Chazaud

| 0 | 100 | 200 | 300 km |
| 0 | 100 | 200 miles |

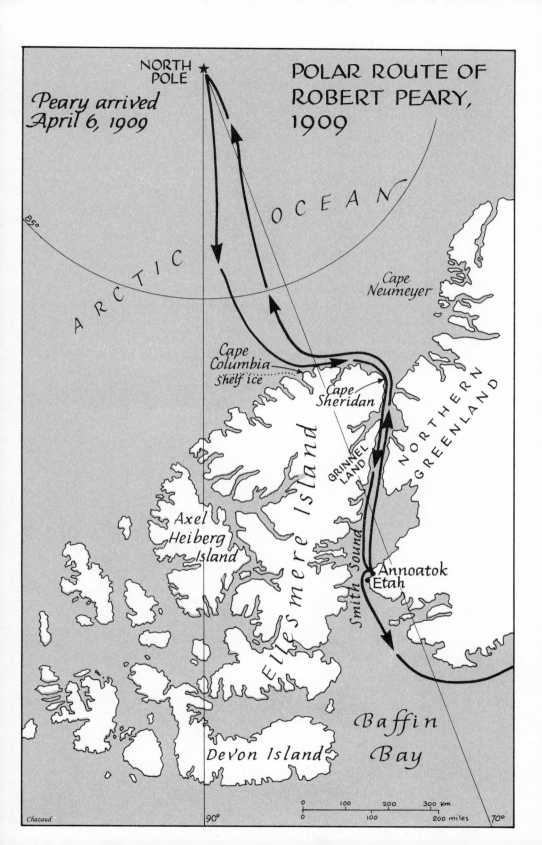

SOURCE NOTES

Complete book publication details are supplied in the bibliography. As for unpublished letters, essays, journals, and other original materials pertaining to Peary and Cook, the former may be found in the Robert E. Peary Collection at the National Archives II, in College Park, Maryland, and the latter in the Frederick A. Cook Collections at both the Library of Congress and the Byrd Polar Research Center at Ohio State University.

Prologue

24   Dialogue between Cook and Whitney: Cook, *Return from the Pole*, pp. 205–9. Further observations of this meeting: Whitney, *Hunting with the Eskimos*, pp. 268–69.

Chapter One   Call of the Northland

29   "the tears and a cold cry": Cook, "Hell Is a Cold Place," unpublished memoir, chap. 1, p. 6.

30   "restless . . . a yearning": Cook, *My Attainment of the Pole*, p. 26.

32   "Passed" and details of Cook ministering to his dying wife: unpublished manuscript by Cook's friend and longtime confidant Milton Lory, "I Knew This Man," Ohio State University Byrd Polar Archives (ca. 1935).

32   "anxiety over the disappearing pennies": Cook, *My Attainment of the Pole*, p. 27.

33   "It was as if a door": Ibid., p. 27.

34   "good times playing": Peary letter to his mother, June 18, 1865.

34   "a never-failing source": Peary essay, Feb. 3, 1872.

35   "I am going to college": Hobbs, *Peary*, p. 14.

35   "Now it is you": Peary letter to his mother, Dec. 7, 1879.

35   "resistless desire to do something": Peary letter to his mother, Aug. 16, 1880.

36   "a respectable job": Stafford, *Discoverer of the North Pole*, p. 35.

36   "I bow to her wishes": Peary diary, Sept. 6, 1880.

36   "whose fame": Peary letter to his mother, Dec. 28, 1884.

36   "a chord had vibrated intensely" and further quotations pertaining to Peary's becoming interested in the Greenland ice cap through Kane's book: Peary, *Northward over the "Great Ice,"* 1:xxxiv.

37   "My last trip": Peary letter to his mother, Feb. 27, 1887.

38   "I have written you": Peary letter to his mother, April 14, 1888.

40   "undigested book knowledge" and further quotations pertaining to Cook's opinion of his education: Cook, "Hell Is a Cold Place," chap. 1, p. 10.

40   "a thoroughly decent fellow": *American Weekly*, July 19, 1925.

41   "The life up there under the Pole" and other dialogue between Cook and Peary: Ibid.

Chapter Two   North Greenland Expedition

43   "First and foremost": Diebitsch-Peary, *My Arctic Journal*, p. 3.

43   "tramping . . . the breath of life": Peary letter to his mother, Nov. 6, 1889.

44   "This is the boy" and further quotations pertaining to Henson meeting Peary: Robinson, *Dark Companion*, pp. 51–52.

44   "body-servant": Peary, *Northward over the "Great Ice,"* 1:46.

45   "without any fingers or toes": Robinson, *Dark Companion*, p. 59.

45   "pioneering along the borders of the unknown": Cook, "Hell Is a Cold Place," chap. 1, p. 12.

45   "obey all directions" and other quotations from the expedition contract: Agreement between F. A. Cook and R. E. Peary, executed on June 4, 1891, and witnessed by Josephine Diebitsch-Peary.

48   "pale as death . . . hurt my leg": Diebitsch-Peary, *My Arctic Journal*, p. 24.

48   "Oh, my dear": Ibid., p. 27.

48   "to some place": Ibid.

Chapter Three   Arctic Tenderfoots

53–55   "Chimo" and other dialogue of first encounter with natives: Cook, "Hell Is a Cold Place," chap. 3, pp. 7–11.

56   "If we have near one family": Ibid., p. 12.

58   "The difference . . . the wisdom": Ibid., p. 13.

60   "in a land where nothing": Frederick A. Cook, "Peculiar Customs regarding Disease, Death, and Grief of the Most Northern Eskimo," *To-day*, June 1894.

60   "covered himself with glory": Peary, *Northward over the "Great Ice,"* 1:149.

61   "White men get scurvy" and other dialogue between Cook and Peary regarding scurvy: Cook, "Hell Is a Cold Place," chap. 5, pp. 11–12.

62   "cold starry heavens . . . a million years or more": Ibid., chap. 7, p. 5.

62   "uncanny feeling . . . everything glistened": Diebitsch-Peary, "Snow Baby," draft chap. 26, p. 6.

62   "queer little people . . . more like wild animals": Ibid.

62–63   "very ancient . . . 'Suna koonah' ": Diebitsch-Peary, "Among the Arctic Highlanders," *Home Queen: A Monthly Journal for Ladies*, Feb. 1896.

64   "one of the most damnable": Cook, "Hell Is a Cold Place," chap. 4, p. 1.

65   "for seldom": Astrup, *With Peary near the Pole*, p. 192.

66   "increasing suspense . . . utterly powerless": Diebitsch-Peary, *My Arctic Journal*, p. 157.

66   "Never in my life": Ibid., pp. 158–59.

Chapter Four   Death on a Glacier

68   "You get nothing": Cook, "Hell Is a Cold Place," chap. 10, p. 9.

68   "a soul of kindness": Ibid., p. 10.

72   "under any circumstances": Diebitsch-Peary, *My Arctic Journal*, p. 177.

72–73   "Well, we'll see . . . disappointment enough . . . without finding that": Ibid., p. 178.

73   "It is time" {footnote}: Cook, "Hell Is a Cold Place," chap. 10, p. 11. Kyo's death in 1902 at the hands of his own tribesman was also reported by Peary in a letter to Josephine, March 5, 1902.

74   "well and hearty": Diebitsch-Peary, *My Arctic Journal*, p. 182.

75   "insularity of Greenland": Peary, *Northward over the "Great Ice,"* 1:438.

76   "free of the rush . . . picnic in the woods": Ibid., p. 387.

76   "on his proposed trip": Ibid., p. 394.

76   "an insurgent type" and other quotations relating to Cook's opinion of Verhoeff: Cook, "Hell Is a Cold Place," chap. 4, p. 6.

76   "I will never go home": Cook, *My Attainment of the Pole*, p. 63 n.

76   "peculiar, sad and mysterious" and other quotations pertaining to Cook's report to Peary on the search for Verhoeff: Cook letter to Peary, Sept. 9, 1892.

Chapter Five   Ruled with an Iron Hand

78   "a fool's paradise . . . We had from a savage": Cook, "Hell Is a Cold Place," chap. 4, p. 4.

79   "This is true of all": Ibid., p. 7.

79   "correctness of [his] theory" and other quotations attributed to Peary in commending members of the expedition: Peary, *Northward over the "Great Ice,"* 1:423–26.

79   "my friends were right": Ibid., p. xlii.

80   "complete the exploration": Peary letter to his mother, Dec. 22, 1892.

80   "ill at ease": Cook, "Hell Is a Cold Place," chapter V, p. 1.

81   "the dogs and sledges": Herbert L. Bridgman, "Peary," *Natural History* 20, no. 1 (1920): 7.

81   "You see, my fingers" and other dialogue between Henson and the naval officer with whom he had a wager: Robinson, *Dark Companion*, pp. 79–80.

82   "I have been thinking": Cook letter to Peary, Jan. 30, 1893.

82   "I have two plans": Cook letter to Peary, Feb. 2, 1893.

82   "The rental of a suitable": Cook letter to Peary, March 7, 1893.

83   "not a word can be published" and other dialogue attributed to Peary when Cook sought permission to publish his Arctic research: Cook, "Hell Is a Cold Place," chap. 5, pp. 1–2.

84   "very glad to hear": Peary letter to Cook, March 21, 1893.

84   "My Dear Mr. Peary": Cook letter to Peary, April 26, 1893.

84   "My dear Doctor": Peary letter to Cook, May 9, 1893.

84   "Thinly scattered": *New York Medical Examiner* 3 (1893): 23–24.

85   "extremely distasteful . . . the quarters of the people": Peary, *Northward over the "Great Ice,"* 1:xiv.

85   "professional engagements": *Brooklyn Standard-Union*, July 11, 1893.

85   "information and suggestions . . . I am sorry": Peary letter to Cook, June 15, 1893.

86   "advise on the treatment . . . feed the brain": Cook, "Hell Is a Cold Place," chap 5, p. 2.

86   "students of nature . . . rapid and flank movement . . . I expect to prove": *Brooklyn Standard-Union*, July 11, 1893.

Chapter Six   The Snow Baby

90   "Everything points to the success": Diebitsch-Peary, *My Arctic Journal*, p. 220.

91   "fates and all hell": Stafford, *Discoverer of the North Pole*, p. 126.

94   "So ends . . . second": Peary diary, Sept. 9, 1894.

95	"cold and cheerless": Peary diary, Dec. 30, 1894.
95	"Lee and Henson alone" [footnote]: Peary, *Northward over the "Great Ice,"* 2:115.
96	"It is the eve of our departure": Peary letter to Josephine, March 31, 1895.
96	"My movements after reaching": Peary letter to "Mrs. Peary or my Representative on the Ship," March 31, 1895.
98	"When you told me": Josephine letter to Peary, June 25, 1895.
99	"a dismal failure": *New York Times*, Oct. 2, 1895.
99	"physically or mentally": Peary, *Northward over the "Great Ice,"* 1:xlvii.
99	"completely crushed": Josephine letter to Morris K. Jesup, Oct. 16, 1895.
99	"Peary's failure": Cook letter to Samuel Entrikin, Sept. 25, 1895.
100	"I shall never see the North Pole": *New York Times*, Oct. 2, 1895.

Chapter Seven   Polar Summer Resort

101	"*EXTRA! Interesting Lecture*": *Brooklyn Standard-Union*, Nov. 14, 1893.
101	"Cook's Expedition . . . intelligent, educated": *Brooklyn Standard-Union*, ca. 1893.
101	"Polar Summer Resort": *New York Journal*, June 17, 1894.
102	"taken very kindly": uncredited newspaper article, June 14, 1894.
102	"ill omen": *New York Sun*, Sept. 21, 1894.
105	"Will you kindly come to our rescue?": Cook letter addressed to "The Captains of American Fishing Schooners," Aug. 16, 1894.
106	"Nelson Greene . . . spleen enlarged": Cook's patient notes, Dec. 18, 1894.
107	"Doctor, I would like to get interested" and other dialogue pertaining to Cook's meeting with Andrew Carnegie: Cook, "Hell Is a Cold Place," chap. 5, pp. 5–6.

Chapter Eight   Bounty Hunting

109	"iron stone": Hobbs, *Peary*, p. 177.
111	"the conquest of the North Pole" and other comments attributed to Peary concerning his polar expedition: Peary's signed draft of his speech delivered to "Mr. President and Members of the Council of the American Geographical Society" on Jan. 12, 1897.
111	"immediate and emphatic": Peary, *Northward over the "Great Ice,"* 1:lii.
111–12	"determined, concentrated": Ibid., p. liii.
112	"*Anything* but that": Green, *Peary*, p. 166.
112	"You remember" and other dialogue pertaining to a discussion with

President McKinley regarding his granting Peary five years leave: Ibid., pp. 166–67.

113   "entirely confidential": Peary's letter "To the Passengers On Board S.S. Hope," Sept. 20, 1897, countersigned by seventeen passengers.

113   "savage stress": Peary, *Northward over the "Great Ice,"* 2:610.

114   "nice warm houses": Berton, *The Arctic Grail*, p. 521.

Chapter Nine   Destination Antarctica

117   "in a flash": Cook, "Hell Is a Cold Place," chap. 5, p. 6.

117   "the dream of my life": Cook, *Through the First Antarctic Night*, p. 48.

119   "shiver because of its force": Ibid., p. 127.

119   "death mask": Frederick Cook, "My Experience with a Camera in the Antarctic," *Popular Photography*, Feb. 1938.

121   "The instinct of any navigator": Amundsen, *My Life as an Explorer*, p. 25–26.

122   "schooled . . . in fighting": Cook, "Hell Is a Cold Place," chap. 12, p. 1.

122   "a truly dreadful": Amundsen, *My Life as an Explorer*, p. 27.

122   "To be caught in the ice": Cook, *Through the First Antarctic Night*, p. 200.

123   "more sense . . . You have a good head": Kugelmass, *Roald Amundsen*, p. 37.

124   "I can breathe lighter . . . His life": Cook, *Through the First Antarctic Night*, pp. 310–11.

124   "The melancholy death": Cook, Ibid., p. 312.

125   "Men, we're going through . . . Open water": Kugelmass, *Roald Amundsen*, p. 41.

125   "a form of anemia": Cook, *Through the First Antarctic Night*, p. 331.

125   "baking treatment": Ibid.

126   "We must have fresh meat": Kugelmass, *Roald Amundsen*, p. 42.

126   "entered into a co-partnership": Cook, *Though the First Antarctic Night*, p. 300.

128   "the principal result": *American Geographical Society Journal* 27 (1895): 61.

128   "discourtesy": Peary, *Northward over the "Great Ice,"* 2:159.

129   "the rest of us": Amundsen, *My Life as an Explorer*, pp. 28–29.

130   "The miracle happened": Ibid., p. 30.

131   "seemed to pine away": *Brooklyn Eagle*, Sept. 5, 1909.

131   "ingenuity . . . saved the day": Amundsen, *My Life as an Explorer*, p. 31.

131   "as modest and unassuming": Pond, *Eccentricities of Genius*, p. 293.

Chapter Ten   The Ice Man

133   "an iron man": Cook, autobiographical sketch (unpublished).

134   "Peary is lost": Cook, "Voyage of the Eric 1901 for the Relief of Peary" unpublished handwritten notes.

135   "The girl . . . belle of the tribe" [footnote]: Herbert, *The Noose of Laurels*, p. 206.

135   "If colonization": Peary diary, 1885.

136   "interfere with [his] work": Josephine letter to Peary, Jan. 23, 1901.

136   "physical wreck . . . love and nurse": Ibid.

136   "aging effect": Cook, "Hell Is a Cold Place," chap. 5, p. 7.

137   "The teeth" and other descriptions and dialogue regarding Cook's examination of Peary: Ibid., chap. 5, p. 9.

138   "nothing should be made": Sverdrup, *New Land*, p. 200.

139   "Sverdrup may at this minute" and other dialogue between Peary and Hensen: Robinson, *Dark Companion*, p. 134.

140   Cook's initial recommendation [footnote]: Minot and Murphy, "Treatment of Pernicious Anemia by a Special Diet," *Journal of the American Medical Association* 87 (1926): 470–75.

140   "I intend to . . . You understand that": *New York Herald*, Nov. 11, 1902.

141   "You will never": *New York Herald*, Nov. 10, 1902.

142   "Next time I'll": Robinson, *Dark Companion*, p. 170.

Chapter Eleven   "Roof of the Continent"

143   "most beautiful thing": Marie Hunt Cook letter to Cook, June 16, 1931.

143   "hypnotized": Marie letter to Cook, May 11, 1931.

145   "long training": *National Geographic Magazine*, Jan. 1903.

145   "for a time . . . twin efforts": Cook, "Round Mount McKinley" (1904), *Bulletin of American Geographical Society* 36, no. 6 (1904).

145   "in their exploits": Cook, *To the Top of the Continent*, p. xvii.

147   "mere tooth of": Ibid., p. 7.

148   "limit her exploring": Ibid., p. 10.

148   "the wildest kind . . . kept one's attention": Ibid., p. 9.

149   "too much and all the time": Dunn, *World Alive*, p. 103.

149   "[Cook's] ways and person": Ibid., p. 109.

149   "I think he would": Ibid., p. 36.

149   "and that makes me": Robert Dunn, "Across the Forbidden Tundra," *Outing Magazine*, Jan. 1904, p. 462.

149   "no respect for anybody" [footnote]: Steffens, *The Autobiography of Lincoln Steffens*, p. 323.

149   "Not much will be" [footnote]: Robert Dunn, "Home by Ice and by
        Swimming from Mt. McKinley," *Outing Magazine*, May 1904, p. 215.

150   "great waving sea": Cook, *To the Top of the Continent*, p. 48.

150   "shingled by plates . . . Here was the roof": Ibid., p. 49.

151   "tortuous course": Ibid., p. 51.

151   "flying machine" [footnote]: Washburn and Cherici, *The Dishonorable
        Dr. Cook*, p. 38.

151   "defeat for our first": Ibid., p. 55.

152   "burst into the arctic": Ibid., p. 62.

153   "I hadn't given": Dunn, *World Alive*, p. 109.

153–54 "My God . . . its glittering spurs . . . trains of rock . . . chaos of awful . . .
        made one's marrow": Cook, *To the Top of the Continent*, pp. 66–67.

154   "Don't pack up": Dunn, *World Alive*, p. 112.

155   "good, faithful animals": Cook, *To the Top of the Continent*, p. 89.

156   "McKinley offers": Cook, "Round Mount McKinley."

Chapter Twelve   Farthest North

157   "had wandered back": Green, *Peary*, p. 233.

157   "black march": Robinson, *Dark Companion*, p. 171.

157   "Ever since my return . . . throw [him]self into . . . first-class": Green,
        Peary, p. 193.

158   "The names of those": Peary letter to Peary Arctic Club members, 1900.

158   "aid and assist . . . the altering of . . . work of propaganda . . . in the
        most favorable . . . complete reversal . . . construction of a vessel":
        Green, *Peary*, pp. 195–96.

159   "the strenuous life": Uberman, *The Presidents and Their Wives*, p. 35.

159   "with characteristic . . . rounded out": Peary, *Nearest the Pole*, pp. 356–57.

160   "The attainment of": Hayes, *Robert Edwin Peary*, p. 54.

160   "I congratulate you": Peary letter to Cook, Dec. 14, 1903.

161   "final . . . Next summer I shall": *New York Sun*, Sept. 15, 1904.

163   "pleasant companion": Peary, *The North Pole*, p. 31.

163   "bowing to the plaudits . . . I am going now": *New York Tribune*, July
        17, 1905.

163   "It would not": *New York Herald*, July 9, 1905.

164   "crucial moment . . . For a minute . . . mighty tremor": Peary, *Nearest
        the Pole*, p. 59.

165   "The battle is on": Green, *Peary*, p. 253.

167   "perfect mesh . . . forced march": Peary journal, April 20,1906.

167   "knot and splice": Henson, *A Black Explorer at the North Pole*, p. 19.

167   "We had at last": Peary journal, April 20, 1906.

168   "thin and pinched . . . sagging jaws": *Harper's Weekly*, July 13, 1907.

168   "cut the margin": Peary, *Nearest the Pole*, p. 135.

168   "We can make' and other dialogue between Peary and Henson: Robinson, *Dark Companion*, pp. 198, 199, 201.

169   "One who can eat": *Harper's Weekly*, July 13, 1907.

169   "To think": Berton, *The Arctic Grail*, p. 561.

170   "distant land": Ibid.

170   "We have got": Bartlett, *The Log of Bob Bartlett*, p. 166.

Chapter Thirteen   "A Crazy Hunger"

173   "breathlessly appreciative": *Seattle Post-Intelligencer*, Nov. 10, 1906.

174   "babies": *New York Herald*, Sept. 12, 1909.

174   "rankest kind of tenderfoot": Cook, *My Attainment of the North Pole*, p. 532 n.

174   "heroic efforts": Parker, "The Exploration of Mount McKinley," *Review of Reviews*, Jan. 1907.

175   "that day . . . twenty-five to fifty": *Seattle Post-Intelligencer*, Nov. 10, 1906.

175   "relay work": Cook, "The Conquest of Mount McKinley," *Harper's Monthly Magazine*, May 1907.

176   "mighty cornice . . . cheerful time . . . almost a hurricane": *Seattle Post-Intelligencer*, Nov. 10, 1906.

177   "as black as": Cook, *To the Top of the Continent*, p. 232.

177   "Sun Sept 16": Ibid., p. 289.

177   "I have been asked": *National Geographic Magazine*, Jan. 1907.

178   "splendid achievement" and other quotations attributed to Cook at the National Geographic Society dinner: Ibid.

178   "year in and year out" and other quotations attributed to Roosevelt: Peary, *Nearest the Pole*, pp. viii–ix.

179   "continued interest" and other quotations attributed to Peary at the National Geographic Society dinner: Ibid., pp. ix, xi.

180   "confinement of prison . . . fretted and chafed": Cook, *My Attainment of the North Pole*, p. 29.

180   "He was to photograph": Bradley, "My Knowledge of Dr. Cook's Polar Expedition," *Independent*, Sept. 16, 1909.

181   "The flag on . . . I shall always remember": Cook, "The Conquest of Mount McKinley."

181   "Why not try for the Pole" and other quotations attributed to Cook and Bradley during their lunch in March 1907: Bradley, "My Knowledge of Dr. Cook's Polar Expedition."

182   "a crazy hunger": Cook, *My Attainment of the North Pole*, p. 30.

182   "The attaining": Ibid., p. 74.

183   "immunity from": *Brooklyn Eagle*, Sept. 10, 1909.

184   "I have hit upon": Cook letter to Herbert Bridgman, Aug. 26, 1907.

Chapter Fourteen   "I Shall Win This Time"

185   "to undertake . . . I believe": Hobbs, *Peary*, p. 319.

185   "last attempt": *Harper's Weekly*, July 13, 1907.

185–86   "a small flood . . . absolutely insure . . . gem of . . . motor cars . . . flying machines . . . submarine . . . how we were": Peary, *The North Pole*, pp. 17–18.

186   "loss with each": Robert Peary, "The Discovery of the North Pole," *Hampton's Magazine*, Jan. 1910.

186   "the greatest . . . Before me": *Harper's Weekly*, July 13, 1907.

187   "an honorable man": *Saturday Review*, Dec. 8, 1951.

188   "sub rosa . . . which has . . . appropriating to . . . under my lead . . . forestall me": Peary letter dated May 1908, published in *New York Times*, Sept. 9, 1909.

188–89   "financially a tower . . . an absolute paralyzing . . . every one . . . lowest ebb . . . munificent . . . in the midst . . . too big . . .": Peary, *The North Pole*, pp. 15–16.

190   "American Route . . . best of all . . . a more rigid massing . . . as happened": Ibid., pp. 4, 5.

190–91   "those frozen spaces . . . face to face . . . my negro assistant . . . his adaptability . . . any other man . . . first and most": Ibid., pp. 19, 20.

191   "disagreeable . . . putting the": Henson, *A Black Explorer at the North Pole*, pp. 24–25.

192   "earnestly and profoundly . . . the most intensely . . . Mr. President . . . I believe": Peary, *The North Pole*, pp. 26–27.

193   "allowing nothing": Herbert Bridgman, "Peary," *National History* 20, no. 1 (1920).

193   "Bully! . . . blessed them": Robinson, *Dark Companion*, p. 211.

Chapter Fifteen   Polar Quest

194   "rewards from . . . the expenditure": Cook, *My Attainment of the Pole*, p. 70.

194   "I'm going" and other dialogue over breakfast between Cook and Bradley: Bradley, "My Knowledge of Dr. Cook's Polar Expedition," *Independent*, Sept. 16, 1909.

195   "how he plays" and other quotations relating to Cook's determination: *New York Herald*, Sept. 2, 1909.

195–96   "could possibly . . . Arctic enthusiast . . . alone with": Cook, *My Attainment of the Pole*, p. 72.

196   "durability of . . . eliminate useless": Ibid., pp. 131 n, 132.

197   "never seemed": Ibid., p. 134.

198   "only safe way": Ibid., p. 78.

198   "I have this": *Boston Herald*, July 12, 1908.

199–200 "the light . . . the pick . . . win the . . . well enough . . . heart": Cook, *My Attainment of the Pole*, pp. 154–56.

199   "the far north . . . change of our . . . much land": Cook letter to Knud Rasmussen, Feb. 1908.

200–201 "the first nights . . . a hopeless jungle . . . ever-hot coffee . . . curious whim . . . modern effort": Cook, *My Attainment of the Pole*, pp. 157–58.

201   "paralyzed the dogs . . . soldiers on": Ibid., p. 161.

202   "Now even . . . existence of": Ibid., p. 185.

203–4   "advanced beyond . . . no trace . . . a garden spot . . . rough and heavy . . . fields of crushed . . . trusted to follow": Ibid., pp. 192–93, 196–97.

204   "a lively interest": Ibid., p. 243.

204   "were to be . . . mere palate": Ibid., p. 199.

205   "dash in as straight": Ibid., p. 194.

205   *"Tigishi ah"*: Ibid., p. 200.

Chapter Sixteen   "Forward! March!"

207   "could hardly . . . a drop of coffee": *Tourist Magazine*, Oct. 1910.

207–8   "Please, dear God . . . This man is": Robinson, *Dark Companion*, p. 213.

208   "incipient scurvy . . . serious mental state": Peary, *The North Pole*, p. 76.

208   "must be our money": Cook letter to Rudolph Franke, March 17, 1908.

208   "In a critical": Rudolph Franke letter to the Department of Justice, Washington, D.C., May 19, 1914.

208   "make the best . . . all the stuff": *New York Times*, Nov. 16, 1908.

209   "just as the enemy" [foonote]: *Tourist Magazine*, Oct. 1910.

209   "a consignment" [footnote]: *Brooklyn Eagle*, Nov. 16, 1908.

209   "home for" [footnote]: *New York Herald*, Sept. 10, 1909.

209   "Franke has now" and other quotations from Peary's letter of instructions: Peary letter, Aug. 17, 1908.

209   "a year's big game": Whitney, *Hunting with the Eskimos*, p. 111.

210   "the Dr. Cook . . . a tangle": Ross Marvin letter to L. C. Bement, Aug. 15, 1908.

210   "This house belongs": *New York American*, Sept. 13, 1909.

211   "sacrificing . . . these descendants . . . work hard": Peary, *The North Pole*, pp. 208, 210.

211   "favorites among": Ibid., p. 246.

211–12   "by the time . . . the iron hand . . . bound for . . . Forward! March!":
           Henson, *A Black Explorer at the North Pole*, pp. 73–75.

212   "brought up the": Peary, *The North Pole*, p. 216.

213   "impinging against": Ibid., pp. 195–96.

213   "dark ominous": Ibid., p. 221.

214   "considerable trouble": Ibid., p. 219.

214   "Because of his" [footnote]: *Boston American*, July 17, 1910.

214   "crossing a river . . . white expanse . . . familiar": Peary, *The North Pole*,
           pp. 222, 225.

215   "worst feature . . . far more troublesome": Ibid., p. 196.

215   "pretending . . . I have. . . . this and . . . seriously puzzled": Ibid., p. 230.

216   "Push on . . . slept like . . . gratuitous . . . a comparatively high": Ibid.,
           pp. 232, 235–36.

216–17   "a sort . . . worth more . . . with almost . . . clouded": Ibid., pp. 238,
           244, 240.

217   "responded like": Ibid., p. 251.

217   "dead reckoning . . . altitude of . . . partly to": Ibid., p. 248.

217   "necessary to check": Ibid., p. 212.

218   "generous contributors": Ibid., p. 252.

218   "advancing with": Ibid., p. 321.

218   "Be careful": Ibid., p. 254.

219   "staggered . . . he did not . . . No human eye" [footnote]: Ibid., p. 318.

219   "the march . . . a good . . . literally to plow": Ibid., p. 256, 257.

219   "creaking and": Ibid., pp. 258, 260.

220   "myth-makers": Ibid., p. 262.

221   "unpleasant possibilities": Ibid., p. 265.

221   "bitter disappointment": *New York Herald*, Sept. 22, 1909.

221   "a little crazy" and other quotations attributed to Bartlett's actions and
           feelings when ordered by Peary to return southward: *New York Herald*,
           Sept. 22, 1909.

222–23   "even more willing . . . He was always . . . blind confidence . . . all the
           impetus . . . others would . . . sweeping over": Peary, *The North Pole*,
           pp. 271, 274.

Chapter Seventeen   "I Have Reached the Pole"

224   "desperate battle . . . suspended on . . . unknown capacity . . . shadow
           of": Cook, *Return from the Pole*, pp. 208–9.

224–25   "with good intentions . . . mirages . . . delusion": Cook, *My Attainment
           of the Pole*, p. 452 n.

224–25   "which every . . . *Noona*": Ibid., p. 206.

225   "Now if": Ibid., p. 444.

225   "honored": *Outing Magazine*, Dec. 1909.

225   "I have reached . . . remarkable . . . no great . . . accomplished no":
        Cook, *My Attainment of the Pole*, p. 437.

226   "a tremendous cut": Ibid., p. 217.

226   "gazed longingly . . . never clearly . . . low mist . . . the Pole": Ibid.,
        pp. 243, 245–46.

227   "equality of the length . . . Lost in a landless": Ibid., p. 271.

227   "the Pole . . . attainment . . . never did . . . that last" and Cook's
        reported dialogue with the Eskimos: Ibid., pp. 272–73.

227   "at a spot": Ibid., p. 287.

228   "hard-fought . . . crushed ice": Ibid., p. 329.

228–29 "secreted for . . . hollow-eyed . . . omen was . . . peace-loving . . . one of
        the most": Ibid., p. 155–57.

229   "slush and . . . nearly as difficult": Ibid., p. 449.

230   "old, rubbed . . . instrumental corrections . . . important for": Ibid., pp.
        497–99.

231   "may remain as": Cook letter to Harry Whitney, April 21, 1909.

231   "gluttonous . . . succumbed . . . principal pastime": Cook, *My
        Attainment of the Pole*, p. 452.

232   "public aspect . . . a three days' . . . done by simpler": Ibid., pp. 454–55.

232–33 "jumped and danced . . . sun glass . . . won the": *Rosary Magazine*, Nov.
        1909.

233   "foretold the . . . considerable financial": Cook, *My Attainment of the
        Pole*, pp. 463–64.

234   "successful and": *New York Sun*, Sept. 9, 1909.

234   "Reached North Pole": *New York Herald*, Sept. 2, 1909.

235   "the Eskimos": *New York Times*, Sept. 2, 1909.

235   "Dr. Cook . . . What evidence": *New York Times*, Sept. 5, 1909.

236   "They had only": Gibbs, *Adventures in Journalism*, p. 46.

236   "dazed . . . clamor . . . moving-picture": Cook, *My Attainment of the
        Pole*, pp. 466–67.

236   "THANK GOD": Original telegram, Sept. 2, 1909, from Brunswick,
        Maine.

237   "naive, inexperienced . . . Why this hurry?": W. T. Stead, "Dr. Cook,
        the Man and the Deed," *Review of Reviews*, Oct. 1909.

237   "down deep . . . I think so" and other direct quotations from the
        Copenhagen news conference: H. M. Lyon, "When Cook Came to
        Copenhagen," *Collier's*, Sept. 25, 1909.

239   "Calm and": *Brooklyn Standard-Union*, Sept. 5, 1909.

239   "He entirely": *New York Times*, Sept. 6, 1909.

239   "It is enough": Stead, "Dr. Cook, the Man and the Deed."

239   "intuition rather": Gibbs, *Adventures in Journalism*, p. 47.

239   "narrative story" [footnote]: Cook, *My Attainment of the Pole*, p. 492.

240   "answers to": *New York Times*, Sept. 5, 1909.

240   "verity . . . as accurate": Ibid., p. 472.

241   "This northward dash": *New York Herald*, Sept. 8, 1909.

241   "an exhaustive . . . Dr. Cook answered": *New York Times*, Sept. 7, 1909.

241   "tremendous offers . . . just as a man . . . by day . . . dreams": Cook, *My Attainment of the Pole*, pp. 470–71.

241   "YOUR OWN . . . WILL YOU . . . MAY WE": Original telegrams, Sept. 1909.

241   "joys of ": Ibid., p. 454.

242   "I can say . . . I can do": *New York Times*, Sept. 11, 1909.

242   "Tired to death": Cook, *My Attainment of the North Pole*, p. 473.

242   "In a wire": *New York Times*, Sept. 7, 1909.

242   "Stars and stripes": Original telegram, Sept. 6, 1909.

243   "I am proud . . . a brave . . . his observations": *New York Herald*, Sept. 8, 1909.

243   "not of envy . . . no rivalry . . . hard, long years . . . might be of . . . discovered new": Cook, *My Attainment of the Pole*, p. 474.

243   "Kindly convey": *New York Herald*, Sept. 7, 1909.

243   "Cook's story": Associated Press, Sept. 8, 1909.

Chapter Eighteen   "Nailed to The Pole"

244   "I have hit upon": Cook letter to Herbert Bridgman, Aug. 26, 1907.

244   "successful trip": Special to *The Record*, Sept. 30, 1909.

244   "way, way north": *Philadelphia Public Ledger*, Sept. 20, 1909.

245   "couldn't talk Eskimo": Bartlett, *The Log of Bob Bartlett*, p. 149.

245   "We pretended": Cook, *Return from the Pole*, p. 221.

245   "rather excited . . . No sabe . . . best dog . . . faster than": Special to *The Record*, Sept. 30, 1909.

245   "no doubt": *New York Herald*, Sept. 27, 1909.

246   "testimony . . . unshaken by . . . threatened them": Statement sworn to and registered by Notary Public, State of New York, Nov. 23, 1909.

246–47 "Have you anything . . . Well, I don't . . . knew well . . . I would not . . . When I said": *New York Herald*, Oct. 1, 1909.

248   "intimated at the time": *New York Herald*, Oct. 12, 1909.

248   "No more Arctic . . . gone beyond": *New York Herald*, Sept. 20, 1909.

248   "had come to . . . half starved": Whitney, *Hunting with the Eskimos*, pp. 268–69.

249   "all claims": Peary Arctic Club agreement signed by William Wallace and Minik Wallace, July 9, 1909.

249   "You're a race": *Evening Mail*, July 9, 1909.

250   "again among his": *New York Herald*, Sept. 20, 1909.

250   "I congratulate you . . . How did": Bartlett, *The Log of Bob Bartlett*, pp. 197–98.

251   "toil, fatigue . . . in practically . . . tracks repeatedly": Henson, *A Black Explorer at the North Pole*, pp. 129–30.

251   "dashed out . . . more than covered . . . not different . . . ": Robinson, *Dark Companion*, pp. 223, 225.

251   "We are now . . . feeling . . . if they had . . . I do not": *Boston American*, July 17, 1910.

252   "limp and lifeless . . . in sparkling . . . nailed to . . . with sun-blinded . . . resolute squaring . . . satisfied . . . confident that . . . a gust . . . in a quavering . . . in a continual . . . practically a dead": Henson, *A Black Explorer at the North Pole*, pp. 133, 135, 140, 130.

252   "utterly exhausted . . . not a thing": Peary, *The North Pole*, pp. 297–98.

252   "Not once . . . in the most": Henson, *A Black Explorer at the North Pole*, p. 153.

252   "life's purpose": Peary, *The North Pole*, p. 287.

253   "Have made good": *New York Times*, Sept. 7, 1909.

253   "big story . . . all editorials": *New York Times*, Sept. 8–9, 1909.

254   "should not be . . . out of sight": Associated Press, Sept. 8, 1909.

254   "ahead of . . . [Marvin] was a very . . . There wasn't" [footnote]: Lewin, *The Great North Pole Fraud*, pp. 160, 164.

255   "Battle Harbor": *New York Herald*, Sept. 11, 1909.

255   "This is a new": Peary, *The North Pole*, p. 334.

255   "Was Dr. Cook" and other quotations attributed to Peary's interview by two Associated Press reporters at Battle Harbour, AP story, Sept. 15, 1909.

256   "every ounce . . . muzzles of . . . from ear . . . Gentlemen": *New York World*, Sept. 20, 1909.

257   "rival expedition . . . It would be": *New York World*, Sept. 16, 1909.

257   "Peary's men": Special Dispatch to the *North American*, Sept. 16, 1909.

258   "Why didn't you . . . Because Dr. Cook": *New York Herald*, Sept. 19, 1909.

258   "the third degree": *New York Herald*, Sept. 22, 1909.

259   "If a man . . . Acting on the advice": *New York Sun*, Sept. 22, 1909.

259   "snapped his great": *New York World*, Sept. 22, 1909.

259   "Concerning Dr. Cook": *New York Times*, Sept. 24, 1909.

Chapter Nineteen   Seized by a "Heartsickness"

261   "anxious to get . . . the ordeal of . . . quickly and . . . When I land . . .
two months . . . official tests . . . as it was": *Pittsburgh Press*, Sept. 21,
1909.

262   "the romance of": *St. Louis Globe Dispatch*, Sept. 24, 1909.

262   "great tooting": *New York Evening Post*, Sept. 21, 1909.

262   "I have come . . . not to enter": *New York Herald*, Sept. 21, 1909.

263   "seeking rest . . . cheerfully to . . . did not depart": *Philadelphia Public
Ledger*, Sept. 23, 1909.

263–64   Quotations from Cook's interview session with forty newspaper
reporters in New York: *Philadelphia Evening Bulletin* and *Philadelphia
Public Ledger*, Sept. 23, 1909.

264   "STARTED FOR HOME": *Philadelphia Public Ledger*, Sept. 27, 1909.

264   "heartsickness . . . very material": Cook, *My Attainment of the Pole*, pp.
497, 499.

265   "observations and . . . that was . . . continuous line . . . I had some":
Ibid., pp. 499, 500.

265   "complicate matters . . . Well, I don't . . . But you have . . . slow in . . .
blank space . . . I had counted . . . Nothing much": *Philadelphia North
American*, Sept. 27, 1909.

265   "strong explicit . . . all would": Cook, *My Attainment of the Pole*, p. 500.

266   "decidedly confirming" [footnote]: *New York Daily Tribune*, Sept. 10,
1909.

267   "I want this": Peary letter to Thomas Hubbard, Sept. 1909.

268   "The Barrill affidavit": *New York Evening Mail*, Oct. 15, 1909.

268   "were the only": *New York American*, Sept. 9, 1909.

268   "this means" [footnote]: *New York Herald*, Oct. 24, 1909.

268   "myself" [footnote]: Original Fidelity Trust Co. draft, Oct. 1, 1909.

268   "will run over" [footnote]: Letter from J. M. Ashton, Tacoma, Wash.,
Sept. 30, 1909.

269   "not conclusive evidence": *Nation*, Oct. 21, 1909.

270   "growing uncertainty . . . mental depression . . . desperate . . . feverish
. . . physical anguish . . . hostility . . . persecuted . . . growing sort . . .
good-natured . . . dangerous": Cook, *My Attainment of the Pole*, pp
504–5.

271   "Not Proven": *New York Herald*, Dec. 22, 1909.

271   "Now I'll be": *Travel Magazine*, June 1910.

271   "foes . . . Such a course": Cook, *My Attainment of the Pole*, p. 501.

271   "My life": *New York Times*, Dec. 27, 1909.

271   "The decision of": Associated Press, Dec. 22, 1909.

Aftermath

273   "a skeptic on the": *New York Times*, Oct. 20, 1909.

273   "perfunctory and hasty . . . veil of secrecy": Private Calendar no. 733, 61st Cong., 3d sess., House Report no. 1961, p. 17.

274   "a paid lobby": *Congressional Record*, 61st Cong., 3d sess., vol. 46, pt. 3, pp. 2701–25.

275   "shows no finger . . . Pemmican is the": *Congresssional Record*, 61st Cong., 3d sess., vol. 46, "Extension of Remarks," Rep. Henry Helgesen, p. 275.

275   "The Pole at last": Peary's handwritten North Pole diary, entry for April 6, 1909.

275   "vague and uncertain . . . We have your word": *Congressional Record*, 61st Cong., 3d sess., 1911, vol. 46, pt. 3, pp. 2701–25.

275   "deep-seated doubts . . . Assuming . . . Arctic exploration": Private Calendar no. 733, 61st Cong., 3d sess., 1911, House Report no. 1961, pp. 23, 1.

277   "her courage and devotion": Associated Press, Dec. 19, 1955.

277   "Through 75 years . . . devoted to a": *National Geographic*, Sept. 1988.

278   "error in so long . . . addressing the . . . strongly influenced": Cook, *My Attainment of the Pole*, p. 554.

278   "made insertions . . . cutting through": Testimony of Lilian Eleanor Kiel, House Committee on Education, Jan. 28, 1915.

278   "Dr. Cook's Confession . . . mental unbalancement . . . After mature . . . insanity plea": *Hampton's Magazine*, Jan. 1911.

278–79   "amazed indignation . . . a sensation-provoking . . . uncertain": Cook, *My Attainment of the Pole*, p. 554.

279   "History demonstrates . . . I have stated": Ibid., p. 566.

281   "tabular bergs . . . flat-topped . . . Neither investigated . . . it is significant": *Seattle Times*, Dec. 6, 1956.

282   "contained some": Cook, *My Attainment of the Pole*, p. 522.

284   "I have observed . . . everyone who had . . . grew bitter . . . an attempt . . . corroborated in . . . sharp backbone . . . difficult to . . . investigated the . . . his discovery . . . suitable design": *Congressional Record*, 63d Cong., 2d sess., April 30, 1914, vol. 51, no. 116, p. 8065.

285   "squelched": *New York Times*, Feb. 2, 1915.

286   "gigantic stock-reloading . . . led to the": *New York Times*, Jan. 11, 1923.

287   "This is one": U.S. District Court record 2273, Fort Worth, Tex.

287   "I agree with" [footnote]: Letter from John M. Killits to Marie Peary Stafford, Jan. 23, 1930.

288   "the finest traveler . . . practical . . . as good as": *New York Times*, Jan. 24, 1926.

288   "yet no person": Letter from Jesse E. Martin, District Attorney, Tarrant County, Fort Worth, Tex., to President Calvin Coolidge, Sept. 1, 1928.

288   "the sentence in the": Letter from U.S. District Court Judge James C. Wilson to Honorable Calvin Coolidge, Aug. 27, 1928.

289   "I am tired": *Seattle Daily Times*, March 10, 1930.

289   "Twenty-eight years": Frederick Cook letter to R. Roland L. Redmond, president, American Geographical Society, Feb. 19, 1936.

290   "Dr. Cook had . . . At that time": *Boston Post*, April 9, 1936.

290   "Thanks. Happy": Associated Press, May 20, 1940.

290   "wishing for you": Frederick Cook letter to Marie Cook, Jan. 23, 1940.

291   "literally gone . . . man of intrepid": *Polar Priorities*, Sept. 1999, p. 3.

BIBLIOGRAPHY

Abramson, Howard S. *Hero in Disgrace: The Life of the Arctic Explorer Frederick A. Cook*. New York: Paragon House, 1991.

———. *National Geographic: Behind America's Lens on the World*. New York: Crown, 1987.

Acheson, Sam Hanna. *Joe Bailey: The Last Democrat*. New York: Macmillan, 1932.

Amundsen, Roald. *My Life as an Explorer*. New York: Doubleday, 1928.

Astrup, Eivind. *A Journey round Melville Bay*. London: Royal Geographical Society, 1895.

———. *With Peary near the Pole*. Philadelphia: J. B. Lippincott, 1898.

Bartlett, Robert A. *The Log of Bob Bartlett: The True Story of Forty Years of Seafaring and Exploration*. New York: G. P. Putnam's Sons, 1928.

Berton, Pierre. *The Arctic Grail: The Quest for the North West Passage and the North Pole, 1818–1909*. Toronto: McClelland and Stewart, 1988.

Borup, George. *A Tenderfoot with Peary*. New York: Frederick A. Stokes, 1911.

Browne, Belmore. *The Conquest of Mount McKinley*. Boston: Houghton Mifflin, 1956.

Bryce, Robert M. *Cook & Peary: The Polar Controversy, Resolved*. Mechanicsburg, Pa.: Stackpole Books, 1997.

Cook, Frederick A. *My Attainment of the Pole*. 1911. Reprint, Pittsburgh: Polar Publishing, 2001.

———. *My Attainment of the Pole*. Revised ed. 1913. Reprint, New York: Cooper Square Press, 2001.

———. *Return from the Pole*. New York: Pellegrini & Cudahy, 1951.

———. *Through the First Antarctic Night*. New York: Doubleday, Page, 1909.

———. *To the Top of the Continent: Discovery, Exploration and Adventure in Sub-arctic*

Alaska: The First Ascent of Mt. McKinley, 1903–1906. 1908. Reprint, Mukileto, Wash.: Alpen Books, 1996.

————. "Hell Is a Cold Place." Unpublished. Frederick Cook Collection, Library of Congress.

Cookman, Scott. *Ice Blink: The Tragic Fate of Sir John Franklin's Lost Polar Expedition.* New York: John Wiley, 2000.

Counter, S. Allen. *North Pole Legacy: Black, White & Eskimo.* Amherst: University of Massachusetts Press, 1991.

Davies, Thomas D. *Robert E. Peary at the North Pole.* Rockville, Md.: Foundation for the Promotion of the Art of Navigation 1989.

Diebitsch-Peary, Josephine. *My Arctic Journal: A Year among Ice-fields and Eskimos.* New York: Contemporary Publishing, 1893.

Driscoll, Charles B. *The Life of O. O. McIntyre.* New York: Greystone Press, 1938.

Dunn, Robert. *The Shameless Diary of an Explorer: A Story of Failure on Mt. McKinley.* 1907. New York: Modern Library, 2001.

————. *World Alive: A Personal Story.* New York: Crown, 1956.

Eames, Hugh. *Winner Lose All: Dr. Cook and the Theft of the North Pole.* Boston: Little, Brown, 1973.

Fleming, Fergus. *Ninety Degrees North: The Quest for the North Pole.* New York: Grove Press, 2001.

Freeman, Andrew A. *The Case for Doctor Cook.* New York: Coward-McCann, 1961.

Gibbs, Philip. *Adventures in Journalism.* New York: Harper & Brothers, 1923.

Gilberg, Aage. *Eskimo Doctor.* Translated by Karin Elliott. New York: W. W. Norton, 1948.

Gillis, Kim Fairley, and Silas Hibbard Ayer III, eds. *Boreal Ties: Photographs and Two Diaries of the 1901 Peary Relief Expedition.* Albuquerque: University of New Mexico Press, 2002.

Green, Fitzhugh. *Peary: The Man Who Refused to Fail.* New York: G. P. Putnam's Sons, 1926.

Guttridge, Leonard F. *Ghosts of Cape Sabine: The Harrowing Story of the Greely Expedition.* New York: G. P. Putnam's Sons, 2000.

Haig-Thomas, David. *Tracks in the Snow.* New York: Oxford University Press, 1939.

Hall, Thomas. *Has the North Pole Been Discovered?* Boston: Gorham Press, 1917.

Harper, Kenn. *Give Me My Father's Body: The Life of Minik, the New York Eskimo.* South Royalton, Vt.: Steerforth Press, 2000.

Hayes, J. Gordon. *The Conquest of the North Pole.* London: Thornton Butterworth, 1934.

————. *Robert Edwin Peary: A Record of His Explorations, 1886–1909.* London: Grant Richards & Humphrey Toulmin, 1929.

Henson, Matthew A. *A Black Explorer at the North Pole.* 1912. Reprint, New York: Walker, 1969.

Herbert, Wally. *The Noose of Laurels: Robert E. Peary and the Race to the North Pole.* New York: Doubleday, 1990.

Hobbs, William Herbert. *Peary.* New York: Macmillan, 1936.

Houben, H. H. *The Call of the North.* Translated by H. J. Stenning. London: Elkim Mathews & Marrot, 1932.

Huntford, Roland. *The Last Place on Earth.* New York: Atheneum, 1986.

Kirwan, L. P. *A History of Polar Exploration.* New York: W. W. Norton, 1959.

Kugelmass, J. Alvin. *Roald Amundsen: A Saga of the Polar Seas.* New York: Julian Messner, 1955.

Lewin, Henry W. *The Great North Pole Fraud.* London: C. W. Daniel, 1935.

Lord, Walter. *Peary to the Pole.* New York: Harper & Row, 1963.

Lory, Milton. "I Knew This Man." Unpublished: OSU Polar Archives, ca. 1935.

MacMillan, Donald B. *Four Years in the White North.* Boston: Medici Society, 1925.

Miller, J. Martin. *Discovery of the North Pole.* N.p.: J. T. Moss, 1909.

Mirsky, Jeannette. *To the Arctic!: The Story of Northern Exploration from Earliest Times to the Present.* Chicago: University of Chicago Press, 1970.

Molett, William. *Robert Peary & Matthew Henson at the North Pole.* Frankfort: Elkhorn Press, 1996.

Morris, Charles, ed. *Finding the North Pole: Dr. Cook's Own Story of His Discovery, April 21, 1908, the Story of Commander Peary's Discovery, April 6, 1909, together with the Marvelous Record of Former Arctic Expeditions.* N.p.: W. E. Scull, 1909.

Mowat, Farley. *The Polar Passion: The Quest for the North Pole.* Toronto: McClelland and Stewart, 1967.

Peary, Robert E. *Nearest the Pole: A Narrative of the Polar Expedition of the Peary Arctic Club in the S.S. Roosevelt, 1905–1906.* New York: Doubleday, Page, 1907.

———. *The North Pole: Its Discovery in 1909 under the Auspices of the Peary Arctic Club.* New York: Frederick A. Stokes, 1910.

———. *Northward over the "Great Ice": A Narrative of Life and Work along the Shores and upon the Interior Ice-cap of Northern Greenland in the Years 1886 and 1891–1897.* 2 vols. London: Metheuen, 1898.

Pond, J. B. *Eccentricities of Genius: Memories of Famous Men and Women of the Platform and Stage.* London: Chatto and Windus, 1901.

Rasky, Frank. *The North Pole or Bust.* Toronto: McGraw-Hill Ryerson, 1977.

Rawlins, Dennis. *Peary at the North Pole: Fact or Fiction?* Washington: Robert B. Luce, 1973.

Roberts, David. *Great Exploration Hoaxes.* New York: Modern Library, 2001.

Robinson, Bradley. *Dark Companion*. New York: Robert M. McBride, 1947.

Sale, Richard. *Polar Reaches: The History of Arctic and Antarctic Exploration*. Seattle: Mountaineers Books, 2002.

Savours, Ann. *The Search for the North West Passage*. New York: St. Martin's Press, 1999.

Shackleton, Ernest. *South: The Endurance Expedition*. New York: Signet, 1999.

Stafford, Marie Peary. *Discoverer of the North Pole*. New York: William Morrow, 1959.

Steffens, Lincoln. *The Autobiography of Lincoln Steffens*. New York: Harcourt, Brace, 1931.

Sverdrup, Otto. *New Land: Four Years in the Arctic Regions*. Translated by Ethel Harriet Hearn. 2 vols. London: Longmans, Green, 1904.

Uberman, C. M. *The Presidents and Their Wives*. Maryland: National Souvenir Center, 1961.

Washburn, Bradford, and Peter Cherici. *The Dishonorable Dr. Cook: Debunking the Notorious Mount McKinley Hoax*. Seattle: Mountaineers Books, 2001.

Weems, John Edward. *Peary: The Explorer and the Man*. Boston: Houghton Mifflin, 1967.

————. *Race for the Pole*. New York: Henry Holt, 1960.

Whitney, Harry. *Hunting with the Eskimos: The Unique Record of a Sportsman's Year among the Northernmost Tribe—The Big Game Hunting, the Native Life, and the Battle for Existence through the Long Arctic Night*. New York: Century, 1910.

Wright, Theon. *The Big Nail: The Story of the Cook-Peary Feud*. New York: John Day, 1970.

INDEX